THE DRAMAS OF LORD BYRON

THE DRAMAS OF LORD BYRON

A Critical Study

by

Samuel C. Chew, Jr., Ph. D.

NEW YORK
RUSSELL & RUSSELL · INC
1964

FIRST PUBLISHED IN 1915
REISSUED, 1964, BY RUSSELL & RUSSELL, INC.
BY ARRANGEMENT WITH LUCY E. CHEW
L. C. CATALOG CARD NO: 64—18596

PRINTED IN THE UNITED STATES OF AMERICA

In Memory of
Horace Howard Furness.

A soul born active, wind-beaten but ascending.
Meredith.

Preface

Most people of culture have read *Manfred* and *Cain*; Byron's other plays are now almost unknown to that portion of the "general public" that reads poetry at all. Yet these plays deserve careful perusal, all but *Werner*, which is about as complete a failure as anything in literature. They are not absorbingly entertaining, but they are provocative of thought. Knowledge of them is essential, moreover, to the appreciation of Byron's entire achievement. There have been many monographs on the individual plays, but the whole group has never been studied with any degree of adequacy.[1] Such a study is here essayed. It is introduced by a brief account of the chief characteristics of the drama of the romantic period, in order that Byron's plays — too often regarded as a group of isolated phenomena — may be related to the general history of dramatic literature.

I planned to print as an appendix to this study a full Thought-Index to Byron's complete works — poems, letters, journals, and scattered prose writings; but it outgrew the space provided for it and shall be published separately.

To record indebtedness is here a pleasure: to Professor J. W. Bright for constant encouragement and criticism; to Professor W. E. Leonard, of the University of Wisconsin, who has read my book in manuscript, for several valuable suggestions; to Mr. John Murray for permission to use the copyright material in the Coleridge-Prothero *Byron*;[2] to Mr. Paul Elmer More and Mr. Richard Edgcumbe for courteous replies to queries; to Mr. George Shipley and Mr. Thomas DeC. Ruth for most welcome aid with the proofs; and to my earliest and best guide in poetry as in all things — my father.

S. C. C., Jr.

---

[1] William Gerard, *Byron Restudied in his Dramas*, London, 1886, is almost worthless.

[2] The abbreviations P. and LJ. are used throughout this book for the *Poems*, edited by E. H. Coleridge, and the *Letters and Journals*, edited by R. L. Prothero, respectively.

Errata.

P. 21, note 2: for "Bryon" read „Byron".
P. 50, line 22: for "he" read "the".
P. 62, note 1: for "Anqlia" read "Anglia".
P. 69, note 1: title should be italicised.
P. 74, last line of note: delete "it".

Contents

Contents

Chapter One.
The Drama of the Romantic Period.

The types of mid-eighteenth century drama disappeared or assumed new forms under the influence of romanticism. As the force of French influence declined, the pseudo-classical play, of which Johnson's *Irene* is a specimen, lost the favor even of the few. The Elizabethanism of Rowe, apparent despite its veneer of classicism, was to be succeeded by a new and sincere revival of interest in the lesser dramatists, who had meanwhile faded almost utterly from the knowledge of play-goers. From the time of Cibber and Steele sentimental comedy had been popular, fostered as it was by the influence of Destouches, Marivaux and Nivelle de la Chaussée, and paralleled later by the sentimentalism of Sterne and Mackenzie. Even the blow dealt at this *genre* by Sheridan in *The Critic* (1779) did not immediately stop the vogue. More genuinely vital was the work of Goldsmith and Sheridan, which derives from Molière and Congreve and passes on the tradition in successive stages of weakness to the school of George Colman the Younger and Thomas Holcroft. The one addition to dramatic types made by the century was the domestic tragedy of George Lillo, which, though descended from an Elizabethan type and related to sentimental comedy, is essentially a new beginning in the dead waste of pseudo-classicism. But such tragedies of common life, often hardly more than dramatized versions of the Newgate Calendar, while an important reform in material and technique, could not raise the standard of dramatic art.[1]

During the eighteenth century the drama dwindled and expired. For it ceased truly to reflect the national life, and

---

[1] For an account of the drama of this time see *The Cambridge History of English Literature*, X (1913), chap. iv.

art cannot exist independently of life. Plays therefore became a "literary by-product".[1] For a brief period at the beginning of the nineteenth century there was a revival of interest in the poetic drama, and it is with this period that I propose to deal in this chapter.

The "Gothic" novel[2] strongly influenced the new romantic drama. The fashion left its mark upon the work of many contemporary writers, including Byron, whose *Lara* especially derives directly from Mrs. Radcliffe's type of hero-villain. It was a crude but authentic manifestation of the time-spirit, and arose from a fundamental deficiency in the eighteenth century. The obtrusion of the reason into those portions of human experience properly the domain of the imagination was abnormal. The imagination, thwarted but restless, was driven forth into barren places. Rationalism produced extravagance because it failed to provide nourishing spiritual food. Not children only need Arabian romances, monkish legends, and "tales that charm away the wakeful night", for

> "something in the shape
> Of these will live till man shall be no more.
> Dumb yearnings, hidden appetites are ours,
> And *they must* have their food."[3]

From the desperate ennui of the time two avenues of escape offered, leading respectively to the remote in space or in time. Hence the popularity of tales of the Orient.[4] To people tired of tea-cups and sedan-chairs the gorgeous East held out the enticement of surprises, mystery, and horror. Hence, too, the renascence of medievalism which is the basis of the "Gothic" revival, the allurement of the remote in time. The impulse had in it the essentials of romanticism: medievalism, the appeal to wonder, the excitation of terror. At best the horrific ele-

---

[1] A. H. Thorndike, *Tragedy*, Boston, Houghton, Mifflin, 1908, p. 321.

[2] See Walter Raleigh, *The English Novel*, New York, Scribner, 1910, p. 221 f.; George Saintsbury, *The English Novel*, New York, Dutton, 1913, p. 155 f. On Walpole's *Castle of Otranto* (1764) see also C. L. Eastlake, *The History of the Gothic Revival*, London, Longmans, 1872, p. 43; Leslie Stephen, *Hours in a Library*, New York, Putnam, 1904, II, 143.

[3] Wordsworth, *The Prelude* V, 504 f.

[4] See M. P. Conant, *The Oriental Tale in English Literature*, New York, Macmillan, p. 247, and for the influence of the *genre* on the drama, p. 76.

ments could be moulded into such a story as *The Fall of the House of Usher*. But the style was on the verge of absurdity, and often, as in Lewis's *Monk*, went far beyond the boundary line.

The license of the mode appeared in the drama as well as in the novel; sensational material was always in demand — ghosts, crime, and horror — and the means employed were coarse and crude. Walpole's *Mysterious Mother*[1] (1768), the earliest and most notable "Gothic" tragedy, was praised by Byron (P. IV, 339) as "a tragedy of the highest order". Coleridge[2], on the contrary, accusing Byron of insincerity, called it "disgusting, vile, detestable." The epithets are justified, for the plot has to do with incest of the most unheard-of sort. The construction of the play is wild and crude; the "Gothic" requisites, a castle falling to ruins, crime, mystery, monks, etc., are abundantly supplied. There is little regard for dramatic development and none for the portrayal of character. The catastrophe alone is pretty well managed. The blank-verse is nearly always sheer bombast.

The number of such terror-dramas was large; novels were dramatized and original plays written in the same style. Of these "Monk" Lewis's *Castle Spectre*[3] is typical. It tells of the attempt of a feudal lord to force his niece to marry him, though she preferred "a basilisk's kiss" to his. "The great run which this piece had", says Genest[4], "is striking proof that success is a very uncertain criterion of merit. . . . How anyone not destitute of sense could write such stuff is wonderful". Byron refers to the piece in *Hints from Horace* (ll. 290, note), and the lines on Lewis in *English Bards* (ll. 269 f.) form a comment on the *genre*.

But upon the stage these extreme examples of the terrific school could obtain no permanent success, for there the chief instrument for the attainment of the effect desired — the use

---

[1] *The Mysterious Mother. A Tragedy.* London, 1781 (ed. Dodsley).

[2] *Table-Talk of the late S. T. Coleridge,* ed. H. N. Coleridge, 1835 II, 154.

[3] *Cumberland's British Theatre* XV.

[4] *Some Account of the English Stage,* Bath, 1832, VII, 332. Cf. *Letters of the Wordsworth Family,* ed. W. Knight, London, Macmillan, I, 114.

of suggestion — was rendered almost powerless. The stage
heightened absurdities and checked the shudder afforded by
solitary perusal "by the light of a candle with a very long
wick".

The motive of terror was combined with that of sentimentality in many plays translated or imitated from the German.
For a while the plays of Kotzebue were immensely popular.
Menschenhass und Reue was produced in 1798, followed a year
later by Sheridan's *Pizarro*[1], a weak version of *Die Spanier in
Peru*. It was a great success.[2] Brandl[3] ascribes the success
of Kotzebue's plays to the fact that "mechanical cleverness
tells more in front of the footlights than all lyrical and philosophical refinements." This technique was employed upon
themes familiar to Englishmen. The sentimentality harmonized
with Holcroftian comedy. The point of view was democratic;
"custom" and "positive law" were denounced in the name of
nature.[4] Thus was the revolutionary thought of the period
voiced; and popularity followed. Southey, whose sole experiment in dramatic form[5] combines the zeal of a republican and
the immature judgment of a boy, wrote[6], "The German plays
have always something ridiculous, yet Kotzebue seems to me
possessed of unsurpassed and unsurpassable genius." Scott, whose
first play was a translation of Goethe's *Götz von Berlichingen*,
pronounced wiser judgment. "The better productions of the
German stage," he says[7], "have never been made known to
us; for by some unfortunate chance the wretched pieces
of Kotzebue have found a readier acceptance, or more willing
translators, than the sublimity of Goethe, or the romantic strength
of Schiller." Nor were others silent in condemnation of the
furore. In the British Museum there is a satirical piece *On*

[1] See further L. Bahlsen, "Kotzebue's Peru-Dramen und Sheridan's Pizarro", Herrig's *Archiv* LXXXI, 354 f.

[2] See Thomas Medwin, *Conversions with Lord Byron*, 1824, p. 189.

[3] Alois Brandl, *Coleridge and the English Romantic School*, London,
John Murray, 1887, p. 171.

[4] C. H. Herford, *The Age of Wordsworth*, London, Bell, 1905, p. 139.

[5] *Wat Tyler*, *Poetical Works*, 1837, II, 1 f.

[6] *A Selection from the Letters of Robert Southey*, ed. J. W. Warner,
London, 1856, I, 68.

[7] Quoted by Bahlsen, p. 379.

the Prevalence of the German Drama on the British Stage, "by a Gentleman", London, 1805 [1], which is interesting as anticipating lines 580 — 5 of *English Bards and Scotch Reviewers.* The "gentleman" thus addresses Sheridan:

"See how thy own, once verdant, laurels fade,
Since thou canst stoop to call in foreign aid,
Since thou canst join the tame translating crew,
And banish Avon's bard for Kotzebue."

He also criticises the German taste for "lawless passion" which drives the "feeling soul" to frenzy, and "sensibility with sickly mien" which "heaves the deep sigh and calls the starting tear". More drastic was the attack by John Styles, whose *Essay on the Character and Influence of the Stage on Morals and Happiness* (second edition, 1807) carries on the tradition of Tertullian and Grosseteste, Prynne and Collier. He writes (p. 47), "The recent introduction of the German drama may be considered a phoenomenon in the world of dissipation. The writings of Congreve and Dryden are absolutely pure, when compared with the vile disgusting offspring of the profligate Kotzebue."

In 1798 appeared *The Rovers,* by Frere and Canning, the *Anti-Jacobin's* famous parody of the German plays. [2] It had much to do with the swift decline of the vogue towards the end of the century. The fashion of tragedy began to change. "Horrors continued to be popular," says Brandl (p. 166), "but less in the way of robbers, ghosts, and tyrants, external miseries, crass romances, and empty tirades, than in inward commotions of the soul." There are attempts at psychological analysis. This tendency is seen in Wordsworth's *Borderers* (1795—6), Lamb's *John Woodvil* (1801), Scott's *Sensuality and Revenge* (1798), and Coleridge's *Osorio.* The new psychological drama is, however, best represented by the series of *Plays on the Passions* by Joanna Baillie.

Lack of space forbids a review of all Miss Baillie's dramas. I therefore select the two praised by Byron: *Ethwald* and *De Montfort.* [3] At the foundation of Joanna Baillie's theories and prac-

---

[1] First noted by Koeppel, *Eng. Stud.* XIII, 530.

[2] *The Poetry of the Anti-Jacobin,* ed. Charles Edmonds, New York, Putnam, 1890, p. 201 f.

[3] Preface to *Marino Faliero,* P. IV, 338.

tice in the drama was a reaction from the "Gothic" vogue,
very similar to that which later led Byron to the "regular"
drama. Byron evidently appreciated the kinship of effort between Miss Baillie and himself. There are, however, only two
important references to her in his writings. He wrote to Miss
Milbanke (LJ. III, 399), "She is our only dramatist since Otway
and Southerne"; and to Moore (LJ. III, 197), "Women (saving
Joanna Baillie) cannot write tragedy: they have not seen nor
felt enough of life for it." While on the Drury Lane Committee,
Byron tried to have *De Montfort* revived, but without success.[1]

Joanna Baillie's design was explained at length in an introductory discourse prefixed to the first instalment of her *Plays
on the Passions*[2] (1798). She declares that the "sympathetic
curiosity" with which man regards his fellow man and which
makes him eager to behold the various and conflicting emotions
that arise in him, and which he governs or is governed by,
is a Godgiven instinct, since "in examining others we know
ourselves" (p. 4). It is the mission of the drama to supply
such situations as will afford opportunity for beneficial observations of passion without the need to seek them out in circumstances of real life. The drama, more than any other branch
of letters, must therefore aim at "the expression of passion,
genuine and true to Nature" (p. 6). The stage has often, and
especially of late, wandered far from this its proper function.
Poets have given their chief attention to emulation and imitation of the masterpieces of the past and "have been tempted
to prefer the embellishments of poetry to faithfully delineated
nature" (p. 8). They have concentrated their efforts on strong
outlines of character, bold features of passion, grand vicissi-
tudes of fortune and striking dramatic situations, "neglecting
the boundless variety of nature" (p. 8). In order to offset this
tendency of the stage Miss Baillie planned to "write a series
of tragedies, of simpler construction, less embellished with
poetical decorations, less constrained by that lofty seriousness
which has so generally been considered as necessary for the
support of tragic, and in which the chief object should be to

---

[1] P. IV, p. 337, note 1.
[2] *The Dramatic and Poetical Works of Joanna Baillie*, 1851.

delineate the progress of the higher passions in the human breast" (p. 10—11). Complementary to the tragedies there was planned a series of comedies illustrating the same passions but "in such situations, and attended with such circumstances, as take off their sublimity" (p. 11). There is very little action in the plays in order that attention may not be distracted from the central passion, and there is extreme simplicity of plot, without episode, sub-plot, or variety of any kind that could interfere with the requisite concentration.

De Montfort is a delineation of the passion of hatred. The protagonist cherishes mortal hate towards Rezenvelt who shortly before the opening of the play had spared his life. When De Montfort hears that Rezenvelt is about to marry his sister Jane, who has been attempting to bring about a reconciliation, he deliberately and cowardly murders him in a lonely forest near a convent. He is captured, but overcome with remorse and shame anticipates justice in the arms of his sister, who pronounces a tribute to his virtues, a lamentation over his one crime, and a solemn warning to others.

Were Miss Baillie's theory of tragedy tenable, *De Montfort* would certainly be a great tragedy. It exhibits the passion of ungovernable and soul-controlling hate with considerable power. By emphasizing the love of De Montfort for his sister and his consequent blind rage at the report of her betrothal to his enemy, it accounts satisfactorily for the murderous impulses which overbear all good instincts. The lack of poetry is in accord with Miss Baillie's design, and in spite of the temptations of the theme there is no bombast. The lesser characters are all given some measure of individuality. The emphasis upon a single passion, the lack of episode, directness of action, simplicity of diction, and individuality of characterization, are certainly well exemplified in this play. Its defects are those inherent in the theory according to which the play was constructed. The pruning away of all supplementary traits from "unaccommodated man" is very faulty psychology. No passion goes "sounding on, a dim and perilous way", subject to none of the cross-currents of conflicting desires nor swerving in its course at the bidding of other instincts. Moreover the attempt to exhibit the subtleties of passion through the words of the

protagonist results in an undramatic monologue during much
of the time. During four acts there is almost complete lack
of action, no goal towards which the purposes of the protagonist are moving; and then in hours of fury the murder is accomplished, the protagonist captured, and an edifying end is made. The
setting in a German town shows the influence of contemporary
fashion. A further concession is the requiem sung by the nuns
over the newly covered grave (Act V, Scene i). The entire fifth
act is, indeed, in a subdued "Gothic" tone. German sentimentality is apparent, with its characteristic readiness to let chari-
table impulses (compare the typical Fielding-esque "goodness of
heart") weigh more in the estimate of a man than his pride,
jealousy, and murderous hate. [1]

Ethwald, an historical play in two parts, portrays the
passion of ambition. The hero is the younger son of a petty
thane, who through bravery and ability comes to be commander
of the Mercian army. Urged on by ambition he visits the
"Mystic sisters" who look "into the stretch of dark futurity"
and prophesy that he shall be king, but shall come to a dire
end. He leads a successful rebellion against the old king, is
crowned, engages in wars of conquest, and at last, weighed
down by enormous crimes, is assassinated. This is the barest
outline of the course of the long story.

The play is too long, but the passion depicted required
a growth of years from vague desire to entire obsession. The
debt to Shakespeare is great [2], and is an interesting illustration
of the power of the native tradition in the midst of the German
furore. The comments which I have made upon *De Montfort*
apply also to *Ethwald*. There is the same simplicity of language,
carried to a point of baldness where the least simile is welcomed. There is the same emphasis upon the central passion.

In her Introductory Discourse, Miss Baillie asked for the

---

[1] Miss Baillie foresaw this ethical objection and attempted to forestall
it in a concluding note (p. 104), but the impression stated in my text remains.

[2] To *Macbeth* throughout the play, especially in the cavern scene with
the "Mystic sisters" and in the final attack upon the castle; to *Hamlet* in
the incident of the appearance of the king's deserted sweetheart gone mad;
to *King John* and *Richard III*, and possibly to Marlowe's *Edward II*, in
the scenes showing the young Edward in prison.

approval rather of her friends than of posterity. Her wish
has been granted. One cannot repeat to-day the praise lavish-
ed on her by some of her contemporaries. I have already
quoted Byron's remarks on her dramas. Scott wrote often and
generously of her, and many others echoed these great plaudits.
Hazlitt was more clear-sighted. "Her tragedies and comedies",
he wrote [1], "are heresies in the dramatic art. She is a Uni-
tarian in poetry. With her the passions are, like the French
Republic, one and indivisible: they are not so in nature, or
in Shakespeare." Joanna Baillie is of considerable significance
in the study of the Byronic drama. Her aim at dignity and
simplicity of style, portrayal of passion rather than external
incident, and directness of plot, is in line with the reform later
advocated by Byron. Her plays are a step in the direction
from superficiality to vital truth. [2]

In the dedicatory Epistle to *The Fall of Robespierre* (1794)
Coleridge admits the influence of the sensational drama, his
aim being "to develope the characters of the chief actors on
a vast scale of horrors". [3] This he fails signally to accomplish.
The play shows, along with some obvious imitation of Shakespeare, a tendency to rhetorical declamation, a portrayal of
the type rather than the individual, and a concentration of
the action immediately before the catastrophe, with narrative
exposition of earlier events, which betray French influence.
Philosophically it is of its time, and should be compared with
Southey's *Wat Tyler* and Wordsworth's *Borderers*. The latter
play depicts the passion of jealousy. Schiller is the inspiration
of its plot and form, Godwin of its philosophy. Individualism,
democracy, the revolt from social conventions, and the return
to nature, are its themes. [4] To the power of Schiller, Coleridge

---

[1] *Lectures on the English Poets*, London, Dent, p. 147.

[2] For convenient analyses of Joanna Baillie's plays see Genest, VIII, 333 f.

[3] *Complete Poetical Works*, ed. E. H. Coleridge, Oxford, The Clarendon
Press, 1912, II, 495.

[4] *Poetical Works*, ed. W. Knight, London, Macmillan, 1896, I, 112 f.
Though written in 1795—6, and therefore important for the study of Wordsworth's development, this play was not published till 1842. It has therefore
no significance for the study of Byron's dramas. On the influence of Schiller,
especially *The Robbers*, see Th. Rea, *Schiller's Dramas and Poems in
England*, London, Unwin, 1906, p. 22 f.

bore testimony in the sonnet *To the Author of "The Robbers"*, in a note to which he tells how he read the play for the first time on "a Winter midnight — the wind high. . . . The readers of Schiller will conceive what I felt. Schiller introduces no supernatural beings; yet his human beings agitate and astonish more than all the *goblin* rout — even of Shakespeare."[1] It was at the height of the German furore that Coleridge translated *The Piccolomini* and *The Death of Wallenstein*, which perhaps rank with Schlegel's *Shakespeare* among the greatest of translations.

Coleridge's most notable play shows a blending of several influences, but it is to be classed with the *Plays of the Passions* as an effort to portray the power of overwhelming emotion. *Osorio* was written in 1797, "expressly for the stage, at the instigation and with the encouragement of Mr. Sheridan, by whom, however, it was not deemed suitable for that purpose."[2] In 1813 it was remodeled and produced at Drury Lane, under the title of *Remorse*,[3] when it had considerable success. Byron was largely responsible for this production.[4] The play stands out in pleasing contrast to the typical stage-play of the time. There are in it numerous passages of genuine and beautiful poetry. It won Byron's support chiefly from its attempt to depict tragic passion, not horrific incident. The error is made of singling out one passion and portraying it as almost wholly unrelated to the complex mass of rival emotions and traits that together make up human nature. The emphasis upon motive is that afterwards adopted by Byron, and the consequence of this emphasis is the same in both cases — almost complete stagnation of the action through long stretches of dialogue.[5] The real action is spiritual, the progress towards remorse of the protagonist's soul. Hence the play at once lost

---

[1] *Complete Poetical Works* I, 72.

[2] *Dramatic Works of S. T. Coleridge*, ed. Derwent Coleridge, p. v. Cf. *Complete Poetical Works*, II, 812.

[3] Both versions are included in *Complete Poetical Works*, II, 518 f. and 812 f.

[4] Wordsworth erroneously ascribed its production to "the kindness of Mr. Sheridan": *Poetical Works*, I, 113.

[5] Two of the situations are dramatically satisfying: Act II, Sc. ii; Act IV, Sc. i.

control of the stage. But this very introspection must have been a factor in winning the approval of Byron. Coleridge did not despise the "Gothic" trappings of the terrific school, and he introduces incantation, paynims, castles, caverns, dungeons, etc. *Remorse* shows also the influence of Schiller[1] and Shakespeare.[2] With this romanticism there is mixed a rather incongruous politico-philosophic strain characteristic at once of Coleridge and of the period. Byron welcomed *Remorse* as the best play "for very many years" (LJ. III, 191), and so it was. Its dignity, its lack of bombast, its real and high poetic merit, its refusal to accumulate horrors on horror's head even while complying with the taste of the time, its aim to present motive instead of mechanical action, to portray, however imperfectly, the struggles of human volition, — all put it on a relatively high level of achievement.

Coleridge's second attempt to win success upon the stage was a failure. At Byron's suggestion that a tragedy might be welcomed by the public (LJ. III, 191), *Zapolya* was submitted to the Drury Lane Committee, but was rejected.[3] The interval of twenty years between the first and second acts destroys the continuity of the action. This Coleridge realized, and sought to shelter himself behind a comparison with *The Winter's Tale* and by dividing the play into two parts. The piece is not without merit. It is a typically romantic play, the action passing in Illyria during the Middle Ages; but it avoids the customary mechanical accessories of the "Gothic" drama. The inspiration of the play is Shakespearean, superficially obvious by the large borrowings from *Cymbeline, As You Like It, The Winter's Tale*, and *The Tempest*, but seen also in the undertone of love and beauty and ripe experience, which connects it with the latest plays of Shakespeare.

---

[1] From Schiller's *Ghostseer* (the source of Byron's *Oscar of Alva*) Coleridge took the story of the man who murders his brother to obtain his bride, but in *Osorio* the victim escapes and returns (as in *The Robbers*). See Brandl, p. 168; cf. Rea, p. 24 f. A like motive is used in Beddoes' *Death's Jest-Book*.

[2] Shakespearean reminiscences abound; there is little direct borrowing.

[3] Cf. LJ. V, 442, and cf. James Gillman, *Life of Coleridge*, London, 1838, I, 266 f.

When *Zapolya* was found not "feasible", Maturin's *Bertram*[1]
was accepted in its stead, largely through the good offices of Scott
and Byron. The latter wrote to Moore (LJ. IV, 90), "I take
some credit to myself for having done my best to bring out
Bertram," and he considered Maturin "a very clever fellow."
It is better fitted than *Zapolya* for the stage though infinitely
below it in poetic merit. The action is direct and swift, the
style in harmony with the prevailing mode. Despite the extra-
ordinary accumulation of "Gothic" accoutrements, amounting
almost to a caricature of the class, there is a feeling for the
fundamental springs of emotion for which one would look in
vain in the plays of Lewis. The play is essentially Byronic
in its unrestrained sweep of passion; the protagonist is another
Lara, though Maturin borrowed the hero-villain type not so
much from Byron as from Mrs. Radcliffe, in whose books he
quarried along with Byron. Of Maturin's later work Byron
thought little. *Manuel*[2] he called "the absurd work of a clever
man" (LJ. IV, 137), "as heavy a nightmare as was ever be-
strode by Indigestion" (LJ. IV, 151).

The success of *Remorse* caused a revival of the poetic
drama in which several streams of influence merged. This
was furthered by the genius and popularity of Edmund Kean,
who made his first London appearance in January, 1814. For
several years there was a temporary compromise between literature and the stage. Younger playwrights were encouraged;
taste was improved to an extent which made the presentation
even of Byron's dramas a matter of financial speculation despite
his own vigorous opposition. It gave Shelley arguments for
the success of *The Cenci*. "I am exceedingly interested", he
wrote[3], "in the question of whether this attempt of mine will
succeed or no. I am strongly inclined to the affirmative at
present, founding my hopes on this, that as a composition, it
is certainly not inferior to any of the modern plays that have

---

[1] *Bertram; or the Castle of St. Aldobrand. A Tragedy. . . . By the
Rev. R. C. Maturin.* Oxberry's edition, London, 1827.

[2] See John Doran, *Their Majesties' Servants*, Boston, Niccolls, III,
303 f., for an account of the failure of *Manuel* on the stage.

[3] *The Letters of Percy Bysshe Shelley*, ed. Roger Ingpen, London
Pitman, 1909, II, 698.

been acted, with the exception of *Remorse;* that the interests of the plot is [*sic*] incredibly greater and more real", etc. Even Keats, though he acknowledges his ambition "to make as great a revolution in modern dramatic writing as Kean has done in acting"[1], must have been encouraged in the composition of *Otho the Great* by the thought that the poetic drama was coming into its own. To the same innovation may be traced the successes of Bulwer-Lytton twenty years later. With the failure of Browning's *Blot on the 'Scutcheon* in 1843 the revival of romantic tragedy came to an end. Now at length in our own day there begin to be fitful signs of its reappearance.

Among the writers of poetic dramas who came into some prominence after 1816 was Henry Hart Milman. Byron had at one time a high opinion of Milman's poetic powers, though he distrusted his politics and profession. Of many references to him, the following are the more notable. "Milman will *do,* if he don't cant too much, nor imitate Southey: the fellow has poesy in him; but he is envious, and unhappy, as all the envious are. Still he is among the best of the day" (LJ. V, 362). "They have brought out *Fazio* with great and deserved success at Covent Garden: that's a good sign" (LJ. IV, 210). *The Fall of Jerusalem* Byron thought a "very noble" poem, adding "I greatly admire Milman" (LJ. V, 54). Later "the impression that Milman had influenced Murray against continuing the publication of *Don Juan*" and "the mistaken belief that it was Milman who had written the article in the *Quarterly* which 'killed John Keats'" occasioned the virulent attack upon the "poet-priest" in a famous passage of *Don Juan.*[2]

Fazio[3] is the story of a wronged woman, who in sudden jealousy betrays the fact that her husband's wealth was acquired by robbery. The momentary impulse past, she pleads for her husband's life. But it is too late; he is executed, and the play ends with the widow's denunciation of her rival, and her death. The play won success on the stage. Indeed even to-day an actress of power might succeed in the part of Bianca.

---

[1] *Letters of John Keats,* ed. H. B. Forman, London, Reeves and Turner, 1895, p. 364.

[2] *Don Juan* XI, 58 and note 1; P. VI, 445.

[3] *Poetical Works of ... H. H. Milman,* 1839, III, 117 f.

In *Fazio* many of the qualities approved by Byron are present;
but its virtues are mainly negative. The passionate subject
is handled with notable restraint; the advance of the action is
regular and the construction logical; the characters are consistently, if feebly, drawn; the verse, though containing no
poetry of great merit, is correct and pure. There is a praise-
worthy moderation of tone at a time when extravagance was
the fashion.

The Fall of Jerusalem[1] is founded largely on Josephus.
It presents only the last stages of the siege and culminates in
the capture of the city. There is no division into acts, but
merely a succession of scenes in and near Jerusalem. There
is an occasional chorus, and the characters break now and
then into lyrical measures. The influence of Greek tragedy is
obvious. The fact that it followed what Byron considered "the
best models" for dramatic composition, that it was confessedly
not designed for the stage, that there was an effort at compression of time, and that the subject was historical, all are
reasons for Byron's commendation of the play.

Among the "intellectual children" of *Remorse* by far the most
important is *The Cenci*. Byron's comments upon this great
play are disappointingly meagre and unappreciative. To Hoppner
he wrote (LJ. V, 74), "His tragedy is sad work; but the subject renders it so", and to Shelley himself (LJ. V, 268), "I read
Cenci — but, besides that I think the *subject* essentially *undramatic*, I am not a great admirer of our old dramatists *as
models*. I deny that the English have hitherto had a drama
at all. Your *Cenci*, however, was a work of power and poetry".
Shelley's comment on this criticism was made in a letter to
Leigh Hunt. "Certainly", he wrote[2], "if *Marino Faliero* is a
drama, *Cenci* is not — but that between ourselves." How
account for Byron's curiously warpt judgment of the greatest
play of the century? It is explicable on several grounds. (i)
The Cenci, though it preserves admirably the essential unity
of interest, is not written in accordance with a narrow interpretation of those dramatic laws which Byron considered irre-

---

[1] *Loc. cit.*, I, 1 f.
[2] *Letters*, II, 910.

fragable. There are only three more scenes than in *Marino Faliero*, but the fourth act passes at the Castle of Petrella, not in Rome. Yet the spirit of the unity of time is preserved, for there is a compression which enables the historical events of more than a year to pass in a few days. (ii) The Elizabethan inspiration is very apparent. The scene in the castle after the murder owes something to *Macbeth*, the curse of the Count on Beatrice is modeled upon Lear's curse, Giacomo's comparison of the dying lamp to his father had its source in *Othello*. Bates thinks he detects indebtedness to Middleton's *Changeling*. The trial of Beatrice certainly resembles that in Webster's *White Devil* (III, i).[1] Such marks of indebtedness to the "set of mountebanks" of course met with Byron's condemnation. (iii) *The Cenci* deals with an abnormal situation, not with average humanity. Here it differs utterly from the Byronic historical plays. Count Cenci is impossibly wicked; he is one of those "outrageous ranting villains" whom Byron expressly abjured. He closely resembles, but in even more exaggerated form, the heroic-villains of the romantic drama, Bertram, Oswald, Conrad, and so many more. (iv) In spite of his own hostile attitude towards the priesthood, Byron was probably suspicious of Shelley's representation of the clergy and certainly objected to his blatant atheism. (v) More technical objections may have occurred to Byron — the substitution of favorite abstract ideas embodied in realistic form for true objective characterization[2], the theatrically impossible length of some of the soliloquies, the halting nature of the action — but to have specified them would have been to expose himself to the same charges. All this explains, but it does not justify, Byron's adverse criticism of the play. His opinion remains a striking instance of failure to do justice to a great work; but it must be added that Byron told Medwin (p. 95) that *The Cenci* was "perhaps the best tragedy modern times have produced."

---

[1] E. S. Bates, *A Study of Shelley's Cenci*, New York, The Columbia University Press, 1908, p. 54 f., where minor parallelisms will also be found. In my discussion of *The Cenci*, I am in several instances indebted to this monograph.

[2] There are critics (e. g. Mr. Clutton-Brock) who consider *The Cenci* almost as thorough an allegory as *Prometheus Unbound*.

The Cenci is one of the large number of plays that show the increasing strength of the native influence. In his preface Shelley wrote, "Our great ancestors the ancient English poets are the writers, a study of whom might incite us to do that for our own age which they have done for theirs." The revival of interest in the lesser Elizabethan dramatists is an important factor in the romantic drama. Throughout the "German" furore the plays of Shakespeare had remained popular, and the pages of Genest record an endless series of revivals. Otway, too, was occasionally performed, as were one or two of the old comedies. Something of the spirit of the old drama begins to come back into the many imitations towards the close of the eighteenth century. William Godwin's *Antonio* was produced by Kemble in 1800, but had no success at all.[1] It is heavy and uninspired and is of historical interest only as an early attempt at the style of the old dramatists. Its successor, *Faulkner* (1807), was equally dull and was never performed.

The Elizabethan revival can be dated from the publication of Lamb's *Specimens of the Dramatic Poets* (1808). It was furthered by Coleridge's lectures in 1810 and later years. Gifford's editions of Massinger, Jonson, and Ford, and his comments on other dramatists, aided in spreading knowledge of these half-forgotten poets. The lectures of William Hazlitt (1817—1821) were also of importance.

Lamb's influence upon the drama was almost wholly due to his ability as a critic, exerted historically in commentaries upon Elizabethan and Restoration plays, and practically in criticisms of current theatrical productions. At his best, as in the great essay *On the Tragedies of Shakespeare*[2], his work, especially in appreciation of nice distinctions of character and motive, is almost unsurpassed, though his thought never reaches the profundity of Coleridge. His experiments in dramatic composition are of little value. *John Woodvil*[3] (1802), the best of his plays, might be classed with the *Plays of the Passions*

---

[1] Cf. Doran, III, 298.
[2] *Collected Works of Charles Lamb*, ed. A. Ainger, New York, Armstrong, 1890, II, 220 f.
[3] *Ibid.*, II, 25 f.

in that it is a study of the workings of a single passion, but
its historical interest is greater as one of the early essays in
the old style. The intermixture of prose and verse, the use
of archaic words and phrases, the lax construction, the employment of types in the *dramatis personae,* are the signs of this
Elizabethanism.[1] The piece may be described as feebly good.
Lamb's other plays need not here be considered at all.

This tentative stage in the revival of the Elizabethan style
passed and the movement gathered force. It is evident in
Coleridge's plays, and still more so in Keats's *Otho the Great*
and his fragment of *King Stephen.* These are both of secondary
importance among Keats's works, serving chiefly to show the
strength of the attraction of the stage for the poets of the
time; and as both remained unpublished till Lord Houghton's
volume of 1848, it is unlikely that Byron so much as knew
of their existence. The strange manner in which *Otho the Great*
was written (C. A. Brown outlined the action and characters,
scene by scene, and Keats endowed his purposes with words)[2]
makes it unlikely that Keats proceeded on any definite plan
of composition or according to any dramatic theory, but the
inspiration is distinctly Elizabethan. Were one ignorant of
the method of composition employed, it would be easier to
take the piece quite seriously. *King Stephen* is a fragment of
fine promise, and in versification and imagination of almost
Shakespearean richness.

With Procter the Elizabethanism becomes very definite.
He is a disciple of Fletcher. Of *Mirandola* (1821), his only
tragedy, Byron wrote (LJ. V, 217), "I just see . . . that there
is a new tragedy of great expectation, by Barry Cornwall. . . .
I liked the Dramatic Scenes. . . . I think him very likely
to produce a good tragedy, if he keep to a natural style, and
not play tricks to form Harlequinades for an audience. . . .
If I had been aware that he was in that line, I should have
spoken of him in the preface to *Marino Faliero:* he will do a
World's wonder if he produce a great tragedy." But when
Procter sent him a copy of *Mirandola* Byron's only comment

---

[1] Cf. Walter Pater, *Appreciations*, London, Macmillan, 1911, p. 113.
[2] See *The Poems of John Keats,* ed. E. de Sélincourt, New York, Dodd,
Mead, 1909, p. 552.

was, "Barry Cornwall will do better by and bye, I dare say,
if he don't get spoilt by green tea and the praises of Penton-
ville and Paradise Row" (LJ. V, 362). It is not remarkable
that Byron showed no enthusiasm over *Mirandola,* which, though
a piece of considerable merit and excellently adapted to the
stage, where it had a successful "run", is constructed, as expressly stated in the Prologue, on the model of the Elizabethans. It is an Italian tragedy of passion, one of the long
series from such plays as Webster's tragedies to Swinburne's
Duke of Gandia. The story is of a father and son, rivals in
love. The effect of the reaction from the bombast and extravagance of the plays produced before *Remorse* is apparent in
Procter's play, which shows much moderation in tone in spite
of the strained and unnatural situation. But there is lack of
insight into the depths of human nature, there is no foundation
in philosophy, and there is hardly any poetry except faint
Elizabethan echoes, little worth, —

"A few plain words, honestly told,
Like those his mightier masters spoke of old."[1]

The *Dramatic Scenes*[2], which Byron "liked", are of less note.
Only the six original scenes are of interest here; many more
were published long after Byron's death. *Ludovico Sforza* tells
of a woman's revenge for the murder of her lover. It is founded on fact. The central situation is copied from *The Maid's
Tragedy,* Act V, Scene ii. *Lisander and Ione* is an attempt in the
pastoral-mythological style, in which Landor was later successful. *Juan* is a study of sudden jealousy, and owes something
to *Othello. The Way to Conquer,* a trifle, shows a magnani-
mous prince forgiving one who had wronged him. *The Broken
Heart* dramatizes Boccaccio's story of the lover who returns
home to find his mistress wedded to another. The title is
borrowed from Ford. *The Falcon*[3] relates the same tale of
Boccaccio afterwards used by Tennyson. Procter's piece is

---

[1] Prologue, p. vi. There is some resemblance between this play and
the *Paolo and Francesca* of Stephen Phillips.

[2] *Dramatic Scenes with other poems* . . . *by Barry Cornwall,*
Boston, 1857.

[3] Compare *The Works of Lord Tennyson,* edited by his son, New
York, Macmillan, 1909, VI, 219 f.

even slighter than Tennyson's. The latter poet must have seen Procter's *Falcon* though he apparently never acknowledged any debt to it.[1]

Shortly before Byron's death the result of this devotion to the older dramatists began to be apparent, and the high tide of Elizabethanism came during the decade before the emergence of Tennyson. This is really beyond the limits of the present study[2], but two more paragraphs will round out the subject. The interest and appreciation of Coleridge, Keats, and Shelley developed into the enthusiastic homage of Procter, Darley, Beddoes, and Wells. Beddoes is no mere imitator; in him one can discern essential kinship of soul with the darkest of the Elizabethans; he is a reincarnation of Webster[3]. There is no parallel during the century to the grimly grotesque strength of imagination, the great clashing epithets, the "storm and wildness" of his masterpiece, *Death's Jest-Book*.[4] It never has been, nor can ever be, popular, but by the few it will always be appreciated. It is a product of the Renascence of Wonder. There are examples of such work in Poe, *The Masque of the Red Death* for instance; and in France, in such a poem as *Une Charogne*[5] Baudelaire got a somewhat similar effect. Though more Websterian than Webster[6], Beddoes disapproved of the

---

[1] "Hazlitt first suggested the story as suitable for stage treatment" (*Works of Lord Tennyson* VI, 539). See further on Procter, Genest, IX, 102; *Letters of the Wordsworth Family*, ed. Knight, II, 145.

[2] The Elizabethan Revival, which I have been able barely to outline, is worthy of careful investigation.

[3] See Henry Wood, "T. L. Beddoes, A Survival in Style," *Am. Jour. Phil.* IV, 445 f.

[4] *The Poetical Works of Thomas Lovell Beddoes*, ed. Edmund Gosse, 1894, II, 1 f. *The Poems of Thomas Lovell Beddoes*, ed. Ramsay Colles, London, Routledge, 1906, p. 1 f. See also T. F. Kensall, "Thomas Lovell Beddoes", *Fortnightly Review*, new series, XII, 51 f., an article devoted almost exclusively to an analysis of *Death's Jest-Book*.

[5] *Les Fleurs du Mal*, éd. déf., Paris, Calmann-Lévy, p. 127.

[6] Beddoes has many of those succinctly sinister turns of thought which one associates with Webster. For example, recent graves, but six feet under earth, are called "the very garrets of death's town" (II, iii); the earth is called "this grave-paved star" (II. iii); ivy is "that creeping darkness" (III, iii); night is the time when

> "half mankind
> Lie quiet in earth's shade and rehearse death" (III, iii).

current imitations of the old dramatists. "Say what you will,"
he wrote[1], "I am convinced the man who is to awaken the
drama must be a bold trampling fellow — no creeper into
wormholes — no reviver even — however good. These reani-
mations are vampire-cold. Such ghosts as Marloe — Webster,
etc., are better dramatists, better poets, I dare say, than any
contemporary of ours — but they are ghosts — the worm is in
their pages. . . . With the greatest reverence for all the
antiquities of the drama, I still think that we had better beget
than revive — attempt to give the literature of this age an
idiosyncrasy and spirit of its own and only raise a ghost to
gaze on, not to live with — just now the drama is a haunted
ruin." In the preface to *The Bride's Tragedy*[2] he writes, "The
Muses . . . have almost deserted the public haunt, and England can hardly boast of anything that deserves to be called
a national stage."

Beddoes' fellows are of less importance and may be dismissed with a few words. George Darley's beautiful *Sylvia,
or the May Queen,*[3] modeled on Fletcher's *Faithful Shepherdess*
and reminiscent of Shakespeare's fairies and of *Comus*, is, with
the possible exception of Hood's *Plea of the Mid-Summer Fairies*,
the best modern effort to fulfil the land once more with "fay-
erye". In *Thomas à Becket*[4] and *Ethelstan*[5] he experimented
rather unsuccessfully in the chronicle play. He is a disciple
of Shakespeare and Fletcher, as Beddoes is of Webster. The
influence of Marlowe is apparent in the eastern pomp, the
gorgeous language, and the titanic conception of Wells' *Joseph
and his Brethren.*[6]

I have now traced to its consummation this important
element in the Romantic drama. It is the very antithesis of
Byron's plays, yet like them it is a movement of reform. And

---

[1] *The Letters of Thomas Lovell Beddoes*, ed. Edmund Gosse, London,
Elkin Mathews and John Lane, 1894, p. 50 f.

[2] *Poems*, ed. Colles, p. 455.

[3] *Poetical Works of George Darley*, ed. Ramsay Colles, London, Routledge, p. 81 f.

[4] *Ibid.* p. 207. Mr. Colles owns a copy of the play given by Darley to
Tennyson, but I have observed no indebtedness in *Becket* to *Thomas à Becket*.

[5] *Ibid.* p. 325 f.

[6] Charles Wells, *Joseph and his Brethren*, London, Frowde, 1908.

it was in harmony, as Byron's foreign theories never were, with the instincts of the British people. The modern poetic drama, if it is to exist at all, must fuse these tendencies, must have something of the classic strength, restraint, and regularity of design, which were the ideals of Byron in his dramatic experiments, and something of the wealth of imaginative poetry, which was apparently beyond his grasp but which alone, as in the case of Beddoes, will not result in great drama.

The closet drama, as stated above, was of increasing importance during the Romantic period. Several of the plays already considered were either not intended for the stage or unsuccessful thereon. Others, now to be mentioned, come under the class rather of "dramatic poems" than of real dramas. *Count Julian*[1] was apparently the only one of Landor's dramatic pieces that came under Byron's notice[2]. Landor himself noted that his "poems in dramatic form" were "no better than *Imaginary Conversations* in metre."[3] *Count Julian* has almost as much obscurity as *Gebir,* the result of a desire to attain an absolute austerity of diction, a classical restraint pushed to its furthest bounds. The reader must have previous knowledge of the story; that requisite complied with, it is possible to admire the subtle delineation of character expressed in compact and polished verse. But most people knew, and know, nothing of

> "The Father by whose wrong revenged, his land
> Was given for sword and fire to desolate."[4]

The appeal of *Count Julian,* as of almost all Landor's poetry, is therefore very limited. It represents the extreme of the reaction from the stage; the closet drama has wandered so far from its source as to cease to be drama at all.

In the preface to *Marino Faliero* (P. IV, 388), Byron wrote, "There is dramatic power somewhere, where Joanna Baillie,

---

[1] *The Works of Walter Savage Landor,* 1853, II, 503 f.

[2] Bryon's only reference to the play (omitted through an oversight from Mr. Coleridge's Index) occurs in a note to the last line of the Dedication of *Don Juan,* P. VI, 9.

[3] *Works,* p. 503.

[4] Swinburne, *Song for the Centenary of Walter Savage Landor,* stanza 13, *Poems,* New York, Harper, 1904, V, 14.

and Milman, and John Wilson exist. *The City of the Plague* and *The Fall of Jerusalem* are full of the best 'matériel' for tragedy that has been seen since Horace Walpole, except passages of *Ethwald* and *De Montfort*." I have touched on all these plays except John Wilson's *City of the Plague*[1]. This pathetic and beautiful poem, though full of genuine tragic feeling, is hardly a real drama. There is no development of character or situation, no progressive action, no protagonist, no catastrophe. It is a succession of historical scenes portraying incidents of the great pest. Two naval officers, Frankfort and Wilmot, come to London to seek the former's mother. She is found dead already. Magdelene, Frankfort's betrothed, is discovered in the city, a ministering angel to the dying and bereaved. The two lovers meet only to die together and to receive quiet burial at the hands of the faithful Wilmot and an aged priest. Despair in all its forms is portrayed, seeking distraction in the prophecies of an astrologer, or in impious revels, or in the crowded streets, or in the sight of the terrible pit; while brightly against the dark London streets and churchyards there shine far-off glimpses of Magdelene's home, the hills and lakes of Westmoreland. The piece lacks inspiration; the imagination seems forced; it does not strike to the roots of terror or of love. Yet as a tribute to self-sacrifice it is a worthy performance, far from deserving the oblivion that has overtaken it. Byron commended it because of its choice of an historical subject, its lack of exaggeration in spite of a theme which lent itself easily to fantastic treatment, its careful composition, and its unsuitability for the stage.

---

[1] *The Works of Professor Wilson ... edited by Professor Ferrier,* 1858, XII, 75 f. *The City of the Plague* is founded upon Defoe's *History of the Plague,* though the chief characters have no analogues in the source. The incidents of the play — the astrologer, the revels, the portents in the skies, such as the line of hearses seen along the clouds, the lunatics running through the streets and sometimes jumping into the pit, the ghosts in the churchyards, the special horror of the Aldgate pit — these and other scenes are found in Defoe's crowded narrative. But the poet has not improved upon his original; the *History* remains the more terrible and the more impressive description of the pest, equaled, if at all, in English (for I leave aside Thucydides and Boccaccio), only by the narrative of the Naples plague in *John Inglesant.*

It is difficult to classify the plays of Sir Walter Scott since he made experiments in nearly every *genre*. His dramas are the least notable part of his achievement, but are not absolutely negligible. Byron must have known of the existence of some of them, but they made no impression on him. Scott's first experiment in dramatic form was a translation of Goethe's *Götz von Berlichingen* (1799), followed the same year by *The House of Aspen*, a prose drama strongly influenced by Goethe and following the traditional methods of the terrific school. At this time, be it remembered, Scott was associated with M. G. Lewis and almost in the position of a disciple. But in December, 1801, he wrote[1], "*The Plays of the Passions* have put me entirely out of conceit with my Germanized brat; and should I ever again attempt dramatic composition, I would endeavour after the genuine old English model." Nevertheless his next attempt was "after" no genuine model of any kind, but was a frankly "illegitimate" composition[2]; *The Doom of Devorgoil*[3] is a melodrama with serio-comic goblins and other supernatural accessories, and the usual accompaniment of songs. It lay for long in manuscript, till, in 1826, it occurred to Scott that "the goblin drama" might be published to help his creditors[4]. It is quite worthless. *Halidon Hill* (1822) was written for a miscellany edited by Joanna Baillie, but when found too long for that purpose, was offered to Constable, .who gave Scott a thousand pounds for it. More than any of the other plays it shows what Scott might have done in this line, with care and time and training.[5] It is a clearly drawn historical sketch, full of stirring sentiments and rapid movement. *Mac-*

---

[1] J. G. Lockhart, *Life of Scott*, London, J. B. Millet Co., II, 63.

[2] The "melo-drama", a new form of dramatic entertainment, was introduced into England from France. It was a medley of dialogue and music, with themes varying from farce to tragedy with more than Elizabethan license. Tales of adventure (many taken from Scott), of terror, and of mystery were drawn upon for materials. The *genre* is of negative importance in this study in that more than anything else it disgusted Byron with the English stage (Cf. LJ. II, 350).

[3] *The Complete Poetical Works of Sir Walter Scott*, ed. J. L. Robertson, London, Frowde, 1894, vol. V. (Contains the four poetical dramas.)

[4] Lockhart, VIII, 193.

[5] Cf. Thorndike, p. 350.

duff's Cross is the dramatization of but a single incident, to
supply the promised contribution to Miss Baillie's collection.
Finally, *Auchindrane*, a composition which Lockhart (IX, 297)
considered "far superior to any of his previous attempts of that
nature", was written in 1830. It is a tale of domestic tragedy and persecution and belongs in the same general class
with *Werner*.

The works of two men must now receive a passing glance,
not for their own merits but because of their connection with
Byron. The Rev. George Croly (the "very Reverend Rowley
Powley" of *Don Juan* XI, 57) was one of Byron's earliest and
most successful imitators, and in turn seems to have in a
slight degree influenced Byron[1]. A reference to "Cambyses'
roaring Romans" in *Don Juan* (XI, 58) is an indication that
Byron had read Croly's one play, *Catiline*[2], a version of his
conspiracy and death infinitely inferior to Ben Jonson's, to
which, however, it owes little, though the debt to Shakespeare
is great[3]. It follows Byron in its exaltation of liberty and
curious mixture of aristocratic and democratic sentiments, but
it is of little consequence. And of even less note is the work of
William Sotheby. In 1814 he published *Five Tragedies*, of
which Byron thought *Orestes* the best[4]. He wrote cordially to
Sotheby several times, and through his influence *Ivan* was accepted at Drury Lane. Genest (X, 233) says, "Some parts of
this T[ragedy] are well written, but on the whole it is an indifferent play — it was rehearsed 3 or 4 times at Drury Lane,
but laid aside, as Kean said he could make nothing of the
character of Ivan — Kean was right". Byron expressed regret
at this *impasse* and, when Maturin's *Manuel* failed, he wrote

---

[1] S. C. Chew, Jr. "Byron and Croly", *Modern Lang. Notes* XXVIII, 201 f.

[2] *Poetical Works of Rev. George Croly*, London, n. d., II, 1 f.

[3] Especially to *Julius Caesar*. Catiline is incited to the conspiracy by
means of a letter sent anonymously; like Brutus he walks in his garden; his
wife is a crude copy of Portia; prodigies are seen in the sky before the rebellion breaks out; two of the rebel leaders quarrel before a battle in which
they are defeated; the mob is like those in Shakespeare's Roman plays.

[4]   "Sotheby, with his damned *Orestes*,
      (Which, by the way, the old Bore's best is)" (LJ. IV, 159).
This couplet is given differently in the *Jeu d'Esprit* (P. VII, 48), and in a
third version by Mr. Prothero (LJ. III, 62, note 1).

(LJ. IV, 95), "The failure of poor M's play will be a cordial to the aged heart of Saul[1] who has been 'kicking against the pricks' of the managers so long and so vainly — they ought to act his *Ivan*." He told Rogers (LJ. IV, 97) that Sotheby "was capriciously and evilly entreated by the Sub-Committee about poor dear *Ivan*, whose lot can only be paralleled by that of his original — I don't mean the author, who is anything but original."

Finally, two dramatists who won notable success upon the stage must be mentioned. Throughout the period those plays which were most successful on the stage are historically of least importance. They were purely ephemeral. Only one thoroughly successful playwright even approaches the domain of letters. This is J. S. Sheridan Knowles. His most important play was *Virginius*[2], which owes much to Webster's *Appius and Virginia*, though it suffers in comparison with it[3]. His plays are chiefly on classical or historical subjects. It is of interest to note why a man of mediocre taste and little poetic ability prospered on the stage where men greatly his superiors had failed. This was due, in the first place, to his practical acquaintance with the theatre. He had been an actor and knew at first hand the requirements of the stage. Moreover Knowles centred his interest in common emotions. In the third and fourth decades of the century the fervor of Romanticism was on the wane and the desire for the portrayal of extra-ordinary passions was not so strong as the appeal to what Horne[4] called the "domestic feeling", which was part of the spirit of the age and which increased in strength during the mid-Victorian period. Here the simplicity and lack of subtlety in the work of Knowles acted in his favor. He was a mean between the superficialities and rant of stage hacks on the one hand, and the nice psychology and metaphysics of the closet dramatists on the other.

---

[1] Sotheby, the allusion being to his poem *Saul*.

[2] *Dramatic Works*, London, 1856, I, 59 f.

[3] See H. B. Baker, *The London Stage: Its History and Traditions*, London, W. H. Allen and Co., 1889, I, 226 f.

[4] R. H. Horne, *A New Spirit of the Age*, London, Frowde, 1907, p. 304.

R. L. Sheil is the same type of writer. His *Evadne*[1] shows
a like dependence upon a Jacobean model (Shirley's *The Traitor*)
and a like familiarity with the stage. Both Knowles and Sheil
point forward to the later successes of Bulwer-Lytton.

From the consideration of all the foregoing dramas and
dramatists some general conclusions shall now be attempted;
and such as are arrived at shall be applied specifically to the
dramas of Byron.

At the beginning of the last century a new audience had
been attracted to the theatres. Till then the low classes had
generally preferred more "manly" amusements — prize-fighting,
cock-fighting, and the like; and the theatres had appealed to
a more educated public. But as the lower orders became less
blind and brutal the managers found it profitable to cater to
their tastes, and the standard of theatrical productions inevitably deteriorated. But the typical stage plays carried the seed
of their own destruction. The craze of one decade became
the laughing-stock of the next; "Monk" Lewis parodied his
own style, and Genest (IX, 318) records a farce called *The
Sorrows of Werter, or Love, Liquor and Lunacy*.

The stage of Byron's time did not reflect the varying
emotions of the period. At a time of general social unrest,
when the Tories were sowing the wind to reap the whirlwind
of 1832, with agitation caused by the Union, by legislation
against Roman Catholics, by the economic revolution and labor
unrest, by a restricted and unfair suffrage, by the spectacle
of Napoleon dominating Europe and threatening to engulf England — at such a time the theatre offered German sentimentality, French flippancy, and native sensationalism. One looks
in vain for that sense of national pride and power which is
the glory of the Elizabethan drama. The sense was not wanting
in England, but it found expression in the *Waverly Novels* and
in the *Sonnets dedicated to National Independence and Liberty*.
In it the theatre had no share.

The experiments in dramatic composition made by the
poets of the age, while but a small appendage to the great

---

[1] Oxberry, *New English Drama* XIV. Cf. *Quart. Rev.* XXII, 407 f.

body of romantic poetry, are more nearly in touch with the time-spirit and more nearly worthy of the traditions of the past. A number of characteristics both as to substance and technique stand out clearly.

"There is", wrote Horne (p. 313), "manifestly the strongest tendency in the present age to be dramatic. . . . To go back no further than Byron, Southey, Shelley, Coleridge, the list includes almost every author eminent in works of imagination and invention." This is the first point to be noticed about the drama of the Romantic period. Every one of the great poets of the time made one or more essays in dramatic composition.

In this whole group of plays there is found, broadly speaking, some aspect or other of revolutionary thought. The demand for liberty was sweeping over Europe; the same movement that culminated in England in the Reform Bill was at the bottom of the long struggle for a constitutional Spain, a free Greece, and a free and united Italy. This aspiration is reflected in Southey's *Wat Tyler,* in Croly's *Catiline,* and in other plays; and especially in those of Lord Byron. Since for the most part the plays considered in this chapter assert the independence of the individual, it is significant of Byron's broadness of vision that in *Marino Faliero* he undertook to present in dramatic form the yearnings of an entire people for liberty. The contrast is seen, with the crudeness of a philosophical formula, in Godwin's dramas; it permeates the early attempts of Wordsworth, Coleridge, and Southey; it receives supreme artistic expression in *The Cenci* of Shelley. Pushed to an extreme it resulted in the crude license of *The Mysterious Mother,* and, when subjected to artistic control, in that philosophic defiance and trust in the self-sufficiency of the human intellect which is the central theme of *Manfred* and of *Cain.* Revolutionary thought, which, deriving from the French materialists, is the foundation of the most typical poetry of the age — *The Prelude, Childe Harold, Prometheus Unbound* — is the primary inspiration of the poetic drama.

This leads to a third point. Interest in the struggle of the peoples for freedom and social betterment makes for a choice of historical subjects. This is especially apparent in Byron; but it caused Scott to dramatize subjects from Scottish history, and in varying degree it influenced Landor, Southey, Shelley, Keats, Milman, Wilson, Croly, and others. This choice of themes was of course furthered by the traditions of the English chronicle play. Italian subjects were very popular, partly because of the example of many Elizabethan plays, partly because Italy was the abode of the chief of living poets, but mainly because of the inherent fascination of the country, which influenced Byron, Shelley, Milman, Croly, Procter, and others, and to which at a later date Landor, Browning, Swinburne and many more have paid their tribute of praise.

The poetic treatment of historic themes is in accord with the revival of interest in the Middle Ages, which is so striking a "note" of the time. Romanticism is all-powerful. The domestic themes that had been employed in a number of plays during the preceding century were quite ignored. None of the poets turned to ordinary, daily modern life for the subjects of their plays. Thus it happens that the poetic drama, though more serious than the stage-plays, was almost equally removed from life; it reflected, inadequately but not distortedly, the thought and aspirations of the age, but it did not afford a criticism of the life of the people. It was as far removed as possible from realism.

This is due, apart from the general tendency of the time, to the fact that the authors of these plays were poets in the first place, and only secondarily dramatists. The tremendous outburst of lyric poetry, intense in its individualism, stunted the growth of the drama. Hardly a poet of the time had any of the objectivity and aloofness of the supreme dramatists. This personal and lyric element, very noticeable in Byron's plays and of frequent occurrence elsewhere, accounts for the chief difference between the attitude of the romantic dramatists and that of their Elizabethan brethren. There is a substitution of spiritual for external action, an increasing interest in the psychology of situation, a growing inattention to mere plot, a new and (judging by old standards) disproportionate insistence upon motive. This is illustrated by Miss Baillie, Coleridge, and others; and especially by Byron. It reaches its climax in Browning's dramas. In *Luria*, for example, there is a minute examination and revelation of every thought and impulse from the moment of its birth, and this in the character, not only of the protagonist but of each lesser person, as his or her deeds affect the significance of the spiritual motive which is behind the mere act.

The individualism, romanticism, and lyrism of these plays are all subordinate to a fourth characteristic. The escape from the world of reality, resulting in the selection of themes often far removed from common sympathy and interest, is a defect inherent in the great inspiration of the period — its idealism, whether expressed in Wordsworthian nature-worship, or Shelley-ian visions of a golden age, or in Byron's practical encouragement and aid extended to actual revolutionaries. Directly from this idealism comes one of the great defects of the romantic drama — its absolute lack of humour. In this respect Shelley is typical. "Humour", it has been well said, "is the joyful acceptance of human imperfections". Such acceptance is never characteristic of the reformer and revolutionary zealot. Humour is always the possession of the conservative element, which seeks in it a weapon against the encroachment of new ideas. The humour of *Beppo* and *Don Juan* and Byron's matchless letters is entirely lacking in his plays[1]; there is not a trace of it in the dramas of Coleridge and Shelley; even Lamb left it behind him, save in feeble imitation of Shakespeare, when he wrote his dramas.

Some of these writers made experiments along different lines of dramatic theory. Miss Baillie's design to illustrate the various passions in a series of plays was, she thought, quite original. Byron attempted to found a "national drama" on the French and Italian model and broke away from English tradition. Shelley's desire was to adapt the Elizabethan model to the requirements of his own day. Scott and others planned a compromise between poetry and the stage. Of all these theories Shelley's was the only one that resulted in a drama of first rank; had he lived, it is not easy to set a limit to what he might have accomplished in restoring the English drama to the dignity of its heritage. This preoccupation with

---

[1] There is but one character in the whole group intended to be humourous (Idenstein in *Werner*) and that is a complete failure.

dramaturgic theory was accompanied by an almost utter lack of experience in stage-craft and of knowledge of technique. The writers of the Romantic drama were amateurs. Hence their enthusiasm for new theories. Hence their openness to influences. Hence the frequently faulty construction of their plays. Byron is a case in point. The partial failure of his dramatic exercises is due largely to lack of purely technical training. He and his fellow writers were further hampered by that devotion to introspection and philosophy which I have noted as one of the characteristics of these dramas. This played havoc with the construction of many of their pieces. The action is halted through long dialogues and soliloquies while the niceties of motive are discussed. Almost always the interest of the poet is obviously in the sentiments more than in the plot.

Byron's dramas can be understood properly only if they are placed in their true light with regard to the other plays of the period. They are closet dramas, never intended for the stage; they are written in accordance with a special theory of dramatic art; they express a revolt from contemporary fashions; they are concerned with the effect of situation on character rather than with the course of external incident; they are the work of a man who was poet first and dramatist afterwards; they show a lack of technical equipment; in them are found traces of various and divergent influences. Far from standing alone they are thus part of the general history of the English drama.

Chapter Two.
Byron and the Contemporary Drama.

The contemporary English stage exerted a great negative influence over Byron. I have described the chief current fashions of the drama, which I have attempted to illustrate by various plays, choosing for that purpose, wherever possible, those with which Byron was himself familiar. Disgust with the extreme license of romanticism was a leading cause, indeed, as I think, the greatest cause, of Byron's abandonment of that romanticism and reliance upon narrow laws in his attempt at the formation of a truly national drama, of a drama of which England should not be ashamed.

During his school and college days Byron attended the theatre with considerable frequency. Of such a visit there is a record in stanzas v and vi of the poem *On a Distant View of Harrow* (P. I, 26). He saw W. H. W. Betty, "the young Roscius," of whose mediocre abilities he made a correct estimate (LJ. I, 63), and in *English Bards* he exclaims "Thank Heaven! the Rosciomania's o'er" (l. 564)[1]. Frequent allusions show his familiarity with the popular farces of the day. Twice, in 1806 and 1808, he took part in private theatricals at Southwell, for the earlier of which performances he wrote an *Occasional Prologue* (P. I, 45), following the conventional type — the request for applause or at least indulgence. Years later he wrote (LJ. V, 445), "When I was a youth I was reckoned a good actor", and Medwin says (p. 134), "perhaps Lord Byron would have made the finest actor in the world." An eye-witness of the earlier of these private performances recorded the impression that Byron acted "inimitably."[2] When only thirteen he attempted to write a drama called *Ulric and Ilvina*, apparently on the the same theme as the later *Werner*, which he had "sense enough to burn" (P. V, 338).

Byron attacked the drama in his first satire (ll. 560 f.), where he deplores "the degradation of our vaunted stage." The specific nature of the criticism shows that the lines are founded upon observation. The chief *genres* then in fashion are referred to contemptuously — "the mummery of German schools;" translations from Kotzebue, especially Sheridan's *Pizarro;* farces displaying "buffoonery's mask"; imitations of Elizabethan tragedy; melodramas; and Lewis's "spectres". Byron laments the scanty appreciation of Shakespeare, Otway, and Massinger, and the loss of George Colman and Cumberland. He exhorts Sheridan to do something worthy of his powers:

"Give, as thy last memorial to the age,
One classic drama, and reform the stage" (ll. 584—5).

While in the East Byron wrote *Hints from Horace,* a kind of

---

[1] On Betty and the "mania" see Doran, III, chap. ix.
[2] Quoted by Mr. Prothero, LJ. I, 108, note.

supplement to *English Bards and Scotch Reviewers*. There are
in it several remarks in disparagement of the drama. In theatres
we can "dispense with common sense" and Wit is the one
thing *not* employed to raise a laugh (ll. 157—60). "Lewis's self,
with all his sprites" is derided, as is the taste for carnage
and ghosts, "French flippancy and German sentiment" (l. 454).
In this poem Byron introduces his earliest references to
dramatic principles. Violent action should not take place upon
the stage;

> "Many deeds preserved in History's page
> Are better told than acted on the stage;
> The ear sustains what shocks the timid eye,
> And Horror thus subsides to sympathy;
> True Briton all beside, I here am French" (ll. 267 f.).

Moreover there must be no action exceeding belief, for an
event may be an historical fact, yet dramatically impossible.
Pomposity and show at the expense of vitality and realism are
to be avoided. The theatre should instruct as well as amuse.
This is significant, for here are opinions developed early in life
that afterwards appear in the three historical plays. It was
evidently through no sudden caprice that Byron elected to
follow the classical model. The precepts are but echoes of
Horace (as the title acknowledges) and Boileau, but it is to be
remarked that already Byron took "hints" from them. There
is the germ of the dramatic theory later exemplified by the two
Venetian plays and *Sardanapalus*. The aim is in the direction
of truth to nature, decorum, and a higher moral purpose.

On his return from the East Byron took up his residence
in London. He was now a constant attendant at the theatre.[1]
The few criticisms of the stage contained in his letters of this
period are uniformly disparaging. "Good plays are scarce", he

---

[1]) Among the plays which he saw before the end of 1813 were: *Corio-
lanus, The Merry Wives of Windsor, Antony and Cleopatra, Richard III*,
and Rowe's *Fair Penitent;* various farces and comedies such as Colman's
Bluebeard; and at least one example of the style of melodrama founded on
Scott's novels and poems, — Morton's *Knight of Snowdoun*, a musical drama
taken from *The Lady of the Lake*. There are many references to other
dramatists and quotations from their works. A partial list of such includes
Congreve, Vanbrugh, Farquhar, Gay, Goldsmith, Foote, Rich; and of foreign
dramatists, Schiller *(The Robbers)*, Alfieri, and Monti.

writes in September, 1811 (LJ. II, 34), and speaks of "our stage in its present state" where the context shows that the reference is to the English lack of regularity. His next actual work in the drama was "a comedy of Goldoni's translated, one scene," which he sent to Dallas in September, 1811 (LJ. II, 43). This has disappeared. On October 12, 1812 Byron's *Address* was spoken at the opening of the new Drury Lane Theatre. There is in it no profound dramatic criticism, but there is the same disapproval of contemporary fashions upon the stage. Byron promises better things in the future: —

> "If e'er Frivolity had led to fame,
> And made us blush that you forebore to blame —
> If e'er the sinking stage[1] could condescend
> To soothe the sickly taste it dare not mend —
> All past reproach may present scenes refute,
> And censure, wisely loud, be justly mute" (ll. 56 f.).

The *Address* is not good verse, but it is a sincere attempt to point the way to a higher dramatic standard, to "Nature for our guide," to make "the Drama be where she hath been" (ll. 72 and 24). This composition brought Byron into close touch with Drury Lane and was a factor in the choice of him as a member of the Committee of Management two years afterwards.

In 1813—14 Byron had "a box at Covent Garden for the season" (LJ. II, 334). This was the time of the Byron furore; he was writing the Eastern Tales. It is not surprising, therefore, that some newspapers declared him to be the author of an anonymous spectacular Oriental melodrama, produced at Drury Lane in November, 1813, for the costumes of which he had furnished some drawings (LJ. II, 288). His comment upon this ascription was, "I wonder what they will next inflict upon me. They cannot well sink below melodrama" (LJ. II, 350)[2]. At this time he was actually at work upon a play. In his journal for November 14 we find, "This afternoon I have burnt the scenes of my commenced comedy" (LJ. II, 314), and three days later: "I began a comedy, but burnt it because the scene

---

[1] This phrase had already been employed in *Eng. Bards*, l. 734.

[2] Compare *The Devil's Drive*, stanza 26; P. VII, 33—34.

ran into *reality*; — a novel for the same reason. In rhyme I
can keep more away from facts" (LJ. II, 323). This last
sentence indicates that, following the mode, the comedy was
to be in prose, for —

> "Modest Comedy her verse foregoes
> For jest and pun in very middling prose." [1]

Another reason for its destruction may be found in the remark,
"A comedy I take to be the most difficult of compositions,
more so than tragedy" (LJ. II, 373). It is notable that at this
date Byron chose for dramatic treatment the *Ethos*, not the
Pathos, of life. Later he put his pictures of manners into
Don Juan and selected the tragic side of existence for dramatic
presentation. In 1814 he was urged by several friends to try
his hand at a tragedy. On January 22 he wrote to Murray,
"Before I left town Kemble paid me the compliment of desiring
me to write a *tragedy*; I wish I could, but I find my scribbling
mood subsiding" (LJ. III, 16). On February 20 he noted in
his journal, "I wish that I had a talent for the drama; I would
write a tragedy *now*" (LJ. II, 387). In an undated letter of
the same year he remarked to Moore, "As it is fitting there
should be good plays, now and then, besides Shakespeare's,
I wish you or Campbell would write one: — the rest of 'us youth'
have not heart enough" (LJ. III, 81). On July 23 Jeffrey wrote
of Byron to Moore, "I want him above all things to write a
tragedy"[2], upon which Byron's comment was, "Jeffrey does me
more than justice; but as to tragedy — um! — I have no time
for fiction at present" (LJ. III, 126).

Towards the end of 1814 Whitbread, the popular manager
of Drury Lane, committed suicide. The noblemen and gentlemen
who were financially interested in the theatre undertook "the
absurd and perilous step" of appointing a sub-committee to
manage the house. For three years these men, one of whom during
1815 was Lord Byron, "made experiments and amused themselves at the same time."[3] Byron was active and enthusiastic
in his share of the work, and considered the management

---

[1] *Hints from Horace*, ll. 121—2.

[2] Quoted by Mr. Prothero, LJ. III, 126, note.

[3] Percy Fitzgerald, *History of the English Stage*, London, Tinsley
Brothers, 1882, II, 384 f.

"really very good fun, as far as the daily and nightly stir of these strutters and fretters go" (LJ. III, 230). He was probably influenced in his decision to write a play by perusal of the tolerable and intolerable attempts that were submitted to the Committee. Long afterwards he told Medwin (p. 89), "When I first entered upon theatrical affairs I had some idea of writing for the house myself, but soon became a convert to Pope's opinion on that subject. Who would condescend to the drudgery of the stage, and enslave himself to the humours, the caprices, the taste or the tastelessness of the age?" Byron probably refers to a remark of Pope's in Spence's *Anecdotes*, which he himself quoted in a letter to Murray (LJ. V, 223): "I had taken such strong resolutions against anything of that kind, from seeing how much everybody that *did* write for the stage, was obliged to subject themselves to the players and the town." He may also have remembered lines 304—337 of the *Epistle to Augustus*. His "idea of writing for the house" went so far as the first draft of the first act of *Werner*, which was certainly at that time designed for the stage. Hoping to take advantage of the "opening for tragedy" (LJ. III, 191), Byron chose a theme suitable to the public taste. The "Gothic" setting in "a ruinous chateau on the Silesian frontier" and the period of the play, at the close of the Hundred Years' War, when Europe was infested with robber-bands of discharged soldiery, both link the play to the popular romantic drama. Ruin, storm, darkness, mystery, and misfortune are all huddled together in the first act. *Werner* avoids the extravagance of emotional horror, but it is in essentials of the school of terror. There are similarities in its elements with *Bertram,* which had recently passed through Byron's hands. The composition of *Werner* was interrupted by Byron's domestic difficulties. "I began that tragedy in 1815," he wrote later (LJ. V, 391), "but Lady Byron's farce put it out of my head for the time of her representation." When he left England the fragment was left behind and was not found until after his death. It is not strange that Byron should have commenced a play of this type in 1815; it *is* strange that after the composition of his classical dramas he should have turned again to the subject and treated it, though perhaps with more technical skill, in

all essentials as he would have finished it in 1815. The significance of *Werner* is that it is Byron's one essay in the popular
mode, his one effort to meet the stage half way.

"Self-exiled Harold wanders forth again." In Switzerland
the pressure of sorrow and remorse, the overwhelming presence
of the mountains and the sky, the crowding associations of
romantic scenery, and the companionship of Shelley combined
to open the flood-gates of lyrical, egotistical commentary upon
man and nature, in which there was nothing of the calm abstracted objectivity requisite for the drama. To this summer
belongs *Manfred*. It is distantly related to the school of terror,
but primarily it is an attempt to give objective expression to
intensely subjective emotion.

Byron's thorough opposition to the stage dates from the
time of his departure from England and is part of his increasing
dislike of all things English. His instinct for classical "regularity," of which more shall be said, was fostered by observation of the extravagance of the stage. From the horrible
he reacted to the heroic, from medieval and exotic settings to
historical, from utter lack of truth to nature to insistence upon
fact, from unrestrained wildness to an almost austere control,
from outworn and often unhealthy harpings upon love to study
of the problems of states. He frequently contrasts his conception of tragedy with that current upon the stage. Thus of
Marino Faliero he writes (LJ. V, 167), "It is too regular — the
time, twenty-four hours — the change of place not frequent
— nothing *melo*-dramatic — no surprises, no starts, nor trap-
doors, nor opportunities 'for tossing their heads and kicking
their heels' — and no *love* — the grand ingredient of a modern
play." And again (LJ. V,243), "There are neither rings, nor
mistakes, nor starts, nor outrageous ranting villains, nor melodrama in it." He speaks (LJ. V, 372) of "simplicity of plot
.... and the avoidance of rant." Upon the appearance of each
of his plays he repeats his disclaimer of any ambition for success upon the stage, and I, for one, see no reason to doubt
his sincerity [1]. Medwin and others also record this detestation

---

[1] The following are the chief references. P. IV, 337; P. V, 9 and
338; LJ. IV, 55, 71, and 137; LJ. V, 81, 167, 218, 221, 223; 228, 257, 295
and 304.

of writing for the stage. This attitude is succinctly expressed when he writes (LJ. V, 231), "I will never have anything to do willingly with the theatres."

In the autumn of 1816, on his way to Venice, Byron met at Milan the Italian dramatist Monti with whose works he was already acquainted. This meeting may, as Mr. Coleridge suggests, have stimulated his interest in the modern pseudo-classical Italian drama. He had been in Venice but a short time when he asked Murray to get Dr. Moore's "account of the *Doge Valiere*" transcribed for him, adding, "I mean to write a tragedy upon the subject which appears to me very dramatic" (LJ. IV, 59). But he for the time abandoned his intention, for there was little opportunity for such work in Venice. It required a complete change of surroundings to fit him for the concentrated effort of tragedy. This change came about in 1819 through his liaison with the Countess Guiccioli, by means of which, as Shelley testifies[1], Byron was "greatly improved in every respect." *Marino Faliero* advanced slowly and sometimes with discouragement, amid revolutionary plans and amatory troubles. That he was seriously essaying a new dramatic *genre* is shown by many passages in his letters. Thus (LJ. V, 218), "I am . . . fully persuaded that this [i. e. to "produce a great tragedy"] is not to be done by following the old dramatists, who are full of gross faults, pardoned only for the beauty of their language; but by writing naturally and *regularly*, and producing *regular* tragedies. . . . I have . . . tried a sketch in *Marino Faliero;* but many people think my talent *'essentially undramatic'*, and I am not at all sure that they are not right." Again he wrote (LJ. V, 347), "My dramatic simplicity is *studiously* Greek, and must continue so: *no* reform ever succeeded at first. I admire the old English dramatists; but this is quite another field, and has nothing to do with theirs. I want to make a *regular* English drama, no matter whether for the stage or not, which is not my object, — but a *mental* theatre."

Concrete examples were of more importance in Byron's mind than abstract theories. Of such examples the most in-

---

[1] *Letters* II, 893.

fluential were the plays of Alfieri. The Italian dramatist has, indeed, been considered by some critics as the chief cause of Byron's adoption of the classical form of drama, but this is, I think, to overestimate that influence.

Byron acquired early an acquaintance with Italian and he had not lost all command of it when he went to Italy in 1817. This previous knowledge is alluded to in various letters[1]. Moreover, it has been remarked, "wie sehr Byron auch sonst in gedanken bei den Italienern weilt, beweisen die vielen italienischen ausdrücke und citate, die sein tagebuch gerade damals aufzuweisen hat. . . . So waren denn Byron's italienische sprachkenntnisse, als er im Oktober 1816 nach Italien kam, schon ziemlich bedeutend."[2]

It were a work of supererogation to state in detail the indebtedness of Byron to the influence of Alfieri, since this has already been done by Anna Pudbres in her article "Lord Byron, the admirer and imitator of Alfieri."[3] I shall here give a summary of her results with certain restrictions, for I think she overestimates the "imitation" and even the "admiration." How, for example, would she account for the following remark, written during the composition of *Marino Faliero,* in which the influence of Alfieri is most marked? "The Italians have as yet *no tragedy* — Alfieri's are political dialogues, except *Mirra*" (LJ. V, 64).

Monti and Alfieri were mentioned in Byron's journal as early as February 20, 1814 (LJ. II, 388), when he contrasts them favourably with Schiller.[4] Alfieri's dramas are modeled upon those of Corneille and Racine. There are the simplicity of plot, the brevity of action (embracing hardly more than the catastrophe), the adherence to the unities, the lack of comic scenes, the abundance of rhetoric, and the general stateliness and monotony, which are characteristic of the French pseudo-classical drama. The marked contrast with the contemporary drama in England impressed Byron, and his admiration for the

---

[1] See, e g., LJ. I, 308 ("tolerably master of .... Italian").

[2] F. Maychrzak, "Lord Byron als übersetzer", *Engl. Stud.* XXI, 393. In this article the subsequent steps of Byron's mastery of Italian are traced.

[3] *Engl. Stud.* XXXIII, 40 f.

[4] See also Fuhrmann, p. 100.

Italian school is recorded in various letters. In *Childe Harold*
(LJ. IV, 54), he mentions Alfieri's among those ashes which
make holier the holy precincts of Santa Croce, and in a letter
(LJ. IV, 114), the tomb of Alfieri, along with those of Machia-
velli, Michael Angelo, and Galileo, is said to make Santa Croce
"the Westminster Abbey of Italy." His letters and journals,
and those of Moore and Hobhouse, record various visits to the
theatre and opera at Venice. On one occasion, at a performance of *Mirra*, he burst into tears (LJ. IV, 339). He was
similarly affected "a Ravenna ad una rappresentazione del
Filippo d'Alfieri."[1] The Countess Guiccioli, Lady Blessington,
and Medwin have recorded other instances of this admiration,[2]
an important cause of which was probably the recurring note
of the love of liberty in the writings of Alfieri.

It is going too far, however, to regard Byron as the "disciple" and Alfieri as the "master."[3] . Pudbres (p. 48 f.) shows
that *La Congiura de Pazzi* served in some degree as the model
of *Marino Faliero*, but the resemblance of the plot of the latter
play to Otway's *Venice Preserved* is even closer, and the parallelisms in structure to Alfieri's play are chiefly such as
would naturally occur between plays on kindred subjects following the lines of the regular drama. In the simplicity of diction,
amounting to baldness, which distinguishes *Marino Faliero* from
Byron's other dramas, there is clearer evidence of the influence
of Alfieri's austere style, but the excess of sheer rhetoric in
both dramatists is a characteristic of all pseudo-classical plays
and derives from the French tragedians and through them
from Seneca. It is folly to attempt to find in Alfieri the
original of the peculiarities of Byron's metre. Such as they
are, and in them there is nothing very striking, they have
abundant English prototypes.

Alfieri's direct influence upon *Sardanapalus* was very slight
Pudbres finds evidence of borrowings from *Filippo*, the character of Myrrha resembling that of Isabella, and of Sardanapalus that of Carlo; but the traditional autobiographical inter-

---

[1] LJ. IV, 339, note, quoting from the Countess Guiccioli.
[2] See Pudbres, p. 42—45.
[3] Cf. Pudbres, *passim*.

pretation of Myrrha as the Countess Guiccioli and Sardanapalus as Byron himself seems to me more nearly correct.
Alfieri may have furnished hints. The name Myrrha was
probably suggested by *Mirra*. Compare, however, Ruskin's
suggestion[1], "Perhaps some even of the attentive readers of
Byron may not have observed the choice of the three names
— Myrrha (bitter incense), Marina (sea lady), Angiolina (little
angel) — in relation to the plots of the three plays." This is
pretty, but fanciful. .

Finally it may be noted that *The Two Foscari* shows no
traces of direct borrowing from Alfieri. Byron's indebtedness
is, then, rather for inspiration than for direct assistance.

Sardanapalus, *The Two Foscari*, and *Cain* followed rapidly
between January and September, 1821. The two former are
further exercises in the regular drama; the last stands apart
and nearer *Manfred*. *Heaven and Earth* is a sequel to *Cain*.
The roughly dramatic form in which these two pieces are cast
shows that the fascination of the drama had not passed, yet
is a token of the reaction from the severe restraint that Byron
had previously imposed upon himself. This reaction goes
further in *Werner*, which Byron now took up once more and
completed along the lines of the Romantic drama.

The Deformed Transformed, which brings to a close the
series of plays, is a formless, chaotic piece, of slight value, in
which it is apparent that Byron had left behind him the desire for classical form and restraint, and was discontented with
the drama as a medium of expression. By this time he had
fully "found himself" and was devoting his energies to his
greatest work — *Don Juan*.

This survey of Byron's development as a dramatist has,
I think, made clear how logical was his advocacy of the "regular" drama. It was a reaction from extravagance and form-
lessness. Away from England, that reaction gradually lost
force, and he wrote first a play in the Romantic manner, then
a semi-dramatic piece, and then ceased writing dramas altogether. The course of this development can well be illustrated
by a diagram, as follows.

---

[1] *Fiction, Fair and Foul*, Library ed. of Works, ed. E. T. Cook and
Alex. Wedderburn, London, Allen, 1903 f., XXXIV, 362, note.

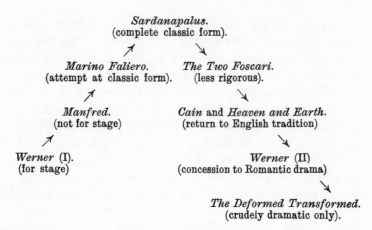

Sardanapalus.
(complete classic form).

Marino Faliero.
(attempt at classic form).

The Two Foscari.
(less rigorous).

Manfred.
(not for stage)

Cain and *Heaven and Earth.*
(return to English tradition)

Werner (I).
(for stage)

Werner (II)
(concession to Romantic drama)

The Deformed Transformed.
(crudely dramatic only).

Chapter Three.
Technique.

Byron's plays are weakest on the technical side. Of this he was probably himself aware. The fact that they violate various principles of technique is a partial explanation of their small vogue at the time of their publication and of the generally low estimate in which they are held. An examination of their technique is therefore instructive for the formation of a correct estimate of the faults and merits of the plays.

The beginning of the struggle in which the will of the protagonist is engaged with an opposing force, must take place either within the confines of the drama itself, or at some time previous to the opening scene. Divergence in this matter sharply differentiates the classical from the romantic drama. In Shakespeare the actual beginning of the conflict is presented in the play. Thus, in *Romeo and Juliet* it does not arise until Romeo, a Montague, falls in love with Juliet, a Capulet. The very moment is indicated by Juliet's words, "My only love born of my only hate." There is shown not merely the clash and result, but the inception and growth, of opposition.

In the "regular" drama, concomitant with the limitation of time, is the almost invariable exclusion from the drama of the beginning of the external conflict. This is one of the great restrictions of the classical model, which cannot portray the causes, in their inception and development, as well as the consequences, of the struggle. In general it may be said that classical tragedy commences at a point immediately before the crisis and thence sweeps down vehemently to the catastrophe. This is the method which Byron employs in his historical plays. All three open with the opposing forces already arrayed. In *Marino Faliero*, had the plot been of Shakespeare's handling, one can imagine an opening scene in which Steno would have been shown scratching his wanton insult upon the wall and revealing incidentally adequate reasons for so doing. This would have been followed by the discovery of the inscription by Faliero. "We cannot but believe," wrote an early critic,[1] "that, if the story of Faliero . . . had fallen into the hands of the barbarian Shakespeare, the commencement of the play would have been placed considerably earlier, that time would have been given for the gradual development of those strong lines of character, which were to decide the fate of the hero," etc. Westenholz[2] signalizes as the greatest flaw in the play "die unklarheit, in welcher wir über die speciellen ursachen der verschwörung, der ja auch der Doge nur beitritt, verbleiben. Wir sehen nichts von den angeblich durch die aristokraten ausgeübten grausamkeiten, und was vollends den Bertram, welchem seine kameraden schon von vornherein 'um seiner sanftmut, nicht seines mangels an treue willen' misstrauen, bewogen hat, dem blutigen und gefährlichen unternehmen sich anzuschliessen, das begreifen wir am allerwenigsten." Had Byron constructed *Sardanapalus* along the lines of English tragedy there might have been an opening scene in which would have been depicted the court of Nineveh darkened only by a distant cloud of discontent; this followed by the representation of Arbaces and Beleses in conference, planning their conspiracy and revealing their motives in undertaking it. But in the play as designed by Byron these events had to be presupposed, and knowledge of them conveyed to the audience[3] in the exposition. So also in *The Two Foscari* the action be-

---

[1] *Quarterly Review*, XXXII, 488.

[2] *Über Byrons historische Dramen*, Stuttgart, 1890, p. 19.

[3] The word "audience" is used purely conventionally and interchangeably with "reader".

gins in the last stages of the conflict.[1] Even in *Werner* the hero has lost his birth-right and been driven from home years before the opening of the play. There is thus at the commencement of Byron's plays a strong obstacle to their success. Readers are asked to interest themselves in the final stages of the fortunes of people with whom they have had no previous acquaintance. This is a serious demand upon patient attention. It results primarily from obedience to the unities,[2] which requires the rejection of all save the last and most indispensable periods of development. This was a reasonable demand upon the Greek audience, for classical tragedy had for subjects myths known to all. The story being familiar, the audience willingly dispensed with the earlier portions and watched the climax and catastrophe. Not so with Byron; his three tragedies upon historical subjects dealt with the fortunes of persons of whom many Englishmen had never heard. It was therefore his duty to cultivate an interest in the character of the protagonist by the gradual development of the tragic situation and the gradual unfolding of the elements of his characters. Instead of so doing, Byron hurls his reader not merely *in medias res* but into the very conclusion of the whole matter. He thus gains that compactness which he sought so anxiously, but he loses more than he gains. He risks the interest of all readers. Of this difficulty he must have been partially aware, for of *Marino Faliero* he wrote, "Recollect that, without previously reading the *Chronicle*, it is difficult to understand the tragedy. So, translate. I had this reprinted separately on purpose" (LJ. V, 62). This is an admission of inadequate technique. A drama ought not to depend upon explanatory extracts from sources. It should be independent of all externals, perfect and entire within itself.

The first part of a drama — the "introduction" or "exposition" — must convey information of events preceding the opening of the play, knowledge of which is needed for an understanding of the situation. It may also be a sort of prelude, serving to indicate the tone of the piece, somewhat as does the "Vorspiel" to an opera. In its primary capacity it is of greater importance in the "regular" drama than in Shake-

---

[1] Cf. *Quarterly Review* XXVII, 506.

[2] See Appendix I.

speare, since there is more information to be conveyed. This may be imparted in various ways: by a prologue more or less disconnected from the actual drama, by a soliloquy delivered by one of the *dramatis personae*, or by dialogue. Of these the second and third methods, and perhaps the first, are employed by Byron.

The prologue-opening developed along several lines in the English drama.[1] The simplest form was the presentation in concise form of the entire course of the action, as in *Romeo and Juliet*, the opening chorus of which is entirely independent of the exposition which follows in the opening scenes. Such a prologue is related to the dumb-show which precedes the spoken play-within-the-play in *Hamlet*. For the most part, however, the Elizabethan prologue became more and more separated from the action, and resolved itself into an address of the poet to the audience, containing greetings and imploring a hearing. Of this type the great opening chorus of *Henry V* is representative. In later times the prologue became increasingly "occasional" and is to-day retained only for special events and gala performances.[2] Of this type is Byron's *Address for the Opening of Drury Lane*, recited in October, 1812, at the first performance in the new theatre.

Though an example of this kind of prologue is numbered among his works, Byron's dramas have none such. But closely connected with the earlier form of the prologue, in which the purpose is to convey information, is the opening soliloquy wherein one of the characters, meditating upon the course of events, imparts knowledge of the state of affairs. The danger of this method is that an audience will not willingly accept a long opening recitative. Shakespeare employs is but once, and then challenges attention by putting the lines into the mouth of the protagonist himself, Richard III, a character in whom the audience is already interested. Byron uses the device twice. In *Manfred*, largely monologue and only pseudo-dramatic, it is the natural way of bringing the reader into

---

[1] See *A Study of the Prologue and Epilogue in English Literature*, by G. S. B., 1884.

[2] A recent example is the prologue written by Mr. Owen Seaman and delivered by Mr. Forbes-Robertson at the royal performance in Coronation Week, 1911.

touch with the situation. Here he had, moreover, the authority
of Goethe. The opening scene of *Sardanapalus* cannot be so
justified. The long soliloquy of Salamenes contains no information that could not be, and hardly any that is not, given in
the following dialogue-scene. Byron had in view a definite dramatic principle and evidently regarded this initial soliloquy as but
half distinct from a prologue directed to the audience and closely
related to the Chorus of *Romeo and Juliet,* which surveys the situation yet tells nothing that is not more fully imparted in the
following expository scenes. This is the "Euripidean" opening.
Confirmation of this view is given by a slight fact to which
attention has not been called. At the conclusion of the soliloquy the entrance of Sardanapalus and his train is marked
"Scene II", after the classical French fashion of numbering
according to important entrances and exits. But throughout
the rest of the play, and in his other regular dramas, Byron
fails so to number the scenes. He seems therefore to have
regarded this soliloquy as a thing apart, and consequently
marked it off from what follows in much the same manner as
the prologues are marked off in Plautus.

Artistic exposition is generally best attained by means
of dialogue. In Shakespearean drama it is almost always
employed, and is often combined with action. The cry "Down
with the Capulets! down with the Montagues!" is heard from
the midst of an exciting brawl, and exposes with the utmost
conciseness the background of the coming conflict. Shakespeare
thus presents "the introduction of his action as an organic
part of the action itself," taking "the spectators *in medias res,*
while he is really building the foundation of his plot."[1] Byron
never reaches such heights of dramatic art. His method is
rather akin to that used in *A Comedy of Errors,* before Shakespeare was a master of technique, and in *The Tempest,* when he
could afford to be careless of such externals. The speeches of Aeg-
eon and Prospero are obviously directed as much to the audience
as to the Duke and Miranda respectively. Byron seldom entirely escapes this difficulty, and he is shadowed by that bane of the
French development of the dialogue-opening, — the *confidant.*

---

[1] A. W. Ward, art. "Drama," *Encyc. Brit.*, 11th. ed., VIII, 477. See
further A. C. Bradley, *Shakespearean Tragedy*, London, Macmillan, 1908, p. 43.

With this preliminary review of expository methods, I proceed to an examination of Byron's expositions in the individual plays, taking them up in chronological order.

Manfred opens with a soliloquy, justified by the all-important character of the protagonist, by the precedent of the English and German *Faust,* and by its service as a key-note, indicating the "Stimmung" of the piece. The essential factors of the situation — sin, loss, and grief, the quest of knowledge and forgetfulness, and the search into the mysteries of life and death — are all alluded to in the opening speech, and while further light is later thrown upon Manfred's life and character, we are at once apprised of the information needed for an understanding of the situation. The simplicity of the action of the piece makes the exposition a matter of little difficulty. The early introduction of the supernatural serves, though in slighter degree, the same purpose as in *Macbeth* and *Hamlet,* viz., to give the proper tone-color and to excite the interest of the audience or reader.

In Byron's first complete drama, *Marino Faliero,* the exposition is accomplished with much skill. It is in dialogue form, and extends through two scenes. The first, a variant of the *confidant* type, presents two minor characters who speak of the "struggling patience" of the Doge, who is awaiting the verdict in the trial of a patrician. That patrician has insulted him, yet because of the privileges of rank, will probably escape serious punishment. Thus in twenty-nine lines the essential elements of the plot are set forth — the overwrought state of Faliero's mind and the boundless license of the aristocracy. At the same time suspense as to the issue of the trial stimulates the interest with which the reader awaits what is to follow. In the second scene the Doge is shown awaiting the result of the trial. With the paltry sentence imposed upon Steno, by which the Senate redoubles the original insult, the tragic conflict, the earlier steps of which do not come within the limits of the drama, reaches an acute stage, and the "rise" of the tragic actions begins.

The opening soliloquy of *Sardanapalus* combines exposition with tone-setting. The central idea of the drama is set forth in these lines:

"If born a peasant he had been a man
To have reached an empire: to an empire born,
He will bequeath none; nothing but a name" (I, i, 14 f.)

The contradictory elements of the king's character are indicated and the nature of the coming conflict is foreshadowed;
but were the entire speech removed and the play made to
begin with the second scene, the portion of the exposition
remaining would suffice to make the play entirely comprehen-
sible. The first scene is therefore a flaw in technique. Such
a recitative cannot but be tedious, and in this case involves
repetition which might well have been avoided.[1]

The exposition of *The Two Foscari* is practically identical
with that of *Marino Faliero*. The conflict has been growing
from a time long before the opening of the play, when we
come face to face with the individual in opposition to the
state. The simple situation is presented through the device
of dialogue between two characters, from which one learns
of the accusations of treason brought against the prisoner, of
the tortures to which he has been subjected, of the "Roman
fortitude" of the Doge who sits at the trial of his only son,
and of the "hereditary hate" of Loredano, who is bent upon
the ruin of the Foscari, and who is one of the speakers in
this expository dialogue — an arrangement which strengthens
the dramatic justification of this opening. Curiosity to see
Jacopo Foscari has in this way been stimulated, and just as
in *Marino Faliero*, when the needed information has been
given the protagonist is revealed, so here attention is promptly
centred upon the younger Foscari. His first words reveal
the motive that guides his conduct throughout the play. He
pays little heed to the words of Barbarigo, but says

"I'm faint;
Let me approach, I pray you, for a breath
Of air, yon window which o'erlooks the waters" (I, i, 86 f.)

As he stands at the window words of remembrance of other
times come to his lips; the very central fact of the entire

---

[1] A minor oversight is the failure to account for Salamenes' knowledge
of the conspiracy at the opening of the play. The king admits that he knows
nothing of how Salamenes came by this knowledge (I, ii, 461), but Byron
should not have left the reader in the same ignorance.

play is conveyed to the reader, not by dialogue or soliloquy, but in a way as simple and inevitable as Nature. A suffering man asks for air, and the sight of Venice, before him in her beauty, brings to his lips the inmost feelings of his soul. It is exposition *within* the action.

An advantage in the choice of subjects founded upon national history or legend, notable in the case of Greek tragedy and the Elizabethan chronicle-play, is that the dramatist may presuppose a certain familiarity on the part of the audience with the theme, and to that extent reduce and simplify the exposition. Byron did not have this advantage in his historical plays and suffered accordingly; but it is well illustrated by *Cain*. There the familiar story does away with the need of any exposition at all, save such as will serve to emphasize distinctions of character. This is accomplished by the opening prayers of Adam and his family (which also serve as a sort of prelude), and by the ensuing dialogue in which the character of Cain is sharply differentiated from the rest. Without further exposition the action then proceeds. *Heaven and Earth*, a dramatic episode only, has like simplicity of exposition; the disobedient love of the two sisters is shown first in dialogue and then by the action of the play.

Both versions of *Werner* employ the dialogue opening, but the more artistic form of this, in which it is carried on between minor characters, thus stimulating interest and expectancy, (e. g., *Antony and Cleopatra*, *Tartuffe*, *The Two Foscari*), is here impossible, since the situation requires that Werner and Josephine be alone. The objection thus arises that Werner recounts to his wife a whole series of events *of which she must be well aware*, but of which it is necessary that the audience be informed. Moreover these facts are set forth at intolerable length, and in one place Werner, speaking *solus*, i. e. meditating,[1] says, "— Kruitzer (such the name I then bore)" (I, i, 568), a fact of which he could have needed no reminder.

---

[1] The soliloquy is, of course. not "talking to oneself", but simply the one means afforded of giving dramatic expression to thought, and as such is a justifiable dramatic convention; though this clumsy way of getting within the mind of a character is a disadvantage of the drama as compared with the epic. When Byron employs it he does so almost always as a sym-

Finally, the exposition of *The Deformed Transformed* is accomplished by means of the action, which explains itself even while getting under way. The crudity of the plot makes the introductory portion very slight, and it is effected in a few lines.

The exposition of a drama is followed by the "rise" towards the climax. This "rise" is sometimes introduced by a brief transition, called the "exciting force" or stimulus. The initial complication commences when first, however obscurely, the protagonist feels that the expression of his individuality clashes with the general good, or rather, — since often he has, or thinks he has, the general good at heart, — with the pervading spirit of his surroundings. This animating force varies greatly in length, in prominence, and in position. It is of note chiefly in the Shakespearean drama, because in the classical mode the "exciting force" has often accomplished its purpose before the beginning of the play. It is sometimes present from the very beginning of the exposition. This is the case in *Richard III*, in which it is the villainy of the protagonist, well defined from the first, that precipitates the tragic conflict. So also in *Sardanapalus*, the self-indulgent ease of the king is the stimulus. In these examples the force is subjective, propelling from within the soul of the protagonist. In others it is objective; as when

bolical means of expressing unspoken thought, and frequently makes this purpose more clear by some reference to "thought," "musing," "meditation," "wrapt in devotions," etc. But where the soliloquy is used in exposition it carries with it an implication of spoken words; it is thus used by Byron only in the opening speech by Salamenes in *Sardanapalus* and in the passage from *Werner* quoted above. The number of monologues in each of Byron's plays, exclusive of brief "asides," is as follows: *Manfred*, 7; *Marino Faliero*, 6; *Sardanapalus*, 7; *The Two Foscari*, 2; *Cain*, 2; *Heaven and Earth*, 3; *Werner*, 8; *The Deformed Transformed*, 1. This enumeration may be compared with the number of soliloquies in a few typical plays, chosen at random: *Hamlet*, 9; *Othello*, 8; *The Duchess of Malfi*, 4; *The Borderers*, 6; *Queen Mary*, 6. The modern stage tends to avoid monologue. Freytag says *(The Technique of the Drama*, trans by E. J. MacEwan, Chicago, Scott, Foresman, [1894], p. 219), "The spectator cares little for the quiet expression of an individual; he prefers to gather for himself the connection and the contrasts of characters, from a dialogue." The best of Byron's soliloquies are not introduced to portray character, but as nature-poetry to afford dramatic relief. See, for example, *Manfred* I, ii; III, ii; III, iv; *Marino Faliero* IV, i; *Sardanapalus* Act II and Act IV.

the thought of killing Caesar is introduced into Brutus' mind, or when Iago tempts and deceives Othello. It is often a matter of gradual growth. Thus the wrongs done the state by the aristocracy have for long weighed upon the mind of Faliero. Yet often some one thing, slight in itself, *added to what has gone before*, becomes the actual exciting power that brings disaster. This is admirably illustrated by the insult offered by Steno to the Doge Faliero. Some critics have complained that the motivation of the play is too petty for tragedy. This is to miss the point. Faliero says:

> "A spark creates the flame — 'tis the last drop
> Which makes the cup run o'er, and mine was full
> Already" (V, i, 245 f.)

Steno's gibe is thus a perfect example of the "exciting force," in itself of little moment, yet fraught with consequence. Shakespeare would have put it at the conclusion of the exposition; Byron has imagined it occurring before the commencement of the play. Its full significance is thus lost, and we are left to gather from dialogue the relation that it bears to the real causes of the Doge's treason. Matters are worse in *The Two Foscari*. Given this theme as a subject for tragedy, he stimulus should obviously be that which should drive Jacopo Foscari, safe in exile, back to Venice and death. There are various possibilities; a rush of home-sickness, induced by the recurrence of some anniversary, or a meeting with some friend from Venice, or false tidings of the relaxation of persecution, etc. But Byron requires that the reader accept the situation and offers no adequate explanation. On the other hand the tragic force in *Cain* is clearly the suggestions by Lucifer of the acceptability of Abel's offerings to God (II, ii, 353). Jealousy is not the motive of the murder; but innuendoes incite Cain thereto.

The "rise" may be quite uniform and consistent; in some dramas it fluctuates, and this fluctuation is an added element of interest. In *Macbeth*, for example, there are alternate moments of doubt and resolution, during which honor and ambition are alternately in control. During this period of the action the fortunes of the *hero* are, on the whole, good. His individual will is making head against the universal norm, till it arrive at a point from whence it is swept down to destruction. But he must not experience unrelieved success during this period of growth. This would occasion two technical flaws; there would be a lack of that interest which change affords, and (what is more important) when at length the fortunes of the hero begin to decline, never to rise again, such a turn of the action would ill consort with previously unfluctuating success. Therefore there are usually a number of more or less clearly defined changes in the position of the hero. This, as an analysis will show, is admirably illustrated by *Sardanapalus*.

The speech of Salamenes with which the play opens shows the peril in which the king stands, and sense of this is increased by the sight of the slothful luxury in which he lives. The peril is made more dire by his refusal to cancel the midnight banquet in the pavilion. Then, at the entreaty of his loved mistress, he abandons this rash purpose. There is a corresponding rise in his fortunes. So ends the first act. The conference between the conspirators, manifesting their bravery and resourcefulness, now forces a sense of the rising of their star; but Balea appears and tells them that the feast is to be, not in the unprotected pavilion which they had planned to attack, but in the hall. This affords relief for concern as to Sardanapalus, which is increased by the arrest of the rebels by Salamanes. This is the highest point reached by the fortunes of the king. The latter's interference in the punishment of the conspirators shows that his soft and yielding nature is the force that is to bring down tragedy upon him. But there is a slight rise when the soldier, touched by the mercy and forebearance of the king, seems inclined to proceed no further in the business. This is for an instant made more apparent when the king's decree of banishment is announced, but this arouses the soldier again. There is a consequent fall in the fortunes of Sardanapalus, the sense of which is made more acute by the ensuing scenes of mercy and love, first between the king and Salamenes, and then between the king and Myrrha.

The period of growth is not always so elaborately developed. In *Marino Faliero* it is much simpler. The fluctuations are psychological rather than in external circumstance. The reader contrasts the growth of the plot with the uneasy doubts and hesitations of Bertram that eventually lead to the discovery, but the chief fluctuations are those in the mind of the Doge, swayed alternately by loyalty to country and to caste. There is here a resemblance to *Macbeth*. *The Two Foscari* exhibits no such rise. Here again the play is badly constructed. The "growth" of the action is absolutely lacking. The fortunes of both Foscaris, from the commencement of the play, sink swiftly to extinction. It is hardly tragic, for there is no resistance; it is not dramatic, for the conflict is one-sided, that is, it is brute force against impotence, which is no true conflict at all. The early part of the action therefore leads to no definite climax. Even more unsatisfactory is *Werner* where the "rise" is but vaguely indicated. It may be said to reach its highest point with Werner's appearance in the garden (III, iv), and with the suspicion of murder directed against him by his own son the decline at once sets in.

The other four dramatic pieces are too irregular to exhibit any clearly marked "rise." *Manfred* is, from one point of view, a continued growth of power over the spiritual world; defiance, first of the spirits of the earth, then of the evil principle itself, and then of death. Or it may be thought of as a steady decline towards death. It has, at any rate, no pretence to the dual movement, first upward and then down, which is characteristic of drama. In *Cain*, Lucifer's efforts are to debase Cain in his own estimation; the movement is therefore persistently down, and lacks the dramatic contrast exhibited by the "casibus illustrium virorum," which is the material of tragedy. *Heaven and Earth* and *The Deformed Transformed* are, to put it succinctly, *all rise*. Both pieces are fragments. The one ends with the disappearance of the angels and rebellious women, defiant and so far triumphant; the other, with Arnold's successful capture of Olimpia and the rejoicing of the peasantry at the close of the war.

The "rise" of the action witnesses the inception or development of the power that is to dominate the second half of the play and is finally to destroy the original aggressive force. This opposition represents the norm; and its rise should be accomplished by degrees so as to forestall objections on the score of *deorum ex machina*. The great example of this is the character of Macduff. His refusal to attend, first the coronation and then the banquet, prepares the mind "for the return action even before it has actually set in."[1] In dramas according to the classical model the opposition may be in force from the very commencement, or before the commencement, of the play, as in *The Two Foscari*. In *Sardanapalus* it fluctuates, in reverse direction, with the fortunes of the king. In *Marino Faliero* it is represented, during the tragic "rise," when the forces of opposition are unaware of the conspiracy, by Bertram who, though one of the plotters, is not with them in heart, and through whom the opposition is aroused.

The climax is the culmination of the rising action. Here occurs that event of utmost significance, through which the forces of opposition win the ascendancy, and gaining on the protagonist, gradually drive him down from the position of vantage which, isolated from the norm, he has been able to assume. The importance of the climax is both psychological and spiritual on the one hand, and external and practical on the other. Psychological, because there is a change or development in the attitude of the hero; spiritual, because he has now to choose finally between opposing loyalties; external and practical, because the forces against him are material and will affect not only character but life itself. To emphasize the importance of this scene, dramatists are accustomed to give to it especial interest; it is brilliant or tremendous in situation and in poetry. Freytag (p. 129) gives as examples — and they cannot be bettered — the banquet scene of *Macbeth* and the storm-and-hovel scene of *King Lear*. The climax must justify its technical name. What of Byron's?

In *Manfred* it is well marked. After lesser exhibitions of power over the world of spirits, by conjuring up the spirits of the universe, and the Witch of the Alps, Manfred penetrates to the abode of the Evil Principle and gains converse with the dead. This is the utmost of his power. Thence by swift decline he goes down to death. He has sought for death; therefore the very moment of the climax may be fixed at

---

[1] E. Woodbridge, *The Drama, Its Law and Technique*, Boston, Allyn and Bacon, [1898], p. 82.

Astarte's words, "To-morrow ends thine earthly ills" (II, iv, 151), while the first indications of the "return action" lie in the words

"This is to be a mortal,
And seek the things beyond mortality" (II, iv, 157—8).

The entrance of the Doge into the house in which the conspirators are met together marks the climax of *Marino Faliero* (III, ii, 90), for with his appearance among them the fortunes of the plot reach the highest point. Already in Calendaro's suspicions of Bertram (II, ii, 67 f.), there have been suggestions of the "return action," and though after Faliero's consent to act as a leader of the conspiracy the outward fortunes of the plot continue to rise, Bertram's treachery soon marks it for failure. Byron has therefore well indicated the highest point of the rising action. He has erred, however, as he often does, in not making it sharp and incisive enough; the Doge "protests too much."

Sardanapalus is better. The climax is a scene of fine theatrical possibilities and appeals to the imagination of the reader. The stage setting of the third act is as follows: "The Hall of the Palace illuminated — Sardanapalus and his Guests at Table. A storm without, and Thunder occasionally heard during the Banquet." Interest in this banquet has already been excited by the part it is known to have in the plans of the conspirators. This is heightened by the incongruity of the voluptuous feast on this night fatal to the Assyrian empire. The clash between individual volition and the general good is here presented in concrete form. There is a sense of "some consequence yet hanging in the stars." This leads to expectancy, so that the sudden entrance of the bloody warrior (line 68) affords a stirring climax to the scene and to the play.

Here, as in almost every technical point, *The Two Foscari* is a failure. There has been no rising action; hence there can be no real climax. The piece has moved downwards towards the destruction of the protagonist. The point that serves as a climax is the announcement of the decree of the Ten that Jacopo Foscari return to Candia. This doom, more dreadful to him than death in Venice, is the immediate cause of his death, and from the time of pronouncement the tragic decline is more swift than during the first portion of the play. But even in this simple matter there is a decided flaw. The climax, such as it is, is spoiled by anticipation. Marina brings the news of the decree to her husband, and he exclaims, "Then my last hope's gone" (III, i, 126). When a few minutes later Loredano brings the official tidings of the same decree, there is nothing left for the doomed man to say; and there is no thrill of emotion left in the breast of the reader.

The action of *Cain* is so simple and it is so far from regular dramatic form that a definite climax is hardly possible. There is a climax in the thought of the poem at the conclusion of the second act, for it is to this position that the arguments of Lucifer have been tending, and it is from his defiant assertion of the powers and privileges of the human mind that the final expression of Cain's revolt comes. *Heaven and Earth* stops at the climax, breaking off at the point of sharpest clash between the will of God and the defiance of the rebels. The catastrophe would have had its beginning at the point where the piece now concludes. *Werner* is as unsatisfactory here as in all other respects. It is difficult to pick out the scene intended for the climax, as all are on the same dead level of attainment, but if the matter must be decided upon, it is obvious that Werner's success is most apparent when he has escaped from the castle to the garden. Then Ulric appears with his feigned suspicions that Werner has been the murderer of Stralenheim. This is the foundation of the catastrophe. It is impossible to find any regular climax in so formless a fragment as *The Deformed Transformed*.

From the climax to the catastrophe the descent is generally more swift than the rising action has been, though this varies in individual plays. The earlier manifestations of the forces of opposition have already been apparent; in the Byronic drama they have been present from the beginning. They now gather head. Thus the third act of *Manfred* opens in an entirely different key from the preceding, and affords a presage of coming calm. In *Marino Faliero* the previously apparent doubts of Bertram are openly expressed in the interview with Lioni (Act IV, Scene i), in which he finally reveals the plot. From this moment one is sure of the coming failure of the conspiracy. Sometimes the dramatist "prepares the mind of the audience for the catastrophe."[1] This is the Shakespearean method. It is employed by Byron in *Sardanapalus* where the dream in Act IV foreshadows the monarch's approaching end. But generally the catastrophe of Byron's dramas is so logically the result of the situation that no such warnings are needed.

In many dramas there is what Freytag (p. 136) calls "the final suspense" immediately before the catastrophe, a point at which a last faint gleam of hope shines in the gloom rapidly enfolding the protagonist. "A slight hindrance, a distant possibility of a happy release, is thrown in the way of the already indicated direction of the end. Brutus must explain that he considers it cowardly to kill one's self; the dying Edmund must revoke the command to kill Lear; Friar Laurence may still enter the monument before the moment when Romeo kills himself." Byron employs this device sparingly. The ringing of the bell in *Marino Faliero* affords a moment's suspense, lest it suffice to arouse the conspirators. But it quickly stops and with its cessation all hope of success is lost. This is the real catastrophe. From now on there is never an instant's doubt as to the outcome; there is no conflict, for the forces of opposition have triumphed. Yet Byron prolongs the play through another act, dull and actionless and utterly undramatic. This is the worst flaw in *Marino Faliero,* and in this respect none of the other plays are equally bad. *Manfred* shows conflict to the last gasp of the protagonist. Sardanapalus fights and foils his enemies even in death. The elder Foscari protests to the last against his fate, but the effect of the end is marred by the certainty of its nature from the commencement of the play. The catastrophe of *Cain* is finely conceived, and veiled in mystery. In all the plays the force of individual will is shown finally succumbing to the power of the norm.

This review of Byron's general constructive abilities in the drama has shown how faulty his technique was. In part this was due to wilful disregard of the rules of the drama, in part to ignorance and inexperience. His lack of success on the formal side of dramatic art is well illustrated by a series of

---

[1] Freytag, p. 135.

diagrams outlining the course of the action of each play.[1]
The obscure motivation of *Werner* makes any attempt at
schematic representation unsatisfactory; and *Heaven and Earth*
and *The Deformed Transformed* can be put in diagrammatic
form merely as upward-slanting lines. These three pieces are
therefore omitted.

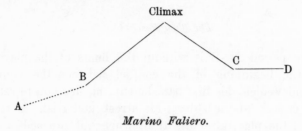

Marino Faliero.

A is the actual beginning of conflict, long before the play
opens; A—B is the period of Faliero's growing resentment.
B is the insult offered him by Steno, the cause of Faliero's
active expression of opposition to the aristocracy, leading up
to the climax, when he joins the conspiracy. There follows
the betrayal of the plot and the "return action," to C, the
arrest of Faliero and his fellows, which is the real catastrophe.
The decline is complete, and the fifth act (C—D) is an undramatic aftermath.

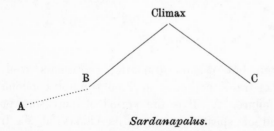

Sardanapalus.

A—B is the period of discontent before the opening of the
play. B is the beginning of the drama and precipitation of
the conflict. The climax follows in due order, whence the
action declines to the catastrophe, C. *Sardanapalus* is a well
constructed play.

---

[1] I have borrowed the idea of these diagrams from Woodbridge, p. 77.

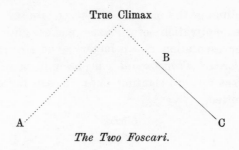

The Two Foscari.

The entire period A—B is without the limits of the play. It
includes the beginning of the conflict between the younger
Foscari and Venice; his first banishment; his decision to return,
the true climax of the story; his arrest and trial. B is the
opening of the play, after the trial, whence it proceeds to the
catastrophe at C. The diagram shows the dramatic possibilities
of the theme; it also shows Byron's failure to avail himself of
these possibilities.

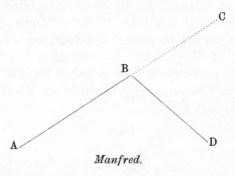

Manfred.

Manfred, though but pseudo - dramatic, represents well the
double nature of tragic action — spiritual triumph concomitant
with material failure. A—B is the period of increasing power
over the world of spirits, reaching its climax at Manfred's
penetration into the Hall of Arimanes. Thereafter the decline
to death is swift (B—D), yet there is a continued spiritual rise
(B—C), culminating in his triumph over the evil spirits who
haunt his death-bed.

In a moment of discouragement Byron wrote (LJ. V, 218),
"Many people think my talent *'essentially undramatic,'* and I
am not at all clear that they are not right." To a great extent

they *were* right; the merits of his dramas are not those which belong exclusively or even chiefly to dramatic literature. Had the same amount of care and energy been expended in work native to his genius — imagine ten more cantos of *Don Juan!* — the world had been the gainer. But Byron chose otherwise; and there is much of worth and wisdom in the result of his choice, worth and wisdom preserved to us though they are through a medium foreign to his genius and faulty in technique.

Chapter Four.
Manfred.

The letters from Switzerland contain no allusion to the composition of *Manfred*. The note attached to *The Incantation*, published with *The Prisoner of Chillon and other Poems*, December 5, 1816, is the earliest reference to it. This note reads: "The following Poem was a Chorus in an unfinished Witch Drama, which was begun some years ago." I think this is sheer mystification. I am not sure that *The Incantation* was originally part of any drama at all; certainly it fits but imperfectly into the context in *Manfred*.[1] Byron later wrote (LJ. IV, 54) that *Manfred* was begun in Switzerland. The composition of the first and second acts may be referred to the latter half of September, during the tour of the Bernese Alps, or just afterwards during the last sojourn at Diodati, before the departure for Italy on October 6, 1816. The bare conception of the poem may be of earlier date (see P. IV, 81),

---

[1] See further H. Varnhagen, *De Rebus quibusdam Compositionem Byronis Dramatis quod Manfred inscribitur*, Erlangen 1909, a monograph of value for the elaborate detail of the "Vorgeschichte" of *Manfred*. Professor Varnhagen finds that one part of the *Incantation* is closely identified in theme and phrase with the rest of *Manfred*, while the other part (stanzas 5, 6, and two lines of 7), metrically distinct from its context, is evidently directed against Lady Byron. He comes to no very satisfactory conclusion as to the meaning of the note originally put under the title of *The Incantation*. It is convenient to add here that in his article "Zur Textkritik von Byrons *Manfred*" *(Byroniana und Anderes*, Erlangen, 1912), Varnhagen fails to note Coleridge's bad misprint of "the" for "thy" in I, i, 242.

but Byron himself records the influence of the Staubbach and the Jungfrau (LJ. IV, 174), and numerous parallels to the Journal-Letter kept during the September tour (LJ. III, 349 f.) date it quite definitely. The third act was composed in Italy. In the abortive first version the inspiration of the earlier acts is markedly lacking and there is evidence of a totally different environment. The second version of Act III was written between April 26 and May 5, 1817 (LJ. IV, 115). *Manfred* was published on June 16, 1817.

The sources of *Manfred*, if we include whatever gave more or less definite suggestions, are numerous. The name of the protagonist Byron probably got from the Manfred of Walpole's *Castle of Otranto*, though there are other possibilities such as Monti's tragedy *Galeotto Manfredi* and the Manfred of *Purgatorio* III, 112 f.

Byron was always so careful by the acknowledgment of obligations to avoid even the appearance of dishonest plagiarism that it is important to note that he refused to ascribe the direct inspiration of *Manfred* to any previous book. "As to the germs of *Manfred*," he wrote (LJ. IV, 174), "they may be found in the journal which I sent to Mrs Leigh . . . when I went over first the Dent de Jamont *(sic)* . . . and made the giro of the Jungfrau, Shreckhorn, etc., etc., shortly before I left Switzerland." And again (LJ. V, 37), "It was the Staubach *(sic)* and the Jungfrau, and something else, much more than Faustus[1], that made me write *Manfred*." The mention of the mountain and the waterfall refers to the influence of nature upon the poet's inspiration, an influence at its height during the Swiss period; the "something else" is that autobiographical background about which speculation has long been rife. To both these subjects I shall return.

The most direct source of *Manfred*, apart from *Faust*, is Chateaubriand's *René*.[2] Of this Chateaubriand seems to have been aware, for he says "Il est vrai que René entrât pour quelque chose dans le fond du personnage unique mis en scène

---

[1] For Byron's borrowings from Goethe's *Faust* in *Manfred* see Appendix II.

[2] I follow Koeppel's admirable study, "Lord Byrons Astarte," *Eng. Stud.* XXX, 195f.

sur des noms diver *(sic)* dans *Childe Harold,* Conrad, Lara, Manfred," etc.[1] Were the similarity only general their connection might be ascribed to the influence of the *maladie du siècle* upon both of them and to their common descent from that source-book of suicidal melancholy *Die Leiden des jungen Werthers,* but in many respects the themes of the two works are identical. René and Manfred have alike had an only love, and that love unlawful in the highest degree. Each has been bound to his sister by conformity of soul, so that the two have grown up together apart from other men. Each is over-thoughtful, and each, through the grief of separation and the pangs of remorse, 'has become misanthropical. Set over against the character of René are the Indian Chactas and the missionary Père Souël; there is something analogous to them in the Chamois-hunter and the Abbot in *Manfred.* For the wildness of the primitive forests where "le Meschacebé roulait ses ondes dans un silence magnifique" there is substituted the wildness of the Alpine crags. There are, of course, in *Manfred* notable divergences from *René.* In place of the tone of Christian submission, typical of the Catholic reaction in France, there is the Byronic "courage never to submit or yield." There is no introduction of the supernatural into Chateaubriand's story. In the character of René there is no trace of the titanic element. Estève[2] summarizes these resemblances and divergencies. "Il y a de singulières analogies de caractère et de situation. Lui aussi [Manfred], ses passions, son genie et ses malheurs l'ont mis en dehors et au-dessus de l'humanité. Mais il la domine de plus haut encore, car son sort est plus affreux; il traîne après lui le remords du crime dont le frère d'Amélie a osé à peine imaginer l'horreur. Et tandis que l'âme ardente et faible de René plie sous le fardeau, Manfred, raidi contre le destin, persiste jusqu'au bout dans son attitude arrogante." That Byron had read *René* admits of no doubt; but in the composition of *Manfred* it exerted, I think, only a sub-conscious influence. Both works are filled with that "malaise inexprimable" which Alfred de Musset describes in the second chapter of the

---

[1] *Essai sur la Littérature anglaise,* Paris, Furne-Jouvet, 1867, p. 314.

[2] Edmond Estève, *Byron et le Romantism francais,* Paris, Hachette, 1907, p. 30.

Confessions d'un Enfant du Siècle. "Beide," says Lohmann,[1] "sind personifikationen des zeitgeistes, und der krankt an dem weltschmerz, welcher alle literaturen Europa's durchzog."

In one important particular, however, the indebtedness to *René* seems to be more than sub-conscious, and that is the incest-*motiv*, an element of much prominence in *Manfred*. Amélie is, as the Germans say, the Ur-Astarte, an Astarte more restrained and finally enskied and sainted. Chateaubriand was the immediate forerunner of Byron, but the theme has been one of wide occurrence in ancient and modern literatures.[2] This fact is ignored by those who see only biographical significance in Byron's employment of it. To say nothing of Euripides, Calderon, Lope de Vega, Racine, Schiller, and Alfieri, there are several dramas on the subject in English. It is the theme of Ford's most famous play. In all essentials, so far as the ethical and psychological problems are concerned, it occurs again in Beaumont and Fletcher's *King and No King*. Dryden's *Don Sebastian* treats of the same sin, though here the lovers are ignorant of their relationship. Walpole's *Mysterious Mother* develops the subject to the wildest extreme of a morbid imagination. As a literary *motiv* it was curiously current during the period of full romanticism, and like the suicidal mania that found expression in *Werther* and of which there is an after-echo in "The Sorrows of Teufelsdröckh," it is one of the pathological extremes of the reaction from classical and rationalistic restraint. Thus Mignon, in Goethe's *Wilhelm Meisters Lehrjahre* (bk. viii, chap. 9), is the daughter of the old wandering musician and his sister, with whom, not knowing who she was, he had fallen in love. The theme laid special hold upon the imaginations of Shelley and Byron. Of the interest which Shelley took in it *Laon and Cythna* (the original form of *The Revolt of Islam*) and *The Cenci* are the main evidences. See also his comments upon Calderon's *Cabellos de Absolom*[3] and compare *Rosalind and Helen*, ll. 146 f. Byron's original plan of *The Bride of Abydos* was to make the lovers brother and sister,

---

[1] O. Lohmann, "Byrons *Manfred* und sein Verhältnis zu Dichtungen Verwandten Inhalts", *Anglia* V, 307.

[2] See Otto Rank, *Das Inzest-Motiv in Dichtung und Saga*, Leipzig, Franz Deuticke, 1912.

[3] *Letters* II, 749.

and as published it resorts to the compromise seen in *A Kinq and No King:* the lovers believe themselves to be, but are not, so related. There is a suggestion of such a love in the plan of Byron's unfinished "tale of terror," *The Vampire.*[1] *Parisina* is in the same class of subject matter. As late as the date of *Cain* Byron's mind seems still to have concerned itself with this obliquity of passion.

Heinrich Gillardon[2] has advanced with much confidence another theory as to the source of *Manfred,* between which and Shelley's juvenile romance *St. Irvyne or the Rosicrucian*[3] "finden sich nun so viele und so auffällige Übereinstimmungen, dass sie mir diesen Roman als die oft vermutete und oft gesuchte Quelle *Manfreds* erscheinen lassen." This assertion is supported by a large number of parallels, in thought or situation, and occasionally in words. He combines the characteristics of the proud, lonely, sinful Wolfstein and of the awful Ginotti — the man who has dived into the mysteries of life and death — and in this combination he arrives at what he considers the Ur-Manfred (p. 112). A difficulty is that these elements of character — sin, mystery, passion, power — are traits of the "Gothic" type of hero in general (compare, for instance, Lewis's Ambrosio or Maturin's Bertram or the Radcliffeian hero), and of the Byronic hero-type in particular. Moreover the one feature that strikingly recalls Ginotti, namely, Manfred's explorations of hidden mysteries, is the one that most probably derives from *Faust.*[4] More fantastic is the complicated combination through which Gillardon obtains his Ur-Astarte. Here he is utterly unconvincing, since nowhere in *St. Irvyne* is there a hint of that which lies at the heart of the mystery of Astarte — the incestuous nature of Manfred's love for her. Such a hint Gillardon (p. 110) attempts t oextract by a non-natural interpretation of one passage (p. 237), of which Koeppel justly remarks[5], "Die

---

[1] See Polidori's outline, LJ. IV, 287, note. See also P. VII, 55, ll. 7 f.

[2] *Shelleys Einwirkung auf Byron,* Karlsruhe, 1898, p. 89 f.

[3] *The Works of P. B. Shelley,* ed. H. B Forman, London, Reeves and Turner, 1880, V, 161 f.

[4] Cf., however, Shelley's *Alastor,* ll. 18 f., quoted below p. 80.

[5] *Eng. Stud.* XXX, 195.

weitere entwicklung der erzählung widerspricht einer solchen annahme durchaus."[1]

Byron had assimilated a large amount of the material common to all extreme romanticism. This is shown not only by the more or less definite indebtedness to *René* and *St. Irvyne,* but by the number of individual suggestions which he got from various and scattered sources.

Walpole furnished more than a name. His romance is the source, direct or indirect, of the taste for Gothic gloom and horror and for the revival of the employment of the supernatural. *Manfred* is in the line of descent from *The Castle of Otranto.* More direct is its descent from Walpole's other essay in Gothicism. *The Mysterious Mother,* a play singled out for Byron's special praise, might well exert some influence, and apparently it does. Like *Manfred* it deals with an incestuous passion, though of an even more horrible kind. After the commission of the crime there follows in each play an ever-present remorse. The emphasis is laid upon the punishment afforded by conscience in this life rather than punishment in any hell hereafter. Such lines as —

> "Memory
> Is full. A head, distract as mine, can hold
> Two only objects, guilt and eternity,"

or —

> "Must I learn
> That minutes stamped with crime are past recall?
> That joys are momentary; and remorse
> Eternal?"

---

[1] A single example of the strain to which Gillardon's theory is put may be given. He quotes from *Manfred:*

> *"Manf.:* I loved her, and destroy'd her!
> *Witch:*   With thy hand?
> *Manf.:* Not with my hand, but heart, which broke her heart;
> It gazed on mine, and withered. I have shed
> Blood, but not hers — and yet her blood was shed;
> I saw — and could not stanch it" (II, ii, 116 f.)

This passage Gillardon derives from the scene in the bed-chamber of Olympia in *St. Irvyne* (p. 228). Wolfstein, the paramour of Megalena, having rejected the advances of Olympia, is forced by his jealous mistress to murder her would-be rival; but, having reached her bed-side, he is unnerved by the sight of her, peacefully asleep, and he throws away his dagger. She wakes and misinterprets the meaning of his presence; a few words pass; again he rejects

might be from Manfred's lips. The protagonist, though in this case a woman, spurns the comfort offered by priests. Dogma and superstition are alike denounced, and the priests are represented as being crafty, worldly, and hypocritical. This last element, though Byronic, hardly enters into *Manfred*. I am inclined to think that Byron drew hints from this play, yet the resemblances may well be from common use of the materials of Romanticism.

The same is true of other plays which Byron had read. There are what seem to me echoes of Coleridge's *Remorse*, [1] and less probably of Maturin's *Bertram*, [2] but in neither case are they sufficiently close to be considered as sources of *Manfred*. They serve to show how closely associated are the individual products of the time, and to what an extent Byron's mind was imbued with romanticism.

There are some minor sources from which Byron certainly derived parts of his material. Eimer [3] declares, "Von Montgomerys Gedicht *The Wanderer in Switzerland* wurde Byron im *Manfred* mehrfach deutlich beeinflusst." This poem [4] is, to borrow Wordsworth's phrase, "thoughts of a Briton on the subjugation of Switzerland." Byron knew Montgomery's work, addressed some verses to him (P. I, 107), and declared "his *Wanderer in Switzerland* is worth a thousand *Lyrical Ballads*." [5] There is, however, nothing in common between it and *Manfred*, except the descriptions of mountain scenery, and its influence must have been small indeed.

From Beckford's *Vathek*, the oriental romance which so powerfully affected Byron's imagination, and of which the influence

---

her advances; in sudden despair she snatches his discarded weapon from the floor and plunges it in her breast. Gillardon's comment (p. 108) is, "Wolfstein hat sie also nicht mit seiner Hand, sondern mit seinem Herzen getödtet, das ihr Herz brach. Er vergoss nicht ihr Blut und doch ward ihr Blut vergossen. Er sah's und konnt's nicht stillen." Here we have *Quellenstudien* forced to a morbid extreme.

[1] Compare *Remorse* III, i, 83 — *Manfred* II, iv, 114; IV. i, 111 — *Manfred passim;* V, i, 60 — Manfred's last words.

[2] Act II, Scene iii is especially Byronic and *Manfred*ian.

[3] M. Eimer, *Byron und der Kosmos*, Anglestische Forschungen, Heft 34, Heidelberg, Carl Winter, 1912, p. 28.

[4] *Poetical Works of James Montgomery*, 1841, I, 1—51.

[5] *English Bards and Scotch Reviewers*, line 425, note.

is especially discernible in *The Giaour* and *The Siege of Corinth*, Byron obtained the "setting" of the Hall of Arimanes. His throne, "a globe of fire," is a replica, so to speak, of that on which "the formidable Eblis" sat.[1]

Lewis's *Monk* may have given suggestions for the last scene. In the last chapter,[2] Ambrosio, about to die for his many crimes, summons Lucifer to rescue him. The "pact" idea is here introduced. The monk at first refuses to sell his soul to perdition, but the extremity of terror overcomes his resolution and he gives himself over to the fiend, who carries him far up on the heights of the Sierra Morena, from whence he is dashed down to death upon the rocks. In the first element of this catastrophe there is a general resemblance to the final scene of *Manfred*. The original grotesque punishment meeted out to the Abbot (in the suppressed first version of act III, P. IV, 122), is a much closer echo of *The Monk*.

There is something Shelleyan in the conference with the Witch of the Alps, the personification of the spirit of Nature, to look upon whose beauty has become Manfred's one desire. Professor Brandl goes so far as to indicate *Queen Mab* and *Alastor* as sources of the second act. Manfred's visit to the Hall of Arimanes vaguely resembles Macbeth's last interview with the Weird Sisters.

Byron, more than most poets, works again and again along the same grooves of thought. This is well illustrated by the recurrence of the Byronic hero-type. This question has received special study by Kraeger, and is of importance here only so far as these typical elements enter into the character of Manfred. Manfred is a solitary, partly by inclination, partly by consciousness of superiority to his fellow-men ("the sense that he was greater than his kind"), partly by the weight of crimes and grief. He is a man of mystery and crime, and linked with these crimes he has, like Conrad before him, the

---

[1] Some critics have traced the epithet "Child of Clay" (I, i, 131) to the words of Eblis, "Creatures of clay, I receive you into mine empire." References to "clay" and "dust" are, however, typically Byronic, and the phrase "creatures of clay" occurs several times in his poetry.

[2] Ed. E. A. Baker, London, Routledge, 1907, p. 348f. The incest *motiv* enters slightly into this story (see p. 354).

questionable virtue of devotion to one only love. This single-
minded devotion and subsequent loss Manfred characterizes as
"the core of my heart's grief" (II, ii, 99). More than almost
anything else this idea is of the very foundation of Byronism.
Manfred is Childe Harold, who "had sigh'd to many though
he loved but one" (I, v); with the Giaour he has learnt "to
die — but know no second love" (l. 1166); like Selim, in *The
Bride of Abydos*, he has experienced "unnumbered perils — but
one only love" (II, 899); like Conrad, in *The Corsair*, there
was in his heart

"love — unchangeable, unchanged,

Felt but for one from whom he never ranged" (I, 287-8).
But in the Eastern tales this One Love had been itself the object
of poetic expression; in *Manfred* Astarte is more than the
heroine of a tragic love tale; she is the formal embodiment,
the concrete presentation, of the abstract mood. Of this I shall
say more. Byron has thus applied a deeper meaning to the
theme. In like manner he has motived the melancholy of
the earlier poems. He lets mystery still hang over the crime,
but explains the grief as the inevitable accompaniment of
knowledge. Manfred is thus the consummation of the Byronic
hero-type. A philosophical meaning, a depth of thought, is
given to the melancholy which in the poems of his youth had
been merely fashionable. The *desenchanté*, the victim of ennui
and unrest, laden with crimes, consumed with vain aspirations
and sterile regrets, had past through many poems; he is now
made the medium of authentic utterance.

In two poems, however, the similarities to *Manfred* are of
a more intimate nature than can be dealt with in generalizations.
These are *The Giaour* and *The Dream*.

The Giaour is the story of an illicit love through which
the womân comes to her death, while the lover, after living
a prey to remorse and yearning for death, dies in a monastery.
Manfred declares, "I loved her and destroy'd her" (II, ii, 116),
and the Giaour says that his love died for him (l. 1034). The
protagonists of both poems have loved not without success.
"My *embrace* was fatal", says Manfred (II, i, 87) and the Giaour,
"I did not vainly seek, nor sigh" (l. 1053). In both cases the
mysterious death of the Beloved drives them to passionate

remorse, and it is in *The Giaour* that, under the simile of the
self-stung scorpion,[1] Byron has best described this passion:

> "So writhes the mind Remorse hath riven,
> Unfit for earth, undoom'd for heaven,
> Darkness above, despair beneath,
> Around it flame, within it death" (l. 435 f.)

Compare Manfred's words:

> "The innate tortures of that deep Despair
> Which is Remorse without the fear of Hell" (III, i, 70 f.)

Shortly before his death the Giaour fancies that he sees the
form of his beloved Leila, who "beckons with beseeching hands"
(l. 1299), just as at the behest of Nemesis the phantom of
Astarte (cf. "the morning *star* of memory") appears before
Manfred with the prophecy that "to-morrow ends thine earthly
ills" (II, iv, 151). The Giaour and Manfred are alike offered
the consolations of religion, and the monk of the earlier poem

---

[1]   "So do the dark in soul expire,
            Or live like scorpion girt with fire" (ll. 433-4)

To these lines Byron added a note, "Alluding to the dubious suicide of the
scorpion." Byron told Dallas that the simile of the scorpion was imagined
in his sleep (*Recollections*, p. 264, cited by E. H. Coleridge, P. III, 107,
note 1). The lines are the first of a series of such similes, employed by
several poets within a few years of the appearance of *The Giaour*. These
are given for the benefit of comparison.
            "The truths of their pure lips, that never die,
            Shall bind the scorpion falsehood with a wreath
                    Of living flame,
            Until the monster sting itself to death."
                    (Shelley, *Queen Mab* VI. 35 f. and cf. IX, 43 f.)
            "And we are left, as scorpions ringed with fire,
            What should we do but strike ourselves to death."
                    (Shelley, *The Cenci* II, ii, 70-1).
            "Mark how the scorpion, falsehood,
            Coils round its own perplexity, and fixes
            Its sting in its own head." (Coleridge, *Zapolya* I, i, 348 f.)
            "Thus to be, like the scorpion, ring 'd with fire,
            Till I sting mine own heart." (Croly, *Catiline* Act II, Sc. ii).
The lines in *Queen Mab* derive from Godwin's *Political Justice* (I, 89):
"Error contains in it the principle of its own mortality". Compare also
Alfred de Vigny's description of the same phenomenon in the "Dernier Nuit
de Travail," prefixed to *Chatterton (Œuvres complètes,* Paris, Delagrave,
Théâtre I, 18) and see Beddoes, *Letters,* p. 114.

foreshadows the Abbot in the later. In both poems these ministrations are rejected. The Giaour exclaims:

"Waste not thine orison, despair
Is mightier than thy pious prayer:
I would not, if I might, be blest;
I want no Paradise but rest" (l. 1267 f.)

This is in exact accord with the prevalent mood of *Manfred*. To the character of the Giaour there were added for the making of Manfred the pantheistic view of Nature, which developed, though already latent in Byron's mind, under the influence of the Alps and the companionship of Shelley; the sense of the vanity of human knowledge, which Byron got from Goethe; and the foundation of personal experience.

Closer yet is the resemblance of *The Dream* to *Manfred*. This poem, the most famous of all Byron's shorter pieces, was composed in July, 1816, probably towards the end of the month, and therefore not long before the commencement of the composition of *Manfred*. The two poems are therefore nearly coincident in time and place of composition, and were the products of much the same mood and environment. That there should be resemblances of theme is but natural, but below the surface similarity there lies a significance that has not been appreciated and that even Mr. Edgcumbe in his discussion of *The Dream*[1] fails to note. *The Dream* and *Manfred* are both, from one point of view, the expression of remorse. The earlier poem is the story of a man's devotion to a woman who did not return his love when first, as a boy, he wooed her. Years passed by and there came the day of parting. The young lover became a wanderer and the Lady of the dream was married to another. After this a mysterious grief came over her, she "changed as by the sickness of the soul", and ended in madness. The Wanderer had meanwhile married another woman, whose

"face was fair, but was not that which made
The starlight of his boyhood" (ll. 147-8.)

That face haunted him perpetually, and when next he appears it is in loneliness and despair. He seems even to have sought for death, but

---

[1] Richard Edgcumbe, Byron: the Last Phase, London, Murray, 1910, p. 289 f.

"lived
Through that which had been death to many men,
And made him friends of mountains: with the stars
And the quick spirit of the Universe
He held his dialogues; and they did teach
To him the magic of their mysteries;
To him the book of night was open'd wide,
And voices from the deep abyss reveal'd
A marvel and a secret" (ll. 193 f.)

The course of Manfred's life is just the same. He had loved
Astarte from his youth up, and had lost her. As in the case
of the Lady there is a mystery surrounding her fate, but in
Manfred the cause of her destruction is known. Manfred says,
"My embrace was fatal." But is Astarte dead? The question
sounds strange; but there are signs that in the biographical
allegory which Byron has assuredly inserted into the play the
idea of actual physical death was not meant to be conveyed.
Manfred, in spite of declaring Astarte innocent, and in spite
of Nemesis' assurance that she "belongs to the other powers,"
speaks of "heaven, *where thou art not*" (II, i, 30)[1]. Again he says:
"What is she now? — a sufferer for my sins —
A thing I dare not think upon — or nothing" (II, ii, 196 f.).
When Nemesis asks him, "Whom wouldst thou uncharnel?"
he replies, "One without a tomb" (II, iv, 81). These phrases,
and especially the last one, mean nothing unless we interpret
them to mean that Astarte is "dead to him", just as the Lady,
married to another and then insane, is dead to the Wanderer.
This idea occurs in several places in Byron's poetry, notably
in a *Fragment* (P. IV, 52) of this same July:

"The absent are the dead,
Who haunt us from tranquillity, and spread
A dreary shroud around us, and invest
With sad remembrancers our hours of rest."

In his *Detached Thoughts* (No. 74, LJ. V, 446), occurs the expression, "Deference to the dead, to the living, and to those
who must be both." It is at least possible that Astarte's
"death" may have the same hidden meaning, particularly since
such an explanation alone satisfies certain statements in the
text of the play.

---

[1] These words, however, perhaps refer to the Chamois-hunter.

The fate of Astarte and of the Lady are explained by mutual comparison. In *The Dream* the *cause* of the Lady's grief and madness is left unrevealed,[1] but the *effect* is plainly told: madness, "the sickness of the soul," as it were a spiritual death. On the other hand, while the *nature* of the catastrophe which overwhelmed Astarte is only hinted at, the *cause*[2] is openly stated to have been Manfred's fatal embrace. After this dim destiny has overtaken the Beloved, the fate of Manfred and the Wanderer is alike. Both have sought for death, and to both the boon has been denied. "I have *wander'd* o'er the earth," says Manfred (II, iv, 143); he breathed "the difficult air of the iced mountain's top" (II, ii, 63), and says:

"The face of the earth hath maddened me, and I
Take refuge in her mysteries, and pierce
To the abodes of those who govern her" (II, ii, 63 f.);

and he holds converse with the "spirits of the unbounded Universe." Compare the last change that came o'er the spirit of the dream. Manfred is "a man of many thoughts", and on the face of the Wanderer "a tablet of unutterable thought was traced." So far as it goes[3] the parallel is exact, and being fairly obvious has been partly noted by Mr. Coleridge in his comments on *The Dream*. It becomes yet more striking when the fact is recalled that the last act of *Manfred* was not written till months later, and that the portion written under the same inspiration that produced *The Dream* ends with Manfred still alive and like the Wanderer in misery. When the Chamois-hunter declares him insane, Manfred exclaims:

"I would I were — for then the things I see
Would be but a distempered dream" (II, i, 61 f.)

In those two earlier poems, then, Byron to some extent anticipated his own later full development of the theme of crime, love, loss, and remorse. In *Manfred* he was therefore working with material already familiar to him, and this fact

---

[1] Why this should be so the biographical references in the poem sufficiently explain, whether we accept Mr. Edgcumbe's theory or not.

[2] Which had to be suppressed in a poem so indiscreet as *The Dream*.

[3] The reservation here has reference to the *Vanitas scientiae* which, as has been said, is part of the indebtedness of *Manfred* to *Faust*, and which does not influence *The Dream*.

should give pause to over-zealous source finders. In the resemblance there is a deeper significance, which links the question to the problem of the autobiographical revelations of *Manfred* and the larger question of the cause of the separation of Lord and Lady Byron.

The autobiographical references in *The Dream* are indisputable in their cogency. The poem is a record of Byron's love for Mary Chaworth. Everyone admits this.[1] The conclusion drawn from the parallels noted above is therefore obvious. "Things equal to the same thing are equal to each other." Since Mary Chaworth is the Lady of *The Dream* and since Astarte's history is identical with that of the Lady, it follows that Astarte and the Lady and Mary Chaworth are one and the same. In Manfred there is an open confession of the wrong done her, the mention of which in *The Dream* would have harmed irreparably that reputation which Byron was so anxious to shield. The confession made in *Manfred* is supplemented by lines 1053 f. of *The Giaour* (a passage added during the summer of 1813 when Byron was in the midst of the mysterious love-affair which is the nucleus of the problem.)

The central difficulty remains. Granting the resemblance in theme of *The Dream* and *Manfred*, there are allusions in the drama that do not, apparently, support the conclusions I have indicated. When Mrs. Stowe made her charges against Byron's memory, she instanced as proof of the truth of them the manifest allusions contained in *Manfred*. So also Lord

---

[1] For the sake of clearness the familiar facts may be repeated. The reference to the hill "crown'd with a peculiar diadem" was so direct that Mr. Musters in wrath had the circular group of tress on a hill near Annesley cut down. The Lady is called "the star-light of his boyhood;" Byron had been accustomed to speak of his "bright, morning star of Annesley." Mr. Edgcumbe has collected the star-similes found in the poems, none of which is without significance as relating to Mary Chaworth. The later incidents in *The Dream*, the period of separation, the last meeting, the final parting, the marriages, the Lady's grief and insanity, and the Wanderer's sojourn among the mountains, are all facts in the lives of Byron and Mary Chaworth, familiar to everyone. There is no external evidence to prove that this was a "boyish passion" (E. C. Mayne, *Byron*, New York, Scribner, 1912, I, 53) only, and there is the testimony of many poems and parts of poems that the love for Mary Chaworth was the love of his life.

Lovelace chose the name *Astarte* as the title of his book.[1]
Mr. Edgcumbe's "reply" to this is a sweeping denial of the
existence of such allusions in the play. "So far as we know,"
he writes (p. 297), "there is nothing in the whole length of
this poem to suggest anything abnormal." This is mere evasion,
since there manifestly *are* such suggestions.[2] I have noted
above (p. 62) earlier examples of the occurrence of the theme
in literature. The presence of suggestions of this sin are in
themselves no warrant for autobiographical interpretations.
Moreover intentional mystification may have been the reason
for their insertion. But the real significance of these passages
is apparent from the following lines in *The Dream:*

> "Her sighs were not for him; to her he was
> *Even as a brother* — but no more: 'twas much,
> For brotherless she was, save in the *name*
> Her infant friendship had bestowed on *him*" (ll. 64 f.)

Here is, perhaps, the core of Byron's mystery. We are told
that Mary Chaworth looked upon him as a brother, and the
fact that he betrayed that confiding friendship made Byron
in *Manfred* record this sin as the "deadliest."

This is the biographical element of *Manfred*, the "something
else" which, together with the mountains, made Byron write
the play. Whether the explanation associated with the names
of Lady Byron, Mrs. Stowe and Lord Lovelace be accepted or
not, every student of the problem must admit that there is a
foundation in actual experience.[3]

---

[1] *Astarte, A fragment of Truth concerning George Gordon Byron,
sixth Lord Byron.* By Ralph Milbanke, Earl of Lovelace. London, The
Chiswick Press, 1905.

[2] See especially II, i, 24; II, ii, 105; III, iii, 47.

[3] Mr. Edgcumbe writes to me: "I most cordially agree with your
excellent reasoning, that Byron's remorse was entirely due to the fact that
he had, in a moment of weakness, abused her faith in him as a *brother.*
The lines you quote are irresistible ... as proof that the crime for which
Manfred reproaches himself is his betrayal of a sister, as mentioned in *The
Dream* — not a sister except in name. That is the germ of previous
misunderstanding, and you will make it clear beyond all doubt." I am
myself not so certain and offer it as a suggestion only. It is an additional
link in the chain of internal evidence put together in Mr. Edgcumbe's *Byron:
the Last Phase,* parts ii and iii. The external evidence of that book is
nearly worthless; Andrew Lang demolished its structure of inference and

More than any other English poem *Manfred* is typical of the Romantic Period; it is an expression of the mood of Romanticism, an epitome of the time.

Study of the sources of *Manfred* has shown that there are three chief elements in the character of the protagonist, distinct but related to each other. These are the themes of

---

surmise (*Fortnightly Review*, August 1910, n. s. vol. LXXXVIII, p. 269 f. See also Augustine Filon, "Le Crime de Lord Byron," *Revue de deux Mondes*, Jan. 15, 1912, p. 387 f.; Mayne, *Byron*, II, 327; Rank, p. 546). The weakest part of Mr. Edgcumbe's book is his contention that Mrs. Musters was the parent of the wretched Medora Leigh, a monstrous fancy that even Mr. Francis Gribble (*The Love Affairs of Lord Byron*, New York, Scribner, 1910, p. 177) does not accept. On the other hand the evidence produced by Lord Lovelace is not complete; his widow and sister should be urged to print the so-called confession of Mrs. Leigh, of 1816, the suppression of which is so fatal a weakness in *Astarte*. Mr. Edgcumbe has done good service in exposing the incorrect deductions and positive misstatements in that book. He here supplements the answer to *Astarte* contributed anonymously by the late E. H. Pember to John Murray's privately printed volume, *Lord Byron and his Detractors*, London, The Roxburghe Club, 1906. It is assuredly deplorable that a stigma should have been put upon the name of a dead woman without absolute proof of its truth. But the internal evidence of his poetry — and with Byron even more than with most poets such evidence may be relied upon — points to Mary Chaworth as the solution of the problem.

Two other notes on this question may be added. (1) In *The Giaour* there are references almost certainly to Mary Chaworth. On this Kölbing says (*Eng. Stud.* XXVI, 289), "Die dafür vorgebrachten beweise wollen wenig bedeuten gegenüber der tatsache, dass des dichters liebe zu Anne Chaworth eine unerwiederte geblieben ist, während der Giaour ausdrücklich hervorhebt 'Come what may I *have been* bless'd'". With ll. 1131 f., added during the summer of 1813, cf. the *Epistle to a Friend* (P. III, 28), where the allusion to Mary Chaworth is indisputable. The resemblances between *Manfred* and *The Giaour* make any allusions in the latter poem significant for the interpretation of the former. — (2) In November, 1813 Byron noted in his journal (LJ. III, 314) that his "second Turkish Tale . . . was written to drive my thoughts from the recollection of — 'Dear sacred name, rest ever unrevealed.'" This is a misquotation of Pope's *Eloisa to Abelard*, 1, 9, the adjective "sacred" being substituted for the original "fatal". I am confident that the fact that *Mary* is a holy name, to which, and to which only, the epithet "sacred" is applicable, made Byron, meditating upon Mary, by a natural trick of memory think that such was the reading of Pope's line.

External and internal evidence are thus contradictory; such antinomies can be solved only "in the dark union of insensate dust." There let us leave   the question.

Prometheus, Don Juan, and Faust. Manfred is a complete representative of no one of these, but includes characteristics of them all.

The basis of the conception is titanic, — the questioning of authority and ceaseless but unavailing revolt. In Manfred there is nothing of the high self-sacrifice of Prometheus, who suffers, Christ-like, for the sake of men, that through his solitary anguish and perpetual war "the sum of human wretchedness" may be rendered less. But like Prometheus he is

"a symbol and a sign
To Mortals of their fate and force;
Like [him] Man is in part divine,
A troubled stream from a pure source."[1]

Manfred echoes these words; "We, half-dust, half-deity!" he exclaims (I, ii, 39 f.) He has the strength of Promethean pride which can make his tortures "tributory to his will" and can wrench a victory from death.

But the conception is Shelleyan rather than Æschylean. A Greek could not forget that Jove was on his throne and that Prometheus was a rebel, punished for offences. This is admirably brought out by the Chorus in the *Prometheus Vinctus*, which, at first overwhelmed with pity for the sufferer, is gradually alienated by his exhibition of mad impiety. It is notable, however, that the character of Zeus, an upstart who is remorselessly cruel and in need of advice from the titan who is his victim, differs widely from the awful majesty of other Æschylean conceptions of the deity. This debasement of the character is of course due to the materials of the myth upon which the dramatist worked. The reverence for authority, apparent in the *Prometheus Vinctus*, is the greatest characteristic of the Middle Ages. Treachery to the State and treachery towards God were sins equally vile, and in Satan's mouths, at the "fondo a tutto l'universo", Brutus and Cassius writhe along with Judas. This "tristo buco" is in the very depths, and into it Dante and Virgil are lifted down by Antaeus, one of a number of giants who are chained around the brink of the pit. This dreadful company, scarce elevated above the

---

[1] Byron, *Prometheus*, ll. 45 f., P. IV, 51.

"fondo d'ogni reo", includes the "giants in those days" of
Genesis and the earth-born titans. As to the cause of their
condemnation Virgil is explicit. Of Ephialtes —

> "'Questo superbo voll' esser esperto
> di sua potenza contra il sommo Giove,'
> disse il mio duca, 'ond' egli ha cotal merto.
> Fialte ha nome; e fece le gran prove,
> quando i giganti fer paura ai Dei.'"[1]

This is the fate of rebels against constituted authority. The
conception is the antithesis of the modern spirit, and is the
link between Æschylus and Shelley. For "authority forgets
a dying king;" after 1789 the medièval spirit is gone forever.
Shelley has nothing of the Dantesque idea. He suppresses
the Æschylean reverence for high Jove, and by emphasizing
the typically Greek humanism, which seeks out the cause of
the titan's rebellion and finds it to be love of man, he enlarges
the admirable qualities of Prometheus so as to harmonize with
the Shelleyan image of perfection. His Prometheus becomes
the suffering fore-seer, the martyr for humanity; his Jupiter
is the "god of the hour", utterly wicked and fated to perish,
the Prince of Evil who from his nature can endure but for a
time. The analogy to *Manfred* is close. For just as Prometheus
is not in revolt against Demogorgon, but rather in harmony
with him, so Manfred breathes no defiance against "the overruling
Infinite", the "other powers", who guard and govern the blessed
and to whom he bids even Arimanes bow. This is apparent
in every interview with the spirits.[2]

The influence of the story of Prometheus upon Byron was
always strong, and while it finds its fullest expression in *Cain*,
it is not absent from *Manfred*. The reviewers were impressed
by the Promethean tone of the piece. Byron himself admitted
the possible indebtedness. "The *Prometheus*, if not exactly in
in my plan, has always been so much in my head, that I can
easily conceive its influence over all or anything that I have
written" (LJ. IV, 174). While at Harrow he had translated
part of a chorus from Æschylus, which he afterwards inserted

---

[1] *Inferno* XXXI, 91 f.

[2] See especially I, i, 152 f.; II, ii, 158 f.; II, iv, 46 f.; and the conclusion
of the poem.

in *Hours of Idleness* (P. I, 14). References to the theme are of frequent occurrence in his writings. Of most importance is the short poem *Prometheus* (P. IV, 48 f.), in which Byron gives splendid utterance to a high and unselfish devotion to humanity. This was written at Diodati in July, 1816, not long before the composition of *Manfred*. Manfred is far less noble a personage than Prometheus; he is not actuated by the desire

"To render . . . less
    The sum of human wretchedness" (ll. 36-7),

but he shares the endless torment and unconquerable mind, the pride, the endurance, and the defiance of the titan. It has been suggested that the scene of Manfred upon the cliffs of the Jungfrau (I, ii) is borrowed from that of Prometheus upon the Caucasus, after the departure of Kratos and Bia; and the close resemblance of the appeals of both protagonists to Earth, the all-bearing mother, makes this indebtedness probable, though it was most likely unconscious. The tie that binds *Manfred* to *Prometheus* is one of kinship of spirit rather than of direct obligation.[1]

The darker aspects of Manfred's character follow the

---

[1] See O. Lohmann, "Byron's *Manfred*", *Anglia* V, 311-2. In spite of Byron's early and life-long interest in the theme, Gillardon (p. 33) is inclined to the belief that the Promethean element in *Manfred* is due largely to the influence of Shelley. "Doch ist im wesentlichen, glaube ich, das Prometheus-Motiv in der Fassung wie sie uns in Byron's Gedicht vorliegt, trotzdem aus Shelley's Dichtung gekommen." He instances especially the Ahasuerus-episode in *Queen Mab* (vii, 67 f.), where we find "das Motiv von dem unbeugsamen Gegner des tyrannischen Prinzips des Bösen, der trotz aller Leiden und Qualen in seinem Widerstand gegen dieses beharrt." On the other hand F. H. Pughe (*Studien über Byron und Wordsworth*, Anglistische Forschungen, Heft 8, Heidelberg, Carl Winter, 1902, p. 99), with the enthusiasm of a disciple, derives Byron's interest in the theme from an unexpected source: "In der annahme von Shelley's einfluss auf die gestaltung von Byron's *Prometheus*, dürfen wir wohl Gillardon zustimmen; nicht unwahrscheinlich ist aber die mitwirkung Wordsworth's auf die gestaltung des gedichtes." In support of this Pughe quotes the words of the Sceptic in *The Excursion*:

"Say why
That ancient story of Prometheus chained
To the bare rock, on frozen Caucasus," etc. (VI, 538 f.).

See the whole context. This is going rather far afield. I do not see that one needs more than Byron's testimony of his interest from boyhood in the theme; but if a source must be found for the renewed interest of 1816, the influence of Shelley is more probable than that of Wordsworth.

tradition of Don Juan. These are the elements of crime, egoism, and pride, accompanied by the power to effect their fullest practical expression. Sganarelle's words can be applied to him. "Un grand seigneur méchant homme est une chose terrible."[1] Manfred and Juan are alike undaunted in the presence of the supernatural; but Manfred drives back the fiends; Juan on the contrary is overpowered and forced down into hell. The sombre imagination of Baudelaire has portrayed Don Juan crossing the Styx[2]; the ghosts of his victims swarm about him or writhe in the black water;

> "Mais le calme héros, courbé sur sa rapière,
> Regardait le sillage et ne daignait rien voir",

a fit comrade of Farinata degli Uberti in the tombs of fire. Manfred has the same power to "overcome the torture by strength of thought." But crime is not the philosophical basis of the poem; the Don Juan elements are incidental, not fundamental. E. H. Coleridge (P. IV, 82) declares that the central motive is remorse for inexpiable crime, a statement that exalts the autobiographical interpretation of the piece out of all due proportion. The crime-element is a concession to literary fashion; Manfred follows the long line of Byronic heroes —

> "A heterogeneous mass of glorious blame,
> Half virtues and whole vices being combined."[3]

But the philosophic conception would have been the same had Manfred been portrayed as free from any stain of sin.

Manfred is more intimately associated with the *Faust*-legend than by mere borrowings from Goethe.[4] The protagonist comes from an intensely aristocratic race and the inherited feelings of caste, strong within him, are increased by the isolation in which he holds himself. He stands above, and aloof from, the ordinary human kind:

---

[1] Molière, *Dom Juan* I, i, 100. Byron may have read Molière's play; it is practically certain that he had not read Cicognani and Giliberto the Italian, and Dorimond and Villiers the French, sources of Molière. He speaks of "the Spanish tradition" (LJ. V, 243), but he had surely not read Tirso's *El Burlador de Sevilla y Convidad de Piedra*. In *Don Juan* (I, i) he refers to "the pantomime" as the source of general knowledge of the legend.

[2] Charles Baudelaire, *Don Juan aux Enfers, Les Fleurs du Mal*, p. 106.

[3] *Don Juan* XV, lvii. Cf. Mayne, II, 110 f.

[4] See Appendix II.

"From my youth upwards
My spirit walked not with the souls of men" (II, ii, 50 f.).

When the Chamois-hunter tells him of the comforts to be found
in the "aid of holy men and heavenly patience", he breaks in
upon him with —

"Preach it to mortals of a dust like thine, —
I am not of thine order!" (II, i, 37 f.)

This is recognized even by the supernatural powers.[1] The
presence of such supermen among the general race of human
beings is an idea of frequent occurrence in Byron's poetry.
The greater intellect "moulds another's weakness to its will"
and "the power of thought — the magic of the mind"[2] binds
to the leader the faith of his followers. This is, as Shelley
records, a strong trait in Byron's own character —

"The sense that he was greater than his kind
Had struck, methinks, his eagle spirit blind
By gazing on its own exceeding light."[3]

Instead of exercising this power along vulgar lines, Manfred,
like Faust, exhibits it in the ceaseless quest after knowledge.
He trusts in the strength of mind to attain to a spiritual
revelation of the mysteries of the universe. Arimanes and his
crew represent the flaming walls of the world within which
his cabined ample spirit is penned, and against which he rebels.
Refusing to submit to such limitations, he reaches out into
communion with the whole. This is of course mysticism, for
he seeks to realize the harmony and unity of nature to which
the mystic aspires. For the attainment of this spiritual communion
Manfred has relied upon knowledge. His mysticism is, like that
of Paracelsus, of an empirical nature and he seeks revelation
through the spiritual interpretation of physical facts. This
leads to a dislike of speculation apart from actual concrete
experience. Manfred therefore seeks the cause of death, not
through abstract speculation, but by study of its effects, an
idea probably suggested to Byron by the opening of Shelley's
Alastor (ll. 18—49). Compare especially:

---

[1] Cf. e. g., II, iv, 51 f.
[2] *The Corsair* I, 182.
[3] *Julian and Maddalo*, ll. 50 f.

"I have made my bed
In charnels and on coffins, where black Death
Keeps record of the trophies won from thee;[1]
Hoping to still those obstinate questionings
Of thee and thine by forcing some lone ghost,
Thy messenger, to render up the tale
Of what we are" (ll. 23—9).

Byron centres Manfred's inquiry upon the mystery of Death, because Death is the very type of the unknown. Inquiry is fruitless; he reaches the boundaries of human nature and human knowledge, and finds there the nothingness of it all. "All that we know is, nothing can be known." "Knowledge is Sorrow", and Science

"But an exchange of ignorance for that
Which is another kind of ignorance" (II, iv, 62 f.)

The secrets of existence remain unfathomed, and even this much gain has been accomplished only by suffering and sacrifice. To win what has proved but dead-sea fruit Manfred had abandoned the society of men. Unlike Paracelsus, he had had "sullen fiends to do his bidding, fallen and hateful sprites" to help him,[2] but their aid had been rejected, because it came with a condition, a pact, which would have broken in upon the untrammelled freedom of his mind.

This rejection of the pact with the spirits of evil is Byron's great alteration of the *Faust*-idea.[3] Manfred retains his independence. There is a variation of the same theme in *Cain* (I, i, 302 f.) and it becomes the central idea of *The Deformed Transformed*, where the devil dispenses with the contract signed in blood, saying,

"You shall have no bond
But your own will, no contract save your deeds" (I, i, 151 f.).

Manfred's quest after knowledge thus ends in failure, and this failure is, as it were, embodied in the character of Astarte. Whatever autobiographical meaning the conception may have, philosophically Astarte is introduced to satisfy the concrete demand for dramatic presentation of the abstract mood of the piece. Her dim and awful history is an instance of the fact

---

[1] Shelley is addressing the "Mother of this unfathomable world."
[2] Browning, *Paracelsus* I, 363 f.
[3] Maturin's *Melmoth the Wanderer* may have furnished him a hint.

that "Knowledge quenches Love," that "Sorrow is Knowledge." There are two other instances in Byron's dramas of this personification of the abstract thought. One is the character of Loredano in *The Two Foscari*, who, besides functioning as the chief factor in the downfall of the Doge and his son, embodies the pride of place, the inexorability, and the injustice of the Venetian aristocracy. The other is Steno in *Marino Faliero*, whose insult to the Doge is the last drop of bitterness which makes his cup overflow, but who is also the concrete embodiment of the vileness of Venetian affairs.

The mood of which Astarte is the concrete expression is that of melancholy begotten of reflexion concerning knowledge under conditions of solitude. The *Manfred*-idea is that knowledge brings trouble and unhappiness. With this is mingled a love of solitude inducing melancholy; and forming the background of the poem, there is a suggestion of Rousseauian "simplicity of life." All these elements are aspects of romanticism. The return to the life of nature is a negation of all government, convention, and society. It is the glorification of exile and solitude. This solitude leads to introspection, brooding melancholy, and that *Weltschmerz* so characteristic of the time. The exaltation of introspection, the constant prying into the secret recesses of the soul, is the cause of that individualism which gives rise to the abundance of personality so obvious in romantic literature. Thus regarded, *Manfred* becomes, as I have said, an epitome of the prevailing thought of the time.

But Manfred does not rest in mere negation; in spite of failure he refuses to abandon the *right to know*. He has "sounded on, a dim and perilous way," and now he scorns to subside into conformity. The obstacles in the way of complete and final knowledge may be insurmountable, but the problem, What is beyond? remains as absorbing as ever. The "obstinate questionings" continue, and the demand for those truths

"Which we are toiling all our lives to find,
In darkness lost, the darkness of the grave."

He is the seeker after absolute truth. Opposed to him are two figures which represent the *doctrinaire* attitude, the acceptance of truth as revealed by authority. The Chamois-hunter, the ordinary man in whom there is more of the dust than of

the deity that commingle in our nature, is yet able to rescue
Manfred and to guide him down in safety to the lowlands.
He is the devotee of a *doctrinaire* religion; he urges Manfred
to seek comfort in the aid of holy men (II, i, 34), and prays
that penitence may restore him to himself (II, i, 88). The
contrast which is hinted at in these scenes with the hunter is
fully expressed later in the poem. The Abbot of Saint Maurice
embodies the implicit acceptance of dogma as opposed to the
search after absolute truth. On his first visit to Manfred he
announces his mission to him:

> "I come to save and not destroy:
> I would not pry into thy secret soul;
> But if these things be sooth, there still is time
> For penitence and pity: reconcile thee
> With the true church, and through the church to
>   Heaven.

> *Manfred:* I hear thee. This is my reply — whate'er
> I may have been, or am, doth rest between
> Heaven and myself — I shall not choose a mortal
> To be my mediator — Have I sinned
> Against your ordinances? prove and punish!

> *Abbot:* My son! I did not speak of punishment,
> But penitence and pardon; — with thyself
> The choice of such remains — and for the last,
> Our institutions and our strong belief
> Have given me power to smooth the path from sin
> To higher hopes and better thoughts" (III, i, 47 f.)

The same dependence upon dogma is characteristic of the monk
in *The Giaour* (ll. 818 f., 1204 f., 1267 f.) and of Adam and Abel
in *Cain*. It is exaggerated to the point of caricature in the
conception of Noah in *Heaven and Earth*. In *Manfred* Byron
gives clearest expression to this opposition to traditionalism.
Trelawny noted that "positiveness and dogmatism irritate him,
he says nothing is certain."[1] But with the sneer at the
priestly attitude there is mingled a sense of the pathos of a
mind confined by authority. This is no mere vulgar attack
on orthodoxy, such as inspired Shelley's youthful work. It is
part of Byron's entire attitude of mind. "The inborn tyranny
of years" and "the omnipotence of opinion" he ceaselessly

---

[1] E. J. Trelawny, *Recollections of Byron, Shelley, and the author*, I, 79.

attacked. The problem is in a way one of epistemology. The eighteenth century combined theoretic intellectual humility with almost boundless practical confidence in the mind. Byron's position is antithetical; though conscious of the limits beyond which the mind has, as yet, failed to penetrate, he continues to assert the boundless possibilities of the intellect.

Manfred is thus the expression of the romantic ideal as opposed to the classic ideal. "Close thy Byron; open thy Goethe," counselled Teufelsdröckh. He had better have left them both unclosed. For Goethe teaches the contented acceptance of limitations; not sluggish ease, but eager effort towards the full realization of definite capabilities, classic finish, rounded wholeness, confined perfection. The choice is the truth rather than the quest of truth. There is danger in this, for in a world where all things are struggling through chaos into harmony nought in which there is life is complete. In death alone is there realization of definite ends. Here is the fundamental distinction between classicism and romanticism. And Byron, in *Manfred* and throughout his poetry, points to an ideal truer and nobler than Goethe's just because it is impossible of accomplishment. Such a doctrine is indeterminate, enormous; but it is full of inspiration.

It is no doctrine of mere negation, such as Carlyle attributes to Byron, and the reader who finds *Manfred* only a poem of revolt has not reached its full meaning. For the final message of the poem is very positive. "Doubt," says Byron in *Don Juan* (XI, 11), is the "sole prism of the Truth's rays," and since "adversity is the first path to Truth" (*ibid.* XII, 50) and Truth is "the grand desideratum" (*ibid.* VII, 81), Manfred bravely faces this doubt and seeks to master it. He shuns nothing; he fears nothing; he will dare "the worst to‾know it,"[1] and though the end is failure, he remains free, — free from alliance with evil, free from submission to pain. *Manfred* is absolutely anti-fatalistic. Byron's opinions on free will and determinism shifted. In *Lara*, for example, there are expressions of a distinctly fatalistic nature, *e. g.* "some mysterious fate" (l. 879), "destiny beset him there" (l. 900); but even Lara, it is said,

---

[1] *Don Juan* XIV, 5.

"at last confounded good and ill,
And *half mistook* for fate the acts of will" (l. 335 f.)

In *Manfred* there are no such doubts. "Man is man and master
of his fate." To the spirits who swarm about him when he
is dying he cries:

"Thou didst not tempt me, and thou couldst not tempt me;
I have not been thy dupe, nor am thy prey —
But was my own destroyer, and will be
My own hereafter. — Back, ye baffled fiends!
The hand of Death is on me — but not yours!"

(III, iv, 137 f.)

Manfred is thus the fullest expression of a doctrine that recurs
constantly throughout Byron's poetry — the doctrine of the
authoritative and reflective principle of conscience, the Categorical Imperative, the affirmation that "Man's Conscience is
the Oracle of God." It is a declaration of moral and spiritual
responsibility; in Meredith's words —

"I take the hap
Of all my deeds. The wind that fills my sails,
Propels; but I am helmsman. Am I wrecked,
I know the devil has sufficient weight
To bear: I lay it not on him, or fate."[1]

To understand and appreciate *Manfred* one must see that
its chief message is one of encouragement and hope. It tells
of the triumph of mind over matter, of soul over body, in that
conflict which a dualistic conception of the universe implies.
Here again is one of the great Byronic "notes," for his poetry
and philosophy are shot through with the idea of this struggle.
In *Manfred*, despite the sense of the clod of clay which clogs
the soul, the final victory is felt to remain with the forces
of good.[2]

---

[1] *Modern Love* xx.

[2] As *Manfred* is Byron's first considerable effort in blank-verse, I have
thought it worth while to scan the entire play. The results of this examination are what one would expect from a poet unaccustomed to blank-verse.
There is but one hypermetric line (III, iii, 9) and there are only three frag-
mentary lines (II, iv, 165; III, ii, 30; III, iii, 59). Of these the last two are
the conventional closing fragments at the end of scenes. All other lines in
the play are quite regular. There are but four cases of epic caesura (I, ii,
52; I, ii, 92; II, i, 87; III, iv, 58). Three of these lines are divided between

Chapter Five.
The Two Venetian Plays.

A trait observable throughout Byron's poetry, often in most unlikely places, is his fidelity to fact. Most of the *juvenilia* have a basis of truth capable of precise determination; as early as 1806 he sent to a friend "a gingle (*sic*) of rhyme ... founded on fact" (LJ. I, 105). Several lines from *Hints from Horace* bear upon this subject.

(1)   "Study Nature's page,
         And sketch the striking traits of every age" (ll. 217 f.)
(2)   "In scenes exciting joy or grief
         We loathe the action which exceeds belief" (ll. 287 f.)
(3) "Fiction does best when taught to look like Truth" (l. 537).
(4) "Expect no credit for too wondrous tales" (l. 539).

The story of *The Giaour* was suggested by an actual adventure (LJ. II, 258 and 311). Byron burnt his early novel and comedy because they "ran into realities" (LJ. II, 337). Of *The Bride of Abydos* he said, "For my *costume* and my *correctness* . . . I will combat lustily" (LJ. II, 283), and that it was "drawn from existence" (LJ. II, 373). *The Corsair* was written "much from existence" (LJ. II, 382). Most of all is this observable in *Don Juan*. "You may rely," he wrote (P. VI, 98), "on my using no nautical word not founded on authority, and no circumstance not grounded in reality." And again (LJ. V, 346), "Almost all *Don Juan* is *real life*, either my own, or from people I knew." Note especially the shipwreck, the siege of Ismail, and the description of Newstead. Note also *Mazeppa, The Prisoner of Chillon, The Island,* the poems founded on events in the lives of Dante and Tasso, and others too numerous to mention.

---

two speakers, which makes more easy the occurrence of the resolved arsis. Caesuraless lines are very few; in fact there is perhaps no line without some interior pause, however light. Harsh and irregular enjambment is avoided, there are very few double feminine endings and weak endings, and the employment of syllabic substitution is very timid. A number of words, however, admit of such scansion, though the elision of one vowel is more probably intended.

This heed for facts is notable in Byron's descriptions of nature, and it has been especially praised by Ruskin. "He is the truest, the sternest Seer of the Nineteenth Century. No imagination dazzles him, no terror daunts, and no interest betrays."[1] "Here at last I had found a man who spoke only of what he had seen and known; and spoke without exaggeration, without mystery, without enmity and without mercy. 'That *is* so — make what you will of it!' . . . The *Arabian Nights* had told me of thieves who had lived in enchanted caves, and beauties who fought with genii in the air; but Byron told me of thieves with whom he had ridden on their own hills, and of the fair Persians or Greeks who lived and died under the very sun that rose over my visible Norwood hills . . . Of all things within the range of human thought he felt the facts and discerned the natures, with accurate justice . . . Even Shakespeare's Venice was visionary; and Portia as impossible as Miranda. But Byron told me of, and reanimated for me, the real people whose feet had worn the marble I trod on."[2]

This rationalistic common sense side of Byron's nature, this anomalous survival of classicism into the heart of romanticism, led him naturally to the historical drama, because of its comparatively slight dependence upon imagination, its harmony with a rationalistic conception of intellectual activity, its basis upon experience. "I could not write upon anything," he told Moore (LJ. III, 254), "without some personal experience and foundation." From Venice he wrote (LJ. V, 93), "I hate things *all fiction;* and therefore the *Merchant* and *Othello* have no great associations to me: but *Pierre* has. There should always be some foundation of fact for the most airy fabric, and pure fiction is but the talent of a liar." These sentiments received their best expression in the two Venetian tragedies.

Marino Faliero.

On February 25, 1817, Byron wrote to Murray (LJ. IV, 58), "Look into 'Moore's (Dr. Moore's) *View of Italy*' for me; in

---

[1] From a suppressed passage in *Fiction, Fair and Foul; Works* XXXIV, 328.

[2] *Praeterita* I, viii; *Works* XXXV, 149—51.

one of the volumes you will find an account of the Doge *Valiere* (it ought to be Falieri) and his conspiracy, or the motives of it. Get it transcribed for me, and send it in a letter to me soon. I want it, and cannot find so good an account of that business here; though the veiled portrait and the place where he was once crowned, and afterwards decapitated, still exist and are shown. I have searched all their histories; but the policy of the old Aristocracy made their writers silent on his motives, which were a private grievance against one of the Patricians. I mean to write a tragedy upon the subject, which appears to me very dramatic; an old man, jealous, and conspiring against the state of which he was actually the reigning Chief. This last circumstance makes it the most remarkable and only fact of the kind in all history of all nations." This letter contains in embryonic form many of the ideas afterwards developed in the play. "But other interests and ideas claimed his attention," says Mr. Coleridge (P, IV, 325), "and for more than three years the project slept." Finally on April 9, 1820, he tells Murray that he has "begun a tragedy on the subject of Marino Faliero" (LJ. V, 7). The drama was finished by July 17 (LJ. V, 52), and the fair copy was in England probably by October 6, 1820 (LJ. V, 86). The play was published early in January, 1821. There was almost immediate trouble with the management of Drury Lane, where the piece was announced for performance. After some delay Byron's solicitors consented to the presentation, but as Byron had foreseen, his play proved quite unsuited to the stage. "I was ill-used in the extreme," he told Medwin (p. 119), "by the Doge being brought on the stage at all, after my Preface."

Byron's primary endeavour in the composition of *Marino Faliero* was for historical accuracy. "History is closely followed," he wrote to Murray (LJ. V, 52). "Dr. Moore's account is in some respects false, and in all foolish and flippant. *None* of the Chronicles (and I have consulted Sanuto, Sandi, Navagero, and an anonymous Siege of Zara, besides the histories of Laugier, Daru, Sismondi, etc.) state, or even hint, that he begged his life; they merely say that he did not deny the conspiracy ... I don't know what your parlour boarders will think of the drama I have founded upon this extraordinary event: the only similar one in history is the story of Agis, King of Sparta, a prince *with* the Commons against the aristocracy, and losing his life therefor; but it shall be sent when copied." E. H. Coleridge (P. V, 326—7) succinctly states the sources employed by Byron, and it is unnecessary to repeat here the list of chroniclers. Nor is it of artistic and poetic importance to note how little actual foundation there is for the legend of the downfall of the traitor Faliero. "The truth of imagination exceeds and transcends at all points the accident of fact."

I have already discussed the influence of Alfieri upon Byron's regular dramas, which is most apparent in *Marino Faliero*. It is remarkable, however, that in spite of his enthusiastic interest in his new foreign model, Byron betrays in *Marino Faliero*, more than anywhere else, his thorough knowledge of Shakespeare.[1] But more direct than the influence of Shakespeare is the influence of Otway's *Venice Preserved*. In a note to *Marino Faliero* V, iii, 8, (P. IV, 454) Byron writes, "I find in reading over (since the completion of this tragedy), for the first time these six years, *Venice Preserved*, a similar reply on a different occasion by Renault, and other coincidences arising from the subject. I need hardly remind the gentlest reader that such coincidences must be accidental, from the very facility of their detection by reference to so popular a play on the stage and in the closet as Otway's chef-d'œuvre." Byron was peculiarly sensitive to the charge of plagiarism, and his word may be taken that the resemblances were coincidences. But he knew Otway's play well In *Childe Harold* (IV, 4) he associated the Rialto with "Shylock and the Moor and Pierre."[2] In two letters he refers to the coincidences between the plays. "I am aware of what you say of Otway," he tells Murray (LJ. IV, 91), "and am a great admirer of his, — all except that maudlin bitch of chaste lewdness and blubbering curiosity, Belvidera, whom I utterly despise, abhor, and detest; but the story of Marino Faliero is different, and, I think, so much finer, that I wish Otway had taken it instead." Again (LJ. V, 89), "Shakespeare and Otway had a million advantages over me, besides the incalculable one of being *dead* from one to

---

[1] See Appendix III.
[2] See also LJ. I, 339; II, 409.

two centuries, and having been both born blackguards (which *are* such attractions to the Gentle living reader): let me then preserve the only one which I could possibly have — that of having been at Venice, and entered more into the local spirit of it. I claim no more."

Hermann Schiff's dissertation[1] is devoted in part to a comparison of *Marino Faliero* and *Venice Preserved*. To his work I am partly indebted in the following paragraphs. Otway's play[2] is so little read that an outline of the plot must be given. *Venice Preserved* is founded on an historical novel by Saint-Réal, *La Conjuration des Espagnols contre la Venise en 1618.*[3] In the play the actual leaders of the historical conspiracy occupy very minor parts and the interest centres in the fortunes of two Venetians, Jaffier and Pierre, who are among the native conspirators with the Spaniards. Belvidera, the daughter of a Venetian senator, has married Jaffier against her father's will, and the two live together in great poverty, shamefully treated by her father. Pierre, one of the plotters, hears of Jaffier's wretched existence and persuades him to join the conspiracy. Jaffier consents and swears secrecy. Pierre stands surety for him, when the other conspirators are suspicious of the son-in-law of a senator. Jaffier himself surrenders his dearly loved wife to one of the band as a guarantee of good faith. The plot is then revealed to him and he learns that his father-in-law is among those to be murdered. This is too great a trial to him, and he forewarns his wife. Moved by her tears and enraged by the insults offered to her by the conspirator who has had her in charge, he betrays the plot to the Senate. Arrests follow; the men are tried and condemned. Jaffier is filled with remorse. When about to die Pierre pardons him for betraying him. Jaffier then, upon the scaffold, stabs Pierre, thus saving him from the disgrace of execution, and kills himself.[4]

---

[1] Hermann Schiff, *Über Lord Byrons "Marino Faliero" und seine anderen geschichtllchen Dramen*, Marburg, 1910.

[2] *The best Plays of Thomas Otway*, ed. Roden Noel, Mermaid Series, London, T. Fisher Unwin, p. 287 f.

[3] See Roden Noel's introduction to the play, p. 288.

[4] There is a comic underplot of a disgusting nature to which there is

In the character of Jaffier there are combined the two
motives that Byron divides between Faliero and Bertram. The
Doge is suspected by the conspirators because he *is* Doge (III,
ii, 90 f.); Jaffier because he is a member of the aristocracy.
Both join the plot because of insults heaped upon them. The
connection between Jaffier and Bertram is even closer. Both
are unable to break loose from private ties; both are moved
to betray their comrades, not by innate treachery, but by compassion. In both plays the conspirators at their trial show a
like scorn of the informer. Compare also the following details.
Calendaro says of Bertram:

> "Yet as he has no mistress, and no wife
> To work upon his milkiness of spirit,
> He may go through the ordeal; it is well
> He is an orphan, friendless save in us:
> A woman or a child had made him less
> Than either in resolve" (II, ii, 79 f.)

Just such motives as those that Calendaro is confident cannot
appeal to Bertram lead Jaffier to betray the plot. Belvidera
tries to get the secret from her husband in much the same
way as Angiola does in *Marino Faliero*. Both poets are here
indebted to the scene between Brutus and Portia in *Julius
Caesar*. Otway admits the resemblance in making Jaffier exclaim,
"O Portia, Portia! what a soul was thine!" (III, ii). Pierre, too,
bears some resemblance to Faliero. He is moved to plot by
the overweening pride of the aristocracy.[1] He has been of
service to the state, and when condemned to death, his speech,
beginning —

> "Are these the trophies I've deserved for fighting
> Your battles with confederated powers?" (IV, ii),

might come from the mouth of Faliero. Faliero's final speech,
"I speak to Time, and to Eternity" (V, iii, 26 f.) may be com-
pared with Jaffier's "Final destruction seize on all the world"
(V, ii, 1 f.), especially with the lines:

> "Let Venice burn
> Hotter than all the rest; here kindle hell
> Ne'er to extinguish" (ll. 6 f.)

---

no parallel in *Marino Faliero*. Otway's introduction of the supernatural
in his final scene likewise offers no analogue.

[1] Cf. Act I, Scene i, *passim*.

But the inspiration of Faliero's terrific denunciation of the "Gehenna of the waters," "the Sea-Sodom," was not literary, but "from the life." It reflects Byron's reaction from the excesses of his Venetian sojourn.[1]

The resemblances between Otway's and Byron's dramas do not extend to the mood and tone of the pieces. Byron is thoroughly in sympathy with the conspirators; here, as always, he is the poet of revolution. Otway rather looks on the fate of Jaffier and Pierre in the light of awful examples. In his dedication he speaks of "the encroachment of republicans," and other expressions betray his royalist sympathies. Byron reflects the ferment and excitement of Italy; Otway covertly satirizes events in English politics of the time.[2] Byron's play is serious from beginning to end; there is no comedy, no humour, hardly a suggestion of Byronic wit. Otway's tragedy is disfigured by scenes of gross comedy, especially those in which the old Senator Antonio[3] appears. The subjective element, so strong in all Byron's verse, is almost entirely absent from Otway, though Schiff (p. 9) says, "Jaffiers Liebe zu Belvidera ist eine Darstellung von Otways Leidenschaft zu Mrs. Barry." Byron's is a tragedy without love — he prided himself on the fact. In Otway's love is the leading *motiv*. Finally, as he himself said, Byron "entered more into the local spirit of it." For Otway's vague and conventional allusions to St. Mark's, the Rialto, the Ducal Palace, Byron substitutes direct and minute references to particular places, local customs, traditions, fashions, and people. "Of the play they may say what they please, but not so of my costume and dram. pers., they having been real existences" (LJ. V, 96).

In *Our Mutual Friend* Dickens contrives that the odour of the slime and scum of the London docks shall never quite be absent from our nostrils. A like effect, in greater degree, is produced in *Measure for Measure*, where one is always

---

[1] Cf. Mayne, II, 161. Cf. also, "Our hatred of that now empty Oyster shell without its pearl — Venice" (LJ. IV, 370).

[2] Cf. the Prologue, p. 293.

[3] The character of Antonio is a disgraceful satire upon the great Earl of Shaftesbury.

conscious of the reek and stench of Vienna. A third instance
of this may be given. Towards the close of *Arden of Faversham*
(IV, ii, 35) Master Arden exclaims, "I am almost stifled in this
fog!" and the reader thinks, not of the sea-mist blowing in
upon Kent, but of that moral fog of sordid gloom and death
that from the commencement of the play has been slowly
enveloping the doomed man. To obtain such effects as these
is indeed to create an *atmosphere* in a work of the imagination.

Byron accomplishes this with singular success in *Marino
Faliero*. Throughout the play there is the impression of the
remorseless power of a corrupt aristocracy. The conflict is
between the patricians and the people, with all right and justice
on the side of the oppressed lower classes. This keynote is
struck at the commencement of the play.

> "*Battista:*   Doubtless 'twas
>   Foul scorn in Steno to offend so grossly.
>   *Pietro:*   Aye, if a poor man: Steno's a patrician,
>   Young, galliard, gay, and haughty.
>   *Battista:*   Then you think
>   He will not be judged hardly?
>   *Pietro:*   'Twere enough
>   He be judged justly" (I, i, 18 f.)

Difference in rank means difference in justice in Venice. There
is an essential flaw in the administration of the state. Again
and again this idea is insisted upon. There is an inward
rottenness, a canker eating the heart out of the ancient insti-
tutions of Venice. When Bertuccio, sounding Faliero as to
the conspiracy, asks him, "Wouldst thou be sovereign lord of
Venice?" "Aye," the Doge answers,

> "If that the people shared that sovereignty,
> So that nor they nor I were further slaves
> Of this o'ergrown aristocratic Hydra,
> The poisonous heads of whose envenomed body
> Have breathed a pestilence upon us all" (I, ii, 418 f.)

The Doge cannot claim the duty of the Senate (II, i, 157); he
is a mere puppet who scarce can obtain right for himself (II,
ii, 32). Musing over Venice he exclaims:

> "Thou must be cleansed of the black blood which makes thee
> A lazar-house of tyranny" (II, i, 8 f.),

these "plague spots," this "Patrician pestilence," must be
done away. It is no matter of pride and vice in certain
individuals;

> "It is not
> Their numbers, be it tens or thousands, but
> The spirit of this Aristocracy
> Which must be rooted out" (III, ii, 38 f.)

"Fatal poison to the springs of Life" is in "the present insti-
tutes of Venice" (III, ii, 316 f.) Thus, when the traitor Bertram
comes to Lioni, the latter believes that he seeks shelter for
some crime, and says:

> "So that thou hast not
> Spilt noble blood, I guarantee thy safety" (IV, i, 144 f.)

Contrast this with the certainty expressed by Pietro in the
first scene that had Steno been a plebian he would have been
condemned.

The theme is the overthrow of the aristocratic oppressors
of the people. The miserable condition of Venice under Austrian
domination greatly influenced Byron in this conception. It is
almost superfluous to recall how constantly the celebration of
political liberty recurs in Byron's verse. From the days of the
first canto of *Childe Harold* to the end of *Don Juan* the note
is constantly struck.

> "Revolution
> Alone can save the earth from hell's pollution." [1]

He believes it a noble task "from foreign yoke to free the
helpless native,"[2] but after all, "who would be free themselves
must strike the blow"[3] — an idea reaffirmed long after in "The
Isles of Greece":

> "In native swords and native ranks,
> The only hope of courage dwells" (stanza 14).

He is confident in the ultimate outcome. The mob are tired of
imitating Job, and "the people by and by will be the stronger."[4]
There is never a sign of despair or of any tendency to subside
into placid acceptance.

---

[1] *Don Juan* VIII, 51.
[2] *Ibid.* XIII, 10.
[3] *Childe Harold* II, 76.
[4] *Don Juan* VIII, 50.

"Yet, Freedom! yet thy banner, torn but flying,
Streams like the thunder-storm *against* the wind."[1]

Finally, and with especial reference to *Marino Faliero*, note
two passages from his journal, written in 1821. *"Onward!* —
it is now the time to act, and what signifies *self,* if a single
spark of that which would be worthy of the past can be
bequeathed unquenchedly to the future? It is not one man,
nor a million, but the *spirit* of liberty which must be spread.
The waves which dash upon the shore are, one by one, broken,
but yet the *ocean* conquers, nevertheless . . . In like manner,
whatever the sacrifice of individuals, the great cause will
gather strength, sweep down what is rugged, and fertilise . . .
what is cultivable" (LJ. V, 163 f.) "It is no great matter, supposing
that Italy could be liberated, who or what is sacrificed. It is
a grand object — the very *poetry* of politics" (LJ. V, 205).

But that clear vision so characteristic of Byron forces him
to see the opposite side of the picture. Though he teaches
the very stones "to rise against earth's tyrants,"[2] though an
absolute autocrat is much worse than a barbarian,[3] he warns
men against the dangers of the opposite extreme.

"It is not that I adulate the people:
Without *me*, there are demagogues enough . . .
. . . . I wish men to be free,
As much from mobs as kings — from you as me."[4]

And again he speaks of —
"The most infernal of all evils here,
The sway of petty tyrants in a state;
For such sway is not limited to kings,
And *demagogues* yield to them but in date
As swept off sooner."[5]

The object of their conspiracy is thus stated by Faliero:
"You are met
To overthrow this Monster of a state,
This mockery of a Government, this spectre,

---

[1] *Childe Harold* IV, 98. Cf. —
        "The thunder comes
     Sullen against the wind" (Keats, *Otho the Great* II, i, 57).
[2] *Don Juan* VIII, 135.
[3] *Ibid.* IX, 23.
[4] *Ibid.* IX, 25.
[5] *The Prophecy of Dante* IV, 117 f.

Which must be exorcised with blood — and then ·
We will renew the times of Truth and Justice,
Condensing in a fair free commonwealth
Not rash equality but equal rights" (III, ii, 164 f.)

This last line is significant. It shows, in contrast to Shelley's
Utopian dream of man "tribeless and nationless," how steadily
Byron held to the *fact*. Such passages show Byron's greatness
as a moral force and a true leader. There are in them no
emotional dreams. Shunning the bugbear of monarchy, he
does not lose himself in the mists of popular theories. He is
practical.

The Doge, Marino Faliero, is almost Byron's ideal of a
hero. History (or legend) records him as being proud, revenge-
ful, jealous; but of history Byron selects only those facts
that accord with his conception.[1] The aristocratic spirit, the
innate feeling of *caste*, of which I have already spoken, is
strong in Faliero. Note the lines (III, ii, 319 f.) in which he
contrasts his position with that of his fellow-conspirators. In-
voluntarily he shrinks from his accomplices, as when Calendaro
cries "Be our general and chief," and he answers:

"Chief! — general! — I was general at Zara,
And chief in Rhodes and Cyprus, prince in Venice:
I cannot stoop — that is, I am not fit
To lead a band of — patriots" (III, ii, 217 f.)[2]

With this aristocratic pride there is mingled an over-sensitive
honor and a habit of command (II, ii, 162 f.) But he is no
tyrant (III, ii, 534 f.) From the moment when, hurrying from
Rome to take up the reins of office, he first experienced the
thwarting, baffling power of the Senate (III, ii, 346 f.), the germ
of revolt had been within him. Before Steno's insult there
had been wrong enough and to spare.

"Begirt with spies for guards — with robes for power —
With pomp for freedom — gaolers for a council —
Inquisitors for friends — and hell for life.
I had one only fount of quiet left,
And *that* they poisoned. My pure household gods
Were shiver'd on my hearth"[3] (III, ii, 358 f.)

---

[1] Cf. Byron's alteration of the traditional motive of the murder in *Cain*.

[2] Cf. also III, i, 65 f. and 99 f.

[3] The parallel passages cited by E. H. Coleridge (P. IV, 404) are not

But it is not mere private wrongs that move him.

"A spark creates the flame — 'tis the last drop
Which makes the cup run o'er, and mine was full
Already"[1] (V, i, 245 f.)

Steno furnishes but the final provocation;

"his offence
Was a mere ebullition of the vice,
The general corruption generated
By the foul Aristocracy" (III, ii 402 f.)

He embodies all that the Doge has to contend with in Venice.
He is a concrete instance of the foulness, injustice, and rank,
weedy growth of the Venetian aristocracy. He resolves the
abstract mood into a situation capable of dramatic treatment.[2]
But Byron, who admits no absolute villain in his plays, gives
him grace at least to express penitence and implore pardon
(V, i, 398 f.)

Faliero feels that many of his wrongs have come upon
him through his pity for the people (III, ii, 195). Even in
moments of passion he puts the public cause before his private
injuries.[3] Bertuccio says:

"His mind is liberal,
He sees and feels the people are oppressed,
And shares their sufferings" (II, ii, 174 f.)

Hence the singular attraction of his character for Byron: an
aristocrat, devoted to the cause of the people.[4] He harkens
to the call of the higher loyalty, and submission to that call
brings with it its reward.

"They never fail who die
In a great cause: the block may soak their gore;
Their heads may sodden in the sun; their limbs

---

very apt. Cf. therefore: "The desolation piled upon me, when I stood alone
upon my hearth, with my household gods shivered around me" (LJ. IV, 262).
"Standing alone besides his desolate hearth,
Where all his household gods lay shivered round him."
(*Don Juan* I, 36, and cf. III, 51).

[1] In Byron's *Reply to Blackwood's Edinburgh Magazine* (LJ. IV,
477) occur almost the same words: "It is the last drop which makes the cup
run over, and mine was already full."

[2] Cf. the character of Astarte in *Manfred*.

[3] Cf. among other places, I, ii, 192 and 316 f.; II, i, 406 f.; III, i, 45 f.

[4] Cf. especially III, ii, 437 f. and V, iii, 16 f.

> Be strung to city gates and castle walls —
> But still their spirit walks abroad. Though years
> Elapse, and others share as dark a doom,
> They but augment the deep and sweeping thoughts
> Which overpower all others, and conduct
> The world at last to freedom" (II, ii, 93 f.)

Noble and impressive words; not those of a jaded egoist,
surely! The moral victory is won long before material success
or failure. The choice of the nobler and manlier part is the
real victory.

> "Is it the *pain* of blows, or *shame* of blows,
> That makes such deadly to the sense of man?"
>
> (II, i, 246 f.)

Byron himself answers Faliero's question —

> "'Tis the cause makes all,
> Degrades or hallows courage in its fall."[1]

Here again is the Byronic exaltation of mind over matter, of
spirit over external circumstance, that essential subjectivity
always apparent in Byron's attitude towards life. Faliero, on
the brink of eternity, declares:

> "We'll meet it
> As men whose triumph is not in success,
> But who can make their own minds all in all
> Equal to every fortune"[2] (IV, i, 276 f.)

Of the minor characters in the play the most notable are
Angiola and Bertram. The conspirators and the senators are
conventional types, and I have already spoken of Steno.

In many respects Angiola is the superior of her husband.
He is drawn into the plot in a moment of passion; Steno can
provoke in her only a scornful smile. Her honor is above the
need of commendation from men. She has —

> "the sense
> Of virtue, looking not to what is called
> A good name for reward, but to itself" (V, i, 417 f.)

Early in the play she tells Faliero that there is no need of
stripes and imprisonment for Steno:

> "There seems to be enough in the conviction
> Of a patrician guilty of a falsehood:

---

[1] *The Island* IV, 261 f.

[2] Cf. Lucifer's last words to Cain, II, ii, 463 f.

All other punishments were light unto
His loss of honour" (II, i, 230 f.)

Her last words of Steno are:

"We leave him to himself, that lowest depth
Of human baseness" (V, i, 457 f.)

These are clear enunciations of the Categorical Imperative. Is
it a low conception of woman that imagines her as depending
upon so lofty a moral code? She is brave and firm; to the
last she supports her husband and presents an unwavering
front to his accusers. "What more pure and lofty than this
character of Angiola . . .?" asks Bulwer.[1] "I know not in
the circle of Shakespeare's women one more true, not only to
nature — that is a slight merit — but to the highest and rarest
order of nature."

Lastly, of Bertram. Byron palliates his treachery. In Act II,
Scene ii, two of the conspirators discuss their plans together.
Calendaro doubts the "hesitating softness" of Bertram (l. 68),
but admits that he fears "less treachery than weakness" (l. 78).
From this conversation the reader is prepared for Bertram's
treachery. His hesitation is displayed when he reports to Calendaro that he has not yet completed the number in his
company (III, ii, 6 f.) and a moment later he asks that some
of the Senators may be spared in the general slaughter (l. 22 f.)
Bertram admits his "natural weakness," his shrinking from
"indiscriminate murder" (l. 64 f.) The rest of the scene passes
without further reference to possible treachery. But the reader
is prepared for what follows. Bertram reveals the plot to
Lioni, having vainly tried to persuade him to remain at home
on the following day. Motives of affection and gratitude force
this treachery upon him (IV, i, 198 f.), and thus mitigate in a
measure the shame of the betrayal of his friends. Bertram is
unequal to the test of the higher loyalty; private obligations
and friendship weigh more with him than the public weal.

"Such ties are not
For those who are called to the high destinies
Which purify corrupted commonwealths;
We must forget all feelings save the one,
We must resign all passions save our purpose,

---

[1] *England and the English* II, 76; cited by Schiff, p. 28.

We must behold no object save our country,
And only look on Death as beautiful,
So that the sacrifice ascend to Heaven,
And draw down Freedom on her evermore" (II, ii, 84 f.)

The Two Foscari.

Byron's second Venetian play is of much less importance
and merit than *Marino Faliero* of the themes of which play it
is largely a re-working. It was begun, according to E. H. Coleridge (P. V, 115), on June 12, and finished on July 9, 1821.[1]
On July 14 Byron sent the new play to Murray (LJ. V, 322).
"The argument . . . Foscolo or Hobhouse can explain to you;
or you will find it at length in P. Daru's history of Venice:
also, more briefly, in Sismondi's *I.R.*[2] An outline of it is in
the *Pleasures of Memory* also." This last passage is quoted in
a note by Mr. Prothero.[3] From it and the note which Rogers
attached to it (p. 94) Byron probably derived his first knowledge of the story. His facts he got from Daru's *Histoire de
la République de Venise* (1821, II, 520 f.) and from Sismondi's
Histoire des Républiques . . . *du Moyen Age* (1815, X, 36 f.)
He does not seem to have gone to original "authorities" as
much as he had done during the composition of *Marino Faliero*.
Schiff (p. 49 f.) gives a considerable number of close parallels
between Daru's narrative and *The Two Foscari*.

The sense of civic corruption, so strong in *Marino Faliero*,
reappears in *The Two Foscari*, but it takes slightly different
shape. In the earlier play the condition of the people had
been considered desperate, but not hopeless. Now, the impression is of a helpless and chaotic mob:

"There's no people, you well know it,
Else you dare not deal thus by them or me.
There is a *populace*, perhaps, whose looks

---

[1] Mr. Coleridge does not state where he finds these exact dates; the
MS. is apparently undated. Moreover, on July 9 Byron had only "nearly
completed the tragedy on the Foscaris" (LJ. V, 322).

[2] The initials apparently stand for "Italian Republic"; Mr. Prothero
offers no explanation of them, nor is the reference included among the "Books
read by Byron" in the index to LJ.

[3] The lines are Part I, ll. 225 f. Cf. Rogers' later and longer version
of the story, in *Italy*, section 19.

> May shame you; but they dare not groan nor curse you,
> Save with their hearts and eyes" (V, i, 257 f.)

It is not merely that the aristocracy have become more powerful.
Their power has become concentrated in the "Ten," who represent and control the state. The state is felt to be possessed
of a mystery, power, and personality. Again and again there
are references to the duties of citizenship. The individual is
as nothing in comparison with the commonwealth.

> "In such a state
> An individual, be he richest of
> Such rank as is permitted, or the meanest,
> Without a name, is alike nothing, when
> The policy, irrevocably tending
> To one great end, must be maintained in vigour"
>   (II, i, 408 f.)

From this sense of the personality of the state there result
two things. On the one hand there is gross abuse of power
by those who, shrouded in the mystery of the commonwealth,
are the real governors. On the other there is implicit obedience and ready sacrifice on the part of citizens. When
Marina, overwrought by the sight of her husband's sufferings,
says:

> "Would he
> But think so, to my mind the happiest doom,
> Not he alone, but all who dwell here, could
> Desire, were to escape from such a land" (II, i, 272 f.),

the Doge replies, *"That is not a Venetian thought,* my daughter."
This furnishes a hint towards the understanding of Jacopo
Foscari's overmastering love of Venice. To Medwin (p. 117)
Byron remarked, "That Faliero should, for a slight to a woman,
become a traitor to his country and conspire to massacre all
his fellow-nobles, and that the young Foscari should have a
sickly affection for his city, were no inventions of mine. I
painted the men as I found them, as they were, — not as the
critics would have them. I took the stories as they were handed
down; and if human nature is not the same in one country
as it is in another, am I to blame? But no painting, however
highly coloured, can give an idea of the intensity of a Venetian's affection for his native city." The reply of the Doge,

quoted above, shows that such a love was not uncommon. In Jacopo's case it is mingled with boyish associations and recollections; his soul is social (III, i, 109) and his mind "sinks in solitude." Away from Venice he yearns for her,[1] and when asked, "Can you so much love the soil which hates you?" he answers:

"The soil! — Oh no! it is the seed of the soil
Which persecutes me: but my native earth
Will take me as a mother to her arms" (I, i, 140 f.)

Nevertheless Byron hardly succeeds in making the character of the younger Foscari convincing.

Just as the state exacts love from the son, so she exacts duty from the father. Once more Byron has a study of the choice of loyalties. The Doge chooses the higher, and presides at the trial and torture of his son. A line in *Parisina* (l. 406) — "To see the son fall by the doom of the Father" — had already touched on this conflict. The theme is of course an old one — as old as the Roman Republic; but that Byron chose such a situation for dramatic treatment and elaborated it with care is proof of the importance which he attached to this doctrine of loyalty to the highest claims upon our allegiance.

Over the lives of these two men the state holds absolute sway. This vague, brooding personality is felt to be full of mystery:

"Men know as little
Of the state's real acts as of the grave's
Unfathom'd mysteries" (I, i, 184 f.)

To this mood Loredano gives concrete expression. He is the embodiment of the inexorable injustice of the Venetian aristocracy. He has its pride of place, its determination, its pitiless grinding of the individual. His moving passions are hatred and revenge. The other men of the play are but shadows.

---

[1] In Foscari's words, "That malady Which calls up green and native fields to view" (III, i, 172), there is a reference to the Falstaffian *motiv*, "babbling of green fields." Compare *The Island* II, 276; *Don Juan* XVI, 46 Coleridge's *Osorio* IV, 213 f.; Keats's *Letters*, ed. H. B. Forman, p. 461. I give these parallels as the expression of this "longing lingering look behind" is not very frequent in literature.

Byron has little of the Shakespearean ability to put individuality into even minor characters.

Marina should be grouped with Angiola and Myrrha. She
has that "tender fierceness of the dove"[1] which will fight to
shield her mate. She is no ignoble creature, for she dares defy
the assembled patricians, the enemies of her family. But her
outlook is limited; she has no conception of that higher loyalty,
that wider view, which is the Doge's guiding motive. Her
husband and children are home and country (V, i, 95); as Adah
with Cain did not much regret the loss of Eden, so with Jacopo Foscari Marina could live in happiness far from Venice.
Nevertheless some of the noblest sentiments of the play come
from her lips. Like Angiola, she has the proud consciousness
of innocence, and that suffices her. Moral superiority is the
feeling on which she builds her hopes and sets her rest. Here
she rises to a height to which her father and husband cannot
attain. Thus, she tells Loredano:

> "You are his equal, as
> You think; but that you are not, nor would be,
> Were he a peasant" (II, i, 290 f.)

Facing the enemy of their house in her husband's dungeon,
when Foscari says that she is of a house as noble as that of
Loredano, she exclaims "Nobler!" "How nobler?" asks Loredano. "As more generous!" is her reply (III, i, 289 f.) As she
sees that the soul is superior to position in life, so she feels
that the mind should rise above the petty woes that afflict the
body. In the dungeon Foscari tells her that he still believes
his life may be taken:

> "*Mar.*:   Thy life is safe.
> *Fos.*:   And liberty?
> *Mar.*:   The mind should make its own."
>   (III, i, 83 f.)

This answer is not unworthy of comparison with that of Isa-
bel to Claudio: "Death is a fearful thing" — "And shamed
life a hateful!"

The technical shortcomings of *The Two Foscari* — and
they are most serious — have been dealt with in an earlier

---

[1] *Childe Harold* I, 57.

chapter. The memorable thing about the piece is that it puts into dramatic form the great Byronic theme of intellectual freedom. Jacopo Foscari could learn from Tasso:

> "I stoop not to despair;
> For I have battled with mine agony,
> And made me wings wherewith to overfly
> The narrow circus of my dungeon wall."[1]

In the *Sonnet on Chillon* (P. IV, 7) Byron invokes the

> "Eternal Spirit of the chainless Mind!
> Brightest in dungeons, Liberty!"[2]

Chapter Six.
Sardanapalus.

There are two circumstances in Byron's life that greatly influenced the composition of *Sardanapalus*. The year 1818, with all its splendid results in poetry, had been morally the lowest in Byron's career. His dissolute, reckless life in Venice was partly a reaction from Shelley's influence in Switzerland, partly his manner of remonstrance against hypocritical cant, partly a way of laughing that he might not weep. The inevitable reaction from this sort of thing was furnished by the liaison with the Countess Guiccioli to whom Byron was introduced in April, 1819. From June till the autumn Byron was with her constantly. A separation resulted in the serious illness

---

[1] *The Lament of Tasso*, ll. 20f.

[2] A note may be added on Miss Mitford's *Foscari* which, though not performed till 1826, was composed before the publication of *The Two Foscari*. The coincidence is of interest. *Foscari* (*Cumberland's British Theatre* XXXVIII) is technically a far better composition than Byron's piece. It is a romantic drama, and not following the rules, has the advantage of beginning the action at an earlier stage of the story, with consequent clearness of motivation. It disregards history recklessly. In place of a younger Foscari accused of treason we have one charged with the murder of his sweetheart's father. In place of Loredano moved by the desire for vengeance, we have Erizzo, moved by low ambition and envy of Foscari. Both father and son are entirely guiltless of wrong-doing. The piece is rather interesting, but tame and quite lacking in poetry and the higher reaches of tragic feeling.

of the Countess, and the only cure was to send for Byron, who was established as a permanent member of the Count's family. Meanwhile he had become interested in the Carboneria[1], and the Count's house in Ravenna became a centre of revolutionists. This, probably, rather than outraged feelings, made him insist upon a separation, which was granted by the Pope in June, 1820. La Guiccioli now retired to her father's house, where Byron visited her, though he continued to live at the Palazzo Guiccioli! In the autumn of 1821 the Gambas were exiled from papal territory and Byron followed his lady to Pisa, where in November, 1821 they took up their abode in the Palazzo Lanfranchi. Here they remained until after Shelley's death, when, partly in consequence of that catastrophe and partly to escape the annoyance of constant surveillance by the Tuscan police, they moved to a villa near Genoa, where they remained till Byron's departure for the East in July, 1823.

Early in 1821, in the midst of his liaison and of public events of the keenest interest, Byron began *Sardanapalus*. Jeaffreson exclaims on the difficulty "to account for an industry so incessant and astoundingly prolific under circumstances so unfavourable to meditation and creative effort."[2] For *Sardanapalus* was but one of many literary projects of these days. In *Don Juan* (II, 207) occur the lines:

> "'Eat, drink, and love, what can the rest avail us?'
> So said the royal sage Sardanapalus."

This had been published in 1819. In his *Reply to Blackwood's Edinburgh Magazine* (LJ. IV, 474 f.), written at Ravenna, March 15, 1820, refuting the charge of certain vices, he says, "With regard to the first sentence, I shall content myself with observing that it appears to have been composed for Sardanapalus, Tiberius, the Regent Duke of Orleans, or Louis XV," etc. These two passages show that the story of the luxurious king was in his mind. The first reference to the play is found in Byron's diary for January 13, 1821 (LJ. V, 172). "Sketched the outline and Drams. Pers. of an intended tragedy of Sardanapalus, which I have for some time meditated. Took the names from Diodorus Siculus, (I know the history of Sardana-

---

[1] See *The Cambridge Modern History*, New York, Macmillan, X, 111 .

[2] J. C. Jeaffreson, *The Real Lord Byron*. 1883, II, 150.

palus, and have known it since I was twelve years old,) and read over a passage in the ninth vol. octavo of Mitford's *Greece*, where he rather vindicates the memory of this last of the Assyrians[1] . . . I carried Teresa the Italian translation of Grillparzer's *Sappho*, which she promises to read. She quarrelled with me because I said that love was *not the loftiest* theme for true tragedy; and, having the advantage of her native language, and natural female eloquence, she overcame my fewer arguments. I believe she was right. I must put more love into *Sardanapalus* than I intended. I speak, of course, if the times will allow me leisure." Following this entry there are many references to the growth of the new tragedy, all summed up in the note at the end of the MS. of *Sardanapalus* (P. V, 112): "Ravenne, May 27th. 1821. Mem. — I began the drama on the 13th. of January, 1821, and continued the two first acts very slowly and at long intervals. The three last acts were written since the 13th. of May, 1821 (this present month, that is to say in a fortnight)." The play was published with *Cain* and *The Two Foscari*, December 19, 1821.

The sources of *Sardanapalus* present no problem. A foreword to the play (P. V, 11), reads, "In this tragedy it has been my intention to follow the account of Diodorus Siculus; reducing it, however, to such dramatic regularity as I best could, and trying to approach the unities." In the second book of the *Bibliothecae Historicae* is found the story of the effeminate, slothful, and debauched king, who, driven to arms by rebellion, committed suicide after exhausting all means of resistance. The pseudo-historical character of Sardanapalus does not concern us, and E. H. Coleridge (P. V, 3 f.) gives all requisite information on the subject.

Of Byron's "regular" dramas *Sardanapalus* is certainly the greatest. It stands somewhat apart from the Venetian plays in that the historical element is slighter. Roden Noel says it "seems to me one of our really excellent plays."[2] Brandes[3] is of the same opinion. George Finley, who saw

---

[1] E. H. Coleridge prints the passage from Mitford, P. V, 23 f.

[2] *Life of Lord Byron*, London, Walter Scott, 1890, p. 160.

[3] *Main Currents in Nineteenth Century Literature*, trans. Diana White and Mary Morison, New York, Macmillan, 1901 f., IV, 336.

Byron at Missolonghi shortly before his death, noted that the poet considered it his best tragedy.[1] The cause of this excellence is two-fold. The remoteness of the theme leaves the mind of the reader open to any impression that the poet desires to convey. Hence, in spite of absurdities arising from strict adherence to the unities, a definite *vraisemblance* remains. There is plenty of action; the characters do not merely plan and talk. But more important than this there is real portrayal of character. "In *Sardanapalus* alone," says Elze, "is there an instance of the development of character."[2]

With the exception of *Manfred* the biographical element enters more largely into *Sardanapalus* than into any of the dramas. Nieschlag[3] devotes a large part of his monograph to establishing the identity of various characters in the play. That the three chief characters are idealized portraits admits of no doubt. I shall briefly indicate the leading points that connect the play with Byron's own life, but this shall be done incidentally in the course of discussion of the chief characters.

Westenholz (p. 45 f.) thinks that the moral awakening which is the key-note of the drama reflects Byron's abandonment of "the mud of Venice" for the more respectable liaison with the Countess Guiccioli.[4] His intense interest in the plots and plans of the Carbonari for the liberation of Italy from the Austrian yoke is the inspiration of the anti-tyrant theme that runs through the play, but the clearer record of this interest is found in the two Venetian plays and has been sufficiently discussed in the last chapter.

Sardanapalus is drawn from the life; he is the idealization of Byron's conception of his own character, — almost an *apologia pro vita sua*. The central trait of his character is put before the reader in Salamenes' opening speech:

"If born a peasant, he had been a man
To have reached an empire: to an empire born
He will bequeath none; nothing but a name" (I, i, 13 f.)

---

[1] Edgcumbe, p. 101.

[2] Karl Elze, *Life of Byron*, 1872, p. 404.

[3] Hermann Nieschlag, *Über Lord Byrons "Sardanapalus,"* Halle, 1900, p. 28 f.

[4] This was of course no new idea; it had been suggested in Galt's *Life of Byron*, 1830, and was probably obvious to the poet's friends.

The latent energies in his nature have been repressed by circumstance, and because ease and pleasure were at hand he has taken his fill of them. The influence of environment upon character is frequently dwelt upon in the poetry of Byron; such phrases as "The influence of the clime,"[1] "As the soil is, so the heart of man,"[2] "Circumstances make men,"[3] are often met with. This becomes an important *motiv* in *Sardanapalus*. "All are the sons of circumstance," says the king (III, i, 320), and again:

> "I am the very slave of circumstance
> And impulse — borne away with every breath!
> Misplaced upon the throne — misplaced in life."
>
> (IV, i, 330 f.)

This, by a natural process of expansion, leads to the affirmation of determinism, not thorough-going, for here Byron's position shifts much, but from time to time confidently asserted. "Fate made me what I am — may make me nothing," says Sardanapalus (I, ii, 627), and Byron himself furnishes the essential comment:

> "Destiny and Passion spread the net
> *(Fate is a good excuse for our own will)*;
> And caught them."[4]

This was written at a later date. The mood of *Sardanapalus* is fatalistic. It is echoed in a remark of about the same date: "I have always believed that all things depend upon Fortune, and nothing upon ourselves" (LJ. V, 451). With this should be compared the long passage in *The Two Foscari* (II, i, 332 f.) in which the sense of the influence of environment gradually develops into the conviction that the governing principle of the universe is determinism.

The admission once made that man is but the sport of circumstance, there is no restraining hand to keep the voluptuous king from full indulgence in sensual selfishness. The resemblance here to *Don Juan* is close. Juan is the most amiable of Byron's heroes. He is no cynic or misanthrope,

---

[1] *Don Juan* III, 56.
[2] *Ibid.* IV, 55.
[3] *Detached Thoughts*, No. 32, LJ. V, 424.
[4] *Don Juan* XIII, 12.

no "perfect Timon not nineteen," but young, enthusiastic, eager to enjoy all things. Taking life as it comes, he accepts the love of Julia and Haidée and Dudu and the Empress and the Duchess, along with shipwreck and slavery and war and diplomacy. He does not seek; things come his way. He has no will in the matter, but is blown resistlessly, if not helplessly, before every wind of chance. Herein lies the moral objection to *Don Juan*; it presupposes, as Mr. Coleridge says (P. VI, xviii), no resistance to temptation, but rather submission to passion. The character of Sardanapalus is very similar. Byron made him "as *amiable* as my poor powers could render him" (LJ. V, 299), "almost a comic character"[1] (LJ. V, 324); but like Juan he is "the sport of circumstances" and is caught in the net spread by passion.

The very traits that result in voluptuous ease are also the cause of that humanitarianism that makes him opposed to war. This is typically Byronic. "Note this main point in Byron's character," wrote Ruskin. "He was the first great Englishman who felt the cruelty of war, and, in its cruelty, the shame. Its guilt had been known to George Fox — its folly shown practically by Penn. But the *compassion* of the pious world had still for the most part been shown only in keeping its stock of Barabbases unhanged if possible: and, till Byron came, neither Kunersdorf, Eylau, nor Waterloo, had taught the pity and the pride of men that —

> 'The drying up a single tear has more
> Of honest fame than shedding seas of gore.'"

In a note Ruskin adds: "Juan VIII, 3; compare 14, and 63, with all its lovely context 61—68; then 82, and afterwards slowly and with thorough attention, the Devil's speech, beginning, 'Yes, Sir, you forget' in scene 2 of *The Deformed Transformed*: then Sardanapalus's, Act I, Scene 2, beginning, 'He is gone and on his finger bears my signet,' and finally the *Vision of Judgment*, stanzas 3 to 5."[2] Nevertheless, if a cause be sanctified by right, then war is justified;[3] otherwise

---

[1] This remark has occasioned some discussion (e. g. by Schiff, p. 37 f.), but it refers, I think, only to the king's frequent sallies of wit.

[2] *Fiction, Fair and Foul, Works* XXXIV, 328.

[3] *Don Juan* IX, 4.

"murder" and "glory" are much the same thing;[1] hence his praise of Leonidas and Washington,

"Whose every battle-field is holy ground,
Which breathes of nations saved, not worlds undone."[2]

This brave hostility to war, in which Byron voices the modern spirit of international understanding, is combined with a clear-sighted knowledge of the ephemeral nature and pettiness of fame and glory, unless won in the cause of freedom. This idea is constantly present in Byron's poetry. It is especially notable in the earlier part of *Sardanapalus* (I, ii, 121 f., 226 f., 259 f., and 548 f.) Yet the king, when aroused, is capable of defending his rights and dies rather than yield. In battle he shows energy that all his "palling pleasures" have not sapped, and his bravery amounts to rashness. He fights, not for love of glory, "that airy lust,"[3] but in defence of the empire. For Byron is careful so to motive the actions of the king's opponents that no sympathy shall be expended upon them. They fight, not for liberty, but for personal aggrandizement.

The keen insight shown by Sardanapalus as to the vanity of glory causes in him a certain contempt for his own kingly position, which he values chiefly as a means to pleasure. Frequently he contrasts his own pleasure-loving life with the career of his ancestress Semiramis. When reminded by Salamenes of her conquest of Bactria, he retorts with a reminder of her miserable retreat with but twenty guards. "Is *this* glory?" he asks (I, ii, 138). He honors Bacchus, not as the conqueror of India, but as the first that

"from out the purple grape
Crushed the sweet poison of misused wine,"

though he would have suppressed the last epithet. After speaking of bloodshed and sepulchres he says:

"I leave such things to conquerors; enough
For me, if I can make my subjects feel
The weight of human misery less, and glide
Ungroaning to the tomb" (I, i, 262 f.)

And at his midnight banquet he asks his guests:

---

[1] *Don Juan* VII, 26.
[2] *Ibid.* VIII, 5.
[3] *Ibid.* IV, 101.

> "Is this not better now than Nimrod's hunting,
> Or my wild grandam's chase in search of kingdoms
> She could not keep when conquered?" (III, i, 5 f.)

Altada praises the king for having "placed his joy in peace —
the sole true glory." Sardanapalus adds:

> "And pleasure, good Altada, to which glory
> Is but the path" (III, i, 12).

With this compare the following entry in Byron's journal (LJ. V,
176). "The only pleasure of fame is that it paves the way to
pleasure" — a remark written two days after Byron began
Sardanapalus.

Analogous to his scorn of kingship and glory is his distrust
of priests. Priests and soldiers are "the most dangerous orders
of mankind" (II, i, 231), but Sardanapalus distrusts the priest
more than the soldier (II, i, 277). Byron's anti-clericalism was
never as violent as Shelley's and among his intimate friends
were curiously enough a number of clergymen (Dallas, Drury,
Hodgson). His attack upon priests in *Sardanapalus* should be
collated with the anti-*doctrinaire* attitude to which there have
been many references in this monograph.

Scorn of war, glory, kingship, and priestcraft all arise from
a fundamental clearness of vision that makes him free from
any illusions. When he wishes to forget that he is a monarch,
the wish is prompted not merely by indolence, for he might
have kept the adornments of station without the cares. He
can see through gaudy robes to the man within. He is not
hoodwinked by pride of place. Even pleasure has drawn no
veil between his eyes and the realities of life. The pathos of
pleasure, the nearness of laughter to weeping, the contrast
between the wine and revel of the banquet and the silence of
the grave that awaits all the revellers, — these things he
realizes to the full, and in this realization he is typical of Byron.
None of the comforts of illusion blind him to the mystery
beyond. Yet —

> "It were to die
> Before my hour, to live in dread of death . . .
> I have loved and lived and multiplied my image;
> To die is no less natural than those
> Acts of this clay!" (I, ii, 393 f.)

When Myrrha reminds him of the death that may be overhanging him, he answers:

"Why let it come then unexpectedly,
Midst joy and gentleness and mirth and love;
So let me fall like the plucked rose — far better
Thus than be withered" (I, ii, 601 f.)

This sentiment is "from the life". In the midst of composition
Byron wrote in his journal (LJ. V, 183), "Met some masques
in the Corso — *Vive la bagatelle!* the Germans are on the Po,
the Barbarians are at the gate, and their masters in council
at Leybach . . ., and lo! they dance and sing and make
merry, 'for to-morrow they may die.' Who can say that the
Arlequins are not right?"

The same scorn of illusion forces Sardanapalus into the
expression of absolute scepticism. Nowhere in Byron does
scepticism so run riot as in this play. So prevalent is it that
it occasions the dramatic flaw of insufficient differentiation of
character. Sardanapalus, Salamenes, Myrrha, Arbaces, all, in
greater or less degree, give expression to doubt. There is no
denial of an overruling Infinite, and the king's repeated scoffing
at the Chaldean worship of the stars represents only the Byronic
scorn of superstition. Here, as elsewhere in Byron, the ag-
nosticism centres in the problem of immortality. It is summed
up in the king's words, "There's something sweet in my un-
certainty" (II, i, 263) — noble words that crystallize the Byronic
refusal of the comforts of conformity and illusion. They may
be supplemented by the following passage from his journal
(LJ. II, 351), "For the soul of me, I cannot and will not give
the lie to my own thoughts and doubts, come what may. If
I am a fool, it is, at least, a doubting one; and I envy no one
the certainty of his self-approved wisdom."

The character of Sardanapalus is more complex than any
other that Byron drew. Those who despise his course of life
accuse him of being effeminate, but he is not really so; his
actions belie their words. Effeminacy in men is not a Byronic
motiv. In only two other places in his poetry is there even a
hint of such a thing: Selim, in *The Bride of Abydos* (see especially l. 99) feigns womanishness, for a definite purpose, and
Julia's maid speaks of Don Juan's "half-girlish face" (I, 171).

When, after buckling on his armour, Sardanapalus calls for a mirror (III, i, 145), the incident is admirably in character, for the king is unconsciously trying to live up to the manner of life that has been his standard. Similarly, when Salamenes congratulates him on the most glorious hour of his life, he adds "And the most tiresome" (III, i, 344). The answer is sincere and not unworthy of his real nobility. He is not flushed with success nor does praise blind him to the vanity of things. The lightness of this reply is typical of what Byron called the "comic" side of his character. Both Byron and Shelley were very successful in reproducing the light small-talk of gentlemen, the finest example of such work being *Julian and Maddalo*. Sardanapalus has a good deal of this easy, well-bred conversation of which it is difficult to give examples since so much depends on the context.[1]

There is a like triviality in the manner in which he regards love. He is far removed from the kind of man (of whom Mark Antony and the Chevalier des Grieux are typical) who sacrifices the world for a woman's sake. His love of Myrrha is patronising; he addresses her as "beautiful thing" (I, ii, 421); when she declares that she will save him, he exclaims:

"*Save* me, my beauty! Thou art very fair,
And what I seek of you is love — not safety" (I, ii, 506 f.)

Note, too, the harsh "You here! Who call'd you?" (IV, i, 437) with which he greets her return after his interview with his wife. *Sardanapalus* is not a love-tragedy, despite the "natural female eloquence" of La Guiccioli.

Finally is to be noted his scorn of the populace. This, too, is typically Byronic.[2] It has been said that Byron's democracy is as though he were saying, "Yes, indeed; we are all brothers, but — ahem! — would you mind sitting on the other side of the table?" Byron is here at one with Shakespeare, who with perfect tolerance of the individual, has nothing good to say of the *crowd*. The mob impressed him with their "rank breaths" and "sweaty nightcaps." Byron has a like feeling. There are various elements in this Coriolanian scorn — (1) the

---

[1] Cf. *e. g.*, I, ii, 563 f.; II, i, 239 f.

[2] See, among other passages, *Childe Harold* III, 113 and IV, 171; and *Sardanapalus* I, ii, 338 f.

caste feeling so remarkable in *Manfred*, (2) knowledge of the fleetingness of fame — fame that is borne abroad upon popular breath, and (3) an ineradicable aristocratic scorn of the *demos* as such.

Sardanapalus is thus another personification of the struggle of the two natures within man. The better traits lie hidden under years of selfish enjoyment, but even his enemies are conscious of their existence.[1] Stress of circumstance forces these nobler qualities to the surface. "Zwei Seelen wohnen, ach! in meiner Brust!" is Faust's cry, and it might be repeated by Sardanapalus. In his nature appears the chaos of

"Light and Darkness —
And mind and dust — and passion and pure thoughts
Mixed and contending without end or order."[2]

From this chaos order comes. There is moral regeneration accomplished by material downfall. He will not purchase life at the price of slavery, but renounces for it the sake of freedom. Like Byron himself, "he passed through the doorway of no ignoble death."

The poet's self-portraiture in the character of Sardanapalus is very evident. His love of pleasure and ease, his selfishness and over-sensuality, his dislike of war and glory, his energy and perfect fearlessness when aroused, his antagonism towards priests and kings, his wit, pride, scepticism, freedom from illusions, and claim to intellectual liberty, are all of the very essence of Byron's complex nature. From the days of Henry Taylor and Carlyle the cry of anti-Byronism has been that the poet drew only his own character. One is tempted to ask whether it is reflected in Faliero, Foscari, Hugo, Salamenes, John Johnson, the Abbot of St. Maurice, Japhet, or Abel! All critics must admit, however, that Sardanapalus is an autobiographic revelation.

In *Marino Faliero* Byron had attempted a tragedy without love (LJ. V, 243). Into his second play, at the behest of his lady, he "put more love." But it is wrong to say that Sardanapalus is "redeemed" through the power of love. His spirit-

---

[1] Cf. II, i, 89 f. and 356 f. Cf. also Salamenes' testimony, I, i, 9 f.
[2] *Manfred* III, i, 163 f.

ual regeneration comes about through the reappearance on
the surface of his nature of those better qualities that have
been hidden beneath, and it is the power of his own will that
urges him on. No word from Myrrha is needed to send him
out to battle. On the contrary, his exhibition of courage inspires *her* to greater love (III, i, 177 f.) Her influence curbs
his rashness, as when she keeps him from going to the pavilion
(I, i, 613), but it dóes not directly bring out his higher qualities.
For example, had Byron wished to make redemption by love
his central theme, he would have arranged matters so that the
suggestion of death by fire, rather than defeat, should have
come from Myrrha. On the contrary, it is he who plans this
without even expecting her to die with him. Love's full force
is spent upon Myrrha. This conception is eminently Byronic,
and analogous passages are numberless, the most famous being
the oft-quoted and very wonderful letter of Donna Julia to
Juan in the first canto of *Don Juan*. Myrrha's words throughout
the play exactly correspond to the tenor of that letter. She
confesses the omnipotence of love. She loves the king despite
country, honor, shame, and everything. Her feelings grow
nobler as dangers gather round him and as he proves to her
how worthy he is of love. Immediately before the end, thinking of the commingling of her lover's ashes and her own, she
says:

> "Pure as is my love to thee, shall they,
> Purged from the dross of earth and earthly passion,
> Mix pale with thine" (V, i, 472 f.)

Surely it is the woman, not the man, who is redeemed through
the greatness of love. The salvation of the king is worked
out independently and by other means. Despite his Countess,
Byron remained firm in his opinion that love was not fit for
the central *motiv* in tragedy. It is the woman's part. But
Myrrha is more than a "blasted flower of love." She is the
finest, as she is the most individual, of Byron's women. It
has been said that Byron's portrayal of women is degrading,
that they are the mere toys of men. To point to Angiola,
Marina, Myrrha, and Haidée is sufficient answer. The mis-
conception arises from Byron's belief that love really was
"woman's whole existence." He tends to exaggerate the de-

pendence of women on men,[1] but in this dependence there is much that is noble and admirable. They minister to their lover, they lighten for him the load of human ills, their instinct is to shield him. This last trait is exquisitely shown in *Don Juan* (IV, 42 – 43), where Haidée, with no thought for herself, throws her body in front of Juan to protect him from her father's pistol. There is no degrading conception of woman in that scene, or in Angiola's appearance in the court-room in *Marino Faliero*, or in Marina's devotion to Foscari.

And love is not Myrrha's nature to the exclusion of all else. She is unselfish; her happiness is in beholding his happiness (I, ii, 25). She is disinterested, loving him more in ill fortune than in good. She is splendidly brave, refusing the guard sent to protect her because his services are needed elsewhere, and extracting unwilling praise even from Salamenes (III, i, 409). Like Sardanapalus, though in less degree, she represents the freedom of the mind. He has never been deceived by the glory of his position; she makes no attempt to gloss over the shame of hers. She submits to none of the illusions that could so easily comfort her and to which she could so naturally become a prey. "To the measure of the light vouchsafed" she is clear-sighted to the end.

There is no doubt that Myrrha's character was copied from La Guiccioli. It is noteworthy that she has no prototype in the narratives of Diodorus and Mitford. There is something of patronage, as I have said, in the attitude of the king towards Myrrha, not unlike the not overstrong bonds that held Byron to his mistress. Galt (p. 238) says that with all her love of Byron, there was mingled in the mind of the Countess much remorse and regret. With this statement compare Myrrha's speech at the close of the first act (ll. 641 f.). But there is a firmness and depth of nature in the slave for which one looks in vain in the Italian lady, and one must conclude that Myrrha is not so much a portrait as she is Byron's ideal of a woman in the position in which he imagines her.

Zarina is a more faintly drawn sketch and is of importance only from the autobiographical point of view. It is

---

[1] Cf. e. g. *The Two Foscari* V, i, 95 f.; *Cain* III, i, 39 f.

unnecessary to review the relations between Byron and his
wife or to point out the analogy between her situation and
that of Zarina in any detail.[1] Galt long ago said (p. 239) that
the scene between Sardanapalus and his wife could not have
been imagined without some thought of Byron's own domestic
disasters. Since Galt's time other students have elaborated the
parallel. Byron seems often to have imagined a meeting with
his wife. Thus in March, 1817, he wrote her (LJ. IV, 66),
"I feel at length convinced that the feeling which I had
cherished through all and in spite of all, namely — the hope
of a reconciliation and a reunion, however remote, — is indu-
bitably useless; and although, all things considered, it could
not be very sanguine, still it was sincere, and I cherished it
as a sickly infatuation: and now I part with it with a regret,
perhaps bitterer . . . [than] that which I felt in parting with
yourself." The manner in which the king greets Zarina, and
his expressions of remorse are characteristic of Byron's better
feelings towards his wife, and should be set off to his credit
against the caricature of her in the portrait of Donna Inez.
Note especially the speech beginning "My gentle, wrong'd
Zarina" (IV, i, 329 f.), of which Galt says (p. 240), "it is impossible to read this speech without a conviction that it was
written to Lady Byron." With it compare the letter to Moore
of March 8, 1816 (LJ. III, 272). There are other personal
"notes" in this scene — with the king's anxiety as to his
children compare Byron's love for Allegra and his frequent
inquiries about Ada. As in the case of Myrrha, Zarina is not
a portrait of Lady Byron, but Byron's ideal of the wronged
and forgiving wife, — with perhaps a touch of veiled satire
in the contrast with reality.[2]

Myrrha has been called "a female Salamenes," — a misnomer,
for their ruling passions are far apart. But in many respects
they are alike. Salamenes is Byron's least unsuccessful attempt

---

[1] See on this, Nieschlag, p. 49 f.

[2] Compare, for example, Zarina's promise that her sons shall know
nothing save what will honor their father's memory (l. 276 f.) with Lady
Noel's directions in her will that her portrait of Byron should not be shown
to Ada till she was of age, and even then only with the permission of Lady
Byron.

to depict a man of a type utterly unlike himself; he is much
more convincing, for example, than John Johnson in *Don Juan*.
He is brave, clear-sighted, level-headed, but with nothing of
the superman, characteristic of Byronic heroes, that is seen
struggling for recognition in the soul of the king. His chief
trait is loyalty; he is another instance of that higher loyalty,
so frequent a theme in Byron. Here the choice is between
personal and public duty and honor, and while Salamenes never
hesitates in what he believes to be the right course, the signs
of the struggle are apparent. Thus, when the king calls him
"brother," he replies:

"The *queen's* brother,
And your most faithful vassal, royal lord" (I, ii, 32 f.)
When Sardanapalus says:

"Get thee hence, then;
And, prithee, think more gently of thy brother,"
he answers, "Sire, I shall ever duly serve my sovereign"
(II, i, 516 f.)

Set off from the king and his party are the figures of the
two conspirators, portrayed with rough, broad strokes. Beleses,
the priest, is the abler of the two, because of his training in
craft and guile. His deceit contrasts with the sterling honesty
of Salamenes, his superstition with the utter lack of superstition
in Sardanapalus. Other traits he has none. Arbaces, the
soldier, is a foil to the other men in the play. In comparison
with Beleses he is open and sincere, and not utterly lacking
in worth. The uses to which he puts his bravery are contrasted
with the loyalty of Salamenes, who, with far greater cause to
rebel, remains faithful unto death. His material success is in
sharp opposition to the spiritual triumph of Sardanapalus.
Byron shows that the king is unfit to rule, but he has no
sympathy with the forces of rebellion, because they are inspired
by unworthy motives. The conspirators are obsessed with the
lust of power. They shake off the yoke of a light tyranny
under which the country has prospered, only to burden it
with a worse.[1]

Lord Morley[2] speaks of the occasionally startling triteness

---

[1] This is shown in the incident of the herald, V, i, 321 f.
[2] *Critical Miscellanies*, London, Macmillan, 1908, I, 249.

of Byron's moral climaxes, and instances *Sardanapalus* IV, i,
432 f. A still better example of such moral bathos is the
following ending of a fine speech:

"Time . . .
Shall spare this deed of mine, and hold it up
A problem few dare imitate, and none
Despise — *but, it may be, avoid the life*
Which led to such a consummation" (V, i, 442 f.)

It needs no ghost, come from the grave, to tell us that! The
real moral of the piece is that material triumph is not necessarily
accompanied by moral elevation and that spiritual victory
surpasses many conquests. Some critics, notably Gerard, interpret the close of the play as Byron's affirmative answer to all
his questionings as to another life. They feel that the exaltation
is incompatible with any emotion save belief that Myrrha and
her lover, "purged from the dross of earth and earthly passion,"
and not merely their pale ashes, will indeed meet and embrace
again. I cannot see that there is here any attempt at such
an answer. Byron is still unable to wrench from death absolute
confirmation of faith.[1] But even though his lovers pass through
fire into nothingness the triumph remains forever.

Chapter Seven.
Cain and Heaven and Earth.
Cain.

The subject of Cain had been in Byron's mind since boyhood.
"When I was a boy," he told Medwin (p. 125), "I studied
German which I have now entirely forgotten. It was very
little I ever knew of it. *Abel* was one of the first books my
German master read to me; and whilst he was crying his eyes
out over its pages, I thought that any other than Cain had
hardly committed a crime in ridding the world of so dull a
fellow as Gessner made brother Abel." "Die erscheinung Cains
in den dichtungen Byron's," says Ackermann,[2] "ist übrigens

---

[1] *Don Juan* V, 38.
[2] *Anglia Beiblatt* VIII, 21.

ebenso vielfach zu finden, wie diejenige des Wandering Jew
in denen Shelley's." Examples of such allusions are as follows:

> "But look — 'tis written on my brow!
> There read of Cain the curse and crime."[1]
> "He reared me, not with tender help,
> But like the nephew of a Cain."[2]
> "By thy delight in others' pain,
> And by thy brotherhood of Cain."[3]

On January 28, 1821, Byron noted in his diary (LJ. V, 189)
that he had "pondered the subjects of four tragedies," one of
which was "Cain, a metaphysical subject, something in the
style of *Manfred,* but in five *acts,* perhaps, with a chorus."
Cain was begun at Ravenna on July 16, 1821, and finished
September 9. On the following day Byron sent it to Murray
with instructions to print it with the two historical tragedies
which he had already sent. "I think it contains some poetry,
being in the style of *Manfred*" (LJ, V, 360). Later letters
contain further references, some of which shall be cited presently.
The "mystery" was published, together with *Sardanapalus* and
The Two Foscari, on December 19, 1821.

The primary and obvious source of *Cain* is the biblical
account in the fourth chapter of *Genesis,* on which narrative
Byron affected absolutely to rest. In his preface he writes
(P. V, 207), "The author has endeavoured to preserve the
language adapted to his characters; and where it is (and this
is but rarely) taken from actual *Scripture,* he has made as little
alteration, even of words, as the rhythm would permit. The
reader will recollect that the book of Genesis does not state
that Eve was tempted by a demon, but by 'the Serpent;' and
that only because he was 'the most subtil of all the beasts of
the field.' Whatever interpretation the Rabbins and the Fathers
may have put upon this, I take the words as I find them, and
reply, with Bishop Watson upon similar occasions, when the
Fathers were quoted to him as Moderator in the schools of
Cambridge, 'Behold the Book!' — holding up the Scripture."
In the elaboration of character he departs much from our

---

[1] *The Giaour,* l. 1057 f.
[2] *The Bride of Abydos,* l. 686 f.
[3] *Manfred,* I, i, 248 f.

preconceived notions, but he inserts nothing absolutely contrary
to the possibilities of the biblical story. By accepting the
outline of the story in Genesis, and especially the account of
the acquisition of knowledge of good and evil, he turns the
orthodox teaching to the advantage of scepticism. As Schaffner
says, "Die Orthodoxie bekämpft er mit ihren eigenen Waffen!"
Scripture tells of the prohibition to eat of the fruit of the
tree which was in the midst of the garden. The consequent
question is —

"Knowledge is good,
And Life is good; and how can both be evil?"

The scepticism is made the logical outcome of the orthodox
doctrine. It is significant that in his care for the literal narrative
Byron goes so far as to include two incidents (perhaps too
familiar to be disregarded), which do not fit perfectly with his
plan. Byron said to Medwin (p. 129), "the mark that was put
upon Cain is a sublime and shadowy act. Goethe would have
made more of it than I have done." Probably; but only by
altering the catastrophe so as to bring out the full force of
the symbolism behind the act. As it is, the "seal" of the
angel is rather of an anticlimax to Eve's curse. So also the
biblical narrative includes the question, "Am I my brother's
keeper?" This is in precise accord with the orthodox tradition,
and is the foundation upon which is reared the structure of
Cain's character in the mysteries; but it fits ill with Byron's
conception, and can be explained only as a flash of defiance
existing along with utter remorse.

The scriptural foundation of the mystery is therefore hardly
more than a *cadre*, furnishing in broad outline the general
situation, the climax and the catastrophe. The action of the
first and second acts has no basis at all in Scripture. The
character of Cain in the Bible is but dimly perceived through
his words and actions, and is as thus imagined utterly different
from that which Byron delineates. The motive of the murder
is indicated only by inference, and from that appears petty and
base. Here Byron departs widely from his source; all his
genius is expended in developing the several causes, which,
when combined with sudden anger, will lead to the commission

of a deed utterly abhorrent to the real nature of the man. He evolves an explanation, almost an excuse.

From the mysteries on the subject of the Death of Abel Byron got nothing save the generic name, which he uses in a way that shows but vague knowledge of the medieval drama.[1] Schaffner[2] suggests that Byron may have obtained his knowledge of the subject from Warton's *History of English Poetry*. This is altogether likely. It is possible that he was indebted to Dodsley's *Old Plays*.[3] Schaffner adduces various parallels between *Cain* and the *Mactacio Abel* of the so-called Towneley cycle,[4] but, besides the fact that this collection was not printed till 1836, there is nothing in common between the passionately speculative Byronic hero and the coarse low hind of the profane and realistic mystery. The resemblances cited are superficial and insignificant. Of even less importance were the other cycles. The Chester Plays were available in the Roxburghe edition of 1818; the Coventry Plays, though represented by a version in Stevens's continuation of Dugdale's *Monasticon*,[5] were probably not easily to be acquired. At all events the indebtedness to these plays was practically nothing. Cain is therein always represented as mean and jealous and foul-mouthed. There is a certain amount of rough comedy. There is no tinge of scepticism.

In his preface (P. V, 208), Byron says that he had not read Gessner's *Death of Abel* since he was eight years old; his already quoted remark to Medwin but imperfectly accords with the statement in the preface that his "general impression" was "delight." Between *Cain* and *Der Tod Abels* the differences are greater than the resemblances.[6] The pastoral character of the German play is faintly reproduced in *Cain*, but the vague motivation and confused characterization has disappeared. The

---

[1] Note the mistaken identification of "mysteries" and "moralities" in the first sentence of Byron's preface (P. V, 207).

[2] Alfred Schaffner, *Lord Byron's Cain und seine Quellen*, Strassburg, 1880, p. 23.

[3] Dodsley (ed. 1749, I, xii) was the first to employ the word "Mystery" to describe a kind of drama.

[4] E. E. T. S., Extra Series, No. lxxi, 1897.

[5] Ed. 1722, I, 139 f. See E. H. Coleridge's note, P. V, 207.

[6] See Schaffner, p. 23-5.

effort of any poet working with the theme must be to establish
an adequate motive for the murder of Abel; the sheer causeless
jealousy implied by the brief biblical story is not sufficient for
the foundation of tragedy. Gessner accepts jealousy as the
basis of the crime, but accounts for it by contrasting the
luxurious and idle life of Abel's family with the toilsome and
wretched existence of Cain's. There is nothing of the Byronic
aspirations of a mind that seeks to outsoar the limitations of
circumstance. Abel is much alike in both plays; Byron merely
puts the characteristics given him by Gessner and inherited
from the mysteries in a less favorable light. He is a long-
winded moralizer. So in less degree is Adam. How much of
this Byron actually recollected from Gessner and how much
was the natural result of the effort to portray antipathetic
characters it is difficult to determine, but I incline to the belief
that much of the resemblance to Gessner is coincidence. The
destruction of Cain's altar by the whirlwind and the substitution
of the Angel of the Lord for God Himself are individual incidents
common to both plays, which Byron probably owed to his
recollection of Gessner.

Of late a new source of *Cain*, overlooked by Schaffner,
has been suggested.[1] This is the apocryphical *Book of Enoch*
which is a source of *Heaven and Earth*. In his dissertation on
that play, Mayn[2] came to the conclusion, accepted by Coleridge,
that while Byron undoubtedly knew the fragment *Concerning
the Watchers*, it was not certain that he knew the complete
book. As early as 1807, when he wrote out a "List of Historical
Writers"[3] he had read, Byron mentions Bruce as one of the
sources of his slight knowledge of Africa. But acquaintance
with Bruce's travels does not prove acquaintance with the
text of the MSS. brought home by Bruce. A translation by
Richard Laurence appeared in 1821. The question whether
or not Byron had seen this Mayn and Coleridge leave unsolved.
Eimer proves that he had. This is not remarkable in so far

---

[1] M. Eimer, "Das apokryphe buch Henoch und Byrons mysterien,"
Eng. Stud. XLIV, 26 f.

[2] George Mayn, *Über Lord Byrons "Heaven and Earth,"* Breslau, 1887.

[3] Mayn, p. 20; Moore's *Life*, ed. 1837, I, 79; Prothero does not reprint
this list.

as it concerns *Heaven and Earth;* but there are notable resemblances to *Cain* also, contained in scattered passages in chapters xvii to xliv, in which it is told how Enoch was taken "to a certain spot, to a mountain, the top of which reached to heaven," where he saw "the spirits of the sons of men who were dead," and heard the voice of Abel accusing Cain. These parallels are summed up by Eimer (p. 29) thus: "Es ist nicht nur die ähnlichkeit der situation, sondern auch eine unverkennbare übereinstimmung des inhalts, was angesichts der hier angeführten stellen des buchs Henoch (bei Laurence) und des *Cain* unmittelbar auffällt. Die immer wiederholte schilderung des weltraumes mit seinen gestirnen, die einblicke in die verborgenen reiche der abgeschiedenen, das durchdringen des weltraums bis in die dunkelsten tiefen, das forschen nach den wundern und rätseln, frage und antwort, die wissbegierde, endlich die anspielung auf die vergänglichkeit der bestehenden welt, — das alles sind ähnlichkeiten, die nicht übersehen werden können."

If when Byron first "pondered" over *Cain,* he planned the flight through the Abyss of Space and Hades, he could not have received any suggestions from the *Book of Enoch* since Laurence's translation was not then published. But by July, 1821, when he actually began the composition of the play, the book might have reached him from England, and the parallels adduced by Eimer establish almost conclusively that it had done so.

From the time of the publication of *Cain* until now, comparisons of Byron's mystery with *Paradise Lost* have been so frequent that it is unnecessary to discuss the matter in great detail. "Of his indebtedness to Milton," says Mr. Coleridge (P. V, 201), "he makes no formal acknowledgment, but he was not ashamed to shelter himself behind Milton's shield when he was attacked on the score of blasphemy and profanity." What he did not see, or affected not to see, was that the motive for the introduction of "blasphemy and profanity" could not be impugned in Milton's case, but might well be in his own. The most obvious, yet least important, connection between the two poems is the very large number of verbal parallels, which show how thoroughly Byron had studied *Paradise Lost* and how retentive was his memory, if, what he declared in his preface ("Since I was twenty I have never read Milton; but I had read him so frequently before, that this may make little difference") be believed. There is close relationship between Milton's Satan and Byron's Lucifer. "Der Miltonische Satan ist seiner äusseren Erscheinung nach kein Teufel . . . mit Klauen, Hörnern, Schwanz und Pferdefuss, sondern eine titanenhafte Gestalt, deren Umrisse zwar menschlich sind, sich aber bis ins Kolossale dehnen und von gewitterhaftem Halbdunkel umwölkt sind."[1] The same remark applies to Lucifer, except that Byron's imagination has failed to render him quite so gigantic a figure as Satan; a fact due also partly to the lack of the intensified human qualities with which Milton has endowed Satan. Lucifer is nearer to pure spirit, more of an abstraction than Satan. Milton has added elements of physical deformity and repulsion, especially in the later appearances of Satan, that are absent from Byron's creation. Yet the chief characteristic of both is the same. The great conception is that of the *fallen archangel*. Their forms have not yet lost all their original lustre. There is still something of celestial brightness hovering about them, though dimmed and changed. Both have in them the spirit of the Titan, the eternal struggle of the individual against omnipotence. Even in *Paradise Lost* there is a suggestion of Manicheism in Satan's words:

"Evil, be thou my Good: by thee at least
Divided empire with Heaven's King I hold,
By thee, and more than half perhaps will reign" (IV, 110f.)

This is echoed in Lucifer's words:

"So that I do divide
His and possess a kingdom which is not
His" (I, i, 552 f.)

Both plan to invade the realm of good and to form a league with mankind, or, if that be impossible, to snare him into evil. The Manicheism of such passages is purely dramatic. In the midst of Tartuffe's casuistry the cautious Molière reminds his readers that "c'est un scélérat qui parle." Those who attacked *Cain* were too apt to lose sight of the dramatic nature of the dialogue and think that the "scélérat" was Byron himself.

Besides part of his conception of the character of Lucifer

---

[1] G. Wenzel, "Miltons und Byrons Satan," Herrig's *Archiv* LXXXIII, 71.

Byron got various details from *Paradise Lost*, of which only
the most important need here be mentioned. The flight through
chaos in the second book furnished suggestions for the flight
of Lucifer and Cain through the abyss of space.[1] To Milton's
description Byron owes at least as much as to the passages
from the *Book of Enoch* already noted. It may be added here
that the flight of the "magic car" in *Queen Mab* also furnished
hints for this scene[2] and much of the speech of Ahasuerus
later in Shelley's poem (VII, 84 f.) is in the mood of Lucifer's
denunciations of Jehovah. Other resemblances are scattered
through *Paradise Lost*. The conversations between Cain and
Lucifer, especially the passages relating to revelations of the
future, owe something to the talks between Adam and Michael
in the eleventh and twelfth books. I cannot see, however,
that the revelation to Adam of the coming murder of Abel
(XI, 429 f.) had any influence upon Byron's choice of the
subject for poetic treatment. Adam's dread, though in ignorance,
of death, expressed in this passage, in IV, 425, and elsewhere,
is reflected in Cain's anxious questionings into the mystery
of death.

With all their points of relationship the basis of the two
poems is antithetical. Milton's is a vindication of divine pro-
vidence while taking into account the existence of evil. He
is therefore *doctrinaire*; and the *doctrinaire* attitude of mind
was an argumentative position which Byron ceaselessly attacked.
Byron is the opponent of dogma; he pleads here as always
for freedom of thought. He seeks, as Schaffner says (p. 32),
"to justify the ways of man to God," to assert man's right to
the employment of the gift of reason. This is Lucifer's final
message to Cain, and Byron's, through his mouth, to humanity:
hold fast to the one good gift — the reason:

---

[1] With the line "His dark materials to create more worlds" (II. 916)
cf. *Cain* I, i, 550 f. and other places. As he journeys Satan sees —

"This pendent World, in bigness as a star
Of smallest magnitude close by the moon" (l. 1052 f.)

Cf. *Cain* II, i, 28 f. There is a serious misprint in Mr. Coleridge's text in
this passage.

[2] Cf. also Astolpho's journey to the moon in the *Orlando Furioso* XXXIV,
stanza 67 f. Byron was well acquainted with Ariosto at the time of the
composition of *Cain*.

> "Let it not be overswayed
> By tyrannous threats to force you into faith
> 'Gainst all external sense and inward feeling:
> Think and endure, — and form an inner world
> In your own bosom" (II, ii, 460 f.)

The same thought runs all through Byron's verse; it is certainly not Miltonic.

It is indeed Promethean. I spoke in the chapter on *Manfred* of the hold which the legend had upon Byron's imagination. In the character of Cain the Promethean element is more apparent than in Manfred, for while the latter has only the pride and resistance of the titanic conception in general, Cain, like Prometheus, suffers not only for himself, but for —

> "All the few that are,
> And all the unnumbered and innumerable
> Multitudes, millions, myriads, which may be,
> To inherit agonies accumulated
> By ages! — and *I* must be the sire of such things!" (I, i, 444 f.)

Thus his is not merely egoistic suffering and rebellion. By anticipation he voices the sorrows of future humanity. Like Prometheus and Faust he is "a symbol and a sign to mortals of their fate and force." He has the instinctive assertion of freedom against the limitations of fate.[1]

The *Faust* element in *Cain* is not confined to the general kinship of their protagonists. There are distinctly Mephistophelean traits mingled with the Satanic attributes of Lucifer. This appears in the occasional outbursts of mockery in the midst of the solemnity and occasional sublimity of his discourse. Schaffner compares the Lucifer-Cain combination with Mephisto-Faust. In both sets of circumstances we see the systematic misleading of a human soul through the representative of the principle of evil. But whereas Goethe has made his Mephisto an abstraction of scorn and denial, ' one among the "Geistern, die verneinen," Byron has endowed Lucifer with personality, even with sympathy. There are critics[2] who compare the position of Adah with relation to Cain to that of Gretchen

---

[1] Schaffner, p. 4.

[2] M. Eimer, "Byrons Beziehungen zur deutschen Kultur," *Anglia* XXXVI, 442 f.

with relation to Faust. Both are in their pious faith in sharp contrast to their lovers who alike express the extreme of scepticism; the innocence of both women forces them instinctively to shun with terror the spirit of evil. Byron himself saw the analogy between the *Faust* and *Cain* themes, but he said, *"Faust* itself is not so fine a subject as *Cain."* [1]

In the seventh canto of James Montgomery's *The World before the Flood,* [2] 1813, Enoch tells Javan of the murder of Abel by Cain. The narrative closely follows the scriptural version. It is quite unimpressive. Byron had probably read it. One of the characters is named Zillah.

To Bayle's *Historical and Critical Dictionary* Byron was indebted for some of his most heterodox opinions. He knew the book well and owned a copy of the English translation of 1734, which was sold with his other books in 1816. He made use of the *Dictionary* in *Childe Harold, The Giaour, The Vision of Judgment,* and other places. That he used a later French edition after his departure from Europe is shown by a note to *Childe Harold* (P. II, 502), in which he quotes a passage in French, and refers to Bayle as "one of the best men, and perhaps the best critic that ever lived — the very martyr to impartiality." The most important ideas abstracted from Bayle were those relating to Manicheism and the origin of evil, especially the article "Paulicians" and the appendix on the Manichees. Bayle is not, however, so much a source of *Cain* as the authority whence Byron derived certain ideas which he incorporated in *Cain.*

In Byron's letters there are two important passages referring to *Cain* that must be quoted at length. "It is in the *Manfred* metaphysical style, and full of some Titanic declamation; — Lucifer being one of the *dram. pers.,* who takes Cain a voyage among the stars, and afterwards to "Hades," where he shows him the phantoms of a former world, and its inhabitants. I have gone upon the notion of Cuvier, that the world has been destroyed three or four times, and was inhabited by mammoths, behemoths, and what not; but *not* by man till the Mosaic period, as, indeed, is proved by the strata of bones found; —

---

[1] Medwin, p. 129.

[2] *Poetical Works,* 1841, II, 1 f. The passage referred to is on p. 91 f.

those of all unknown animals, and known, being dug out, but none of mankind. I have, therefore, supposed Cain to be shown, in the *rational* Preadamites, beings endowed with a higher intelligence than man, but totally unlike him in form, and with much greater strength of mind and person. You may suppose the small talk which takes place between him and Lucifer upon these matters is not quite canonical. The consequence is, that Cain comes back and kills Abel in a fit of dissatisfaction, partly with the politics of Paradise, which had driven them all out of it, and partly because (as it is written in Genesis) Abel's sacrifice was the more acceptable to the Deity. I trust that the Rhapsody has arrived — it is in three acts, and entitled *"A Mystery,"* according to the former Christian custom, and in honour of what it probably will remain to the reader" (LJ. V, 368). The other passage is more significant. "Cain is a proud man: if Lucifer promised him kingdoms, etc., it would *elate* him: the object of the Demon is to *depress* him still further in his own estimation than he was before, by showing him infinite things and his own abasement, till he falls into the frame of mind that leads to the catastrophe, from mere *internal* irritation, *not* premeditation, or envy of Abel (which would have made him contemptible), but from the rage and fury against the inadequacy of his state to his conceptions, and which discharges itself rather against Life, and the author of Life, than the mere living" (LJ. V, 470).

"The inadequacy of his state to his conceptions" — in a few words Byron has comprehended the central idea of the poem. Cain is one of those —

> "Whose intellect is an o'er mastering power
> Which still recoils from its encumbering clay."[1]

At the foundation of his character and of the poem is the theme of the ceaseless struggle of mind and matter which forms so important an element of Byron's conception of tragedy and which is dwelt upon in *Manfred*. Closely connected with it is the constant lingering on the thought of frail mortality. A verbal concordance to Byron would show many occurrences of the words "dust" and "clay." In *Cain* the former word

---

[1] *The Prophecy of Dante* IV, 21 f.

occurs sixteen times and the latter nine. Nature has given a
form of flesh only, it would seem, that thereby the soul may
be clogged.[1] The finest expression of this struggle of the soul
against the barriers of human life, against the limitations of
mortality, occurs in *Childe Harold:*

> "There is a fire
> And motion of the Soul which will not dwell
> In its own narrow being, but aspire
> Beyond the fitting medium of desire" (III, 42).

Lucifer finds Cain in such a mood.

> "I look
> Around a world where I seem nothing, with
> Thoughts which arise within me as if they
> Could master all things" (I, i, 175 f.)

Lucifer essays to intensify this mood. The journey across the
Abyss of Space and through Hades sets, not only Cain's passions
and desires, but the very earth of which he is but a fragment
of dust, against the background of eternity and infinite space.
This is finely imagined. As they recede from the earth it is
seen first as a small circle with the moon beside it (II, i, 25 f.),
then as a faint spark no bigger than a fire-fly (II, i, 123), and
at last it disappears altogether (II, i, 145 f.) Cuvier's theory,
referred to in the first passage quoted above, is made use of
to increase this sense of the littleness of humanity. Lucifer
constantly reiterates the mightiness of the former world of
which our world is but the wreck.[2] Thus Cain's mind is
brought through successive stages of abasement. At first he
is conscious, like Manfred (II, ii, 110), of "a mind to comprehend
the universe." He tells Lucifer:

> "I see thy power,
> And see thou showest me things beyond my power,
> Although inferior still to my desires
> And my conceptions" (II, i, 79 f.)

But when he sees the insignificance of himself and his world
"when placed in competition with the mighty whole, of which

---

[1] *Lara*, l. 333.

[2] The foundation of this idea in Byron's poetry is, I think, the frequent
references to the Preadamite sultans in Beckford's *Vathek*, a book which
influenced Byron greatly.

it is an atom" (LJ. II, 222), when the noisy years of human
life are reduced to moments in the being of the eternal silence,
Cain is brought to admit that he seems "nothing;" to which
Lucifer replies:

> "And this should be the human sum
> Of knowledge, to know mortal nature's nothingness"
> (II, ii, 421 f.)

It is in such a mood that Cain, in slaying Abel, vents his rage
against the Author of life. The same sort of sudden impulse,
swiftly changing to an outburst of lyrical tenderness, had
previously appeared when he threatened to dash his child
against the rocks rather than let him live to propagate misery
(III, i, 125).

For Cain is no murderer at heart; he is, one must repeat,
as far as possible from the jealous ruffian of earlier conceptions
of the character. There is much of gentleness and nobility
in his nature, and his love is always apparent. In the first
scene, despite the adverse position which he takes as to the
worship of Jehovah, he tells Abel and his sisters, "Your gentleness
must not be harshly met" (I, i, 61). His heart leaps "kindly
back to kindness." [1] His love of Adah (see especially II, ii, 255 f.)
resists the Mephistophelean insinuations of Lucifer (II. ii, 323 f.)
His love of the beauties of the natural world is unfailing,[2] and
his discontent is in no wise with that world. His inclinations
and desires are for the good; "I thirst for good!" he cries
(II, ii, 238). His selfcontrol is perfect when Abel urges him
to the sacrifice (III, i, 188 f.), and there is no sign of jealousy.
It is therefore, I think, an artistic flaw of some magnitude
that Byron introduces the incident of Cain's agitation at Lucifer's
suggestion that Abel's sacrifices are the more acceptable (II, ii,
353 f.) This derives from the conception of jealousy as the
motive of the murder, which Byron deliberately discarded, and
it should not have been employed.

The chief flaw in the poem from the technical point of
view is that Lucifer is but a glorified Cain, "changed not in
kind but in degree." There is no dramatic contrast, no struggle

---

[1] *Childe Harold* III, 53.
[2] See especially I, i, 281; II, i, 98; II, ii, 124.

between good and evil. Lucifer does not have to win Cain
over to his side. This has been frequently commented upon;
a single illustration of Cain's accord with Lucifer may be
given.

> "*Cain:* Dost thou love nothing?
> *Luc.:*   What does thy God love?
> *Cain:* All things, my father says; but I confess
>   I see it not in their allotment here" (II, ii, 310f.)

There is no *conflict* here, as there would have been had the
last clause of Cain's reply been assigned to Lucifer, who is
trying to convince Cain. Here and in many other places
tempter and tempted are absolutely at one. Both oppose,
while acknowledging His existence, the Principle of good.

Byron's contention that Lucifer's exaltation of the "two
Principles" was merely dramatic, that he was speaking *in
character*, was, I think, a point well taken. Nowhere else in
his poetry is there any sign of belief in the co-eternal existence
of good and ill, "both infinite as is the universe."[1] The
Manicheistic doctrine of the principles of light and darkness,
good and evil, had been hinted at in *Manfred*.[2] Elsewhere
Byron says:

> "That same devilish doctrine of the Persian,
> Of the two principles, but leaves behind
> As many doubts as any other doctrine."[3]

Manicheism becomes a leading motive in *Cain*. Lucifer alone
(not a disinterested witness) promulgates the doctrine, but no
attempt is made to refute it through the mouth of any of the
other characters. Byron had progressed far since the composition of *Manfred*. There, as I have noted, the revolt is against
the forces of evil that govern the world, and there is no
rebellion against the "other powers." The implied Manicheism
is now open and there is deliberate questioning of the justice
and love of the self-proclaimed Principle of good.

Yet Byron had been "bred a moderate Presbyterian"[4]
and the earliest references to the Deity in his poems are

---

[1] Shelley, *Prometheus Unbound* I, i, 294 — a line which is contradicted
by the spirit and meaning of the entire drama!

[2] Note especially II, iv, 114 f.

[3] *Don Juan* XIII, 41.

[4] *Ibid.* XV, 91.

pious and orthodox! "I'll ne'er submission to my God refuse,"
he writes (P. I. 6), and again:

"I ne'er shall presume to arraign the decree
Which God has proclaim'd as the fate of his creatures"
                                                    (P. I, 24).

In the list of books read by Byron (1807), printed by Moore
(I, 79—81), the entry under "Divinity" is as follows: "Blair,
Porteus, Tillotson, Hooker, — all very tiresome. I abhor books
of religion, though I reverence and love my God, without the
blasphemous notions of sectaries, or belief in their absurd and
damnable heresies, mysteries, and Thirty-nine Articles."

The Prayer of Nature shows an early drift towards
Pantheism, but this poem I believe to be an imitation of Pope.
While in the East Byron went through a period of pronounced
scepticism, with special reference to the immortality of the
soul, the chief record of which is the opening of *Childe Harold*
II (stanzas 1 to 9). The drift is towards deism, for he never
denied the existence of God and remained sceptical as to
immortality. During the Swiss sojourn he again experienced a
period of pantheism, but this, as I shall show in a later chapter,
was due to external influences and never became part of his
real convictions. The pantheistic fervor passed and left Byron,
as it found him, a deist. In *Sardanapalus* there is constant
and remarkable expression of scepticism as to immortality,
but in his latest opinions (e. g. LJ. V, 456 f.) there is evidence
of gradual growth of his belief in immortality. It is significant
that both *Manfred* and *Cain* emphatically affirm the immortality
of the soul and its personal identity and responsibility in
another existence. "Nothing is more common," he wrote late
in life (LJ. V, 490), "than for the early sceptic to end in a
firm belief." The assault in *Cain* is made, not against religious
belief, but against orthodoxy as proclaimed by priests, who,
with soldiers, composed "the most dangerous orders of mankind."
The mood, though less scathing, is that of Swinburne's *Before
a Crucifix:*

"Because of whom we dare not love thee;
Though hearts reach back and memories ache,
We cannot praise thee for their sake."

For *Cain,* like *Manfred,* is the antithesis of the *doctrinaire* attitude of mind. Cain refuses, even before the visit of Lucifer, to be forced into faith against external sense and inward feeling. When to all his questions Adam and the rest give the pious answer, "'Twas *his* will and *he* is good," he replies with a new question, "How know I that?" Adam and Abel, like the Abbot of Saint Maurice, typify obedience to traditionalism and passive acceptance of dogma. Set over against them is Cain, proudly conscious of the power of mind and imperiously asserting his right to make use of that power.

There is a further contrast between Cain and Adah. She is the typical Byronic woman[1], finding her happiness in the man she loves and concerned only for his welfare. The small duties of daily life make up her world. As Adam and Abel represent the intellectual abasement of mere conformity, so Adah represents the attractions of comfortable acquiescence.[2] All the force of her sweet nature is put forth in the effort to make Cain happy in little joys of common life and to make him renounce the vision of infinity that is constantly before his eyes. The temptation is an ethical one. On the one hand is verity and freedom, accompanied by hardship and perhaps despair, on the other placid conformity, submission to comfortable illusion at the sacrifice of intellectual freedom. Cain's choice is Byron's choice. He exhibits the same integrity, candor, and "fierce intrepid scorn of compromise and comfort,"[3] which informs the poetry of Byron with its "splendid and imperishable excellence of sincerity and strength."

Is not this the final message of *Cain?* Is it not an inspiring one? The intellectual position taken is removed as far as possible from that of the easy optimist who cultivates his garden in tranquillity, unmindful of the problems of the universe. Comfortable acquiescence can be bought only at the price of stilling the ceaseless and restless activity of the intellect. Such a prostitution of the reason Byron never submitted to.

---

[1] I may here note that I think Byron's original plan was to contrast the characters of Adah and Zillah in the same way as he later did those of Anah and Aholibamah. One cannot else account for the *tone* of Zillah's first speech (I, i, 18 f.)

[2] See George Rebec, "Byron and Morals," *International Journal of Ethics* XIV, 39 f.

[3] *Ibid.*, p. 50.

" 'Tis a base
Abandonment of reason to resign
Our right of thought — our last and only place
Of refuge; this, at least, shall still be mine."[1]

No suffering, no sacrifice is too great:

"To die
Is nothing; but to wither thus — to tame
My mind down from its own infinity —
To live in narrow ways with little men"[2] —

this Byron never brought himself to do. And, as Mr. Rebec
says (p. 53), "amid the slip-shod complaisant millions of us,
the meed of praise be his for it!"

Heaven and Earth.

Byron's unfinished second Mystery is a further study of
the same themes that inspired *Cain*. Perhaps the most notable
thing about the piece is that it should have been one of four
poems on the same subject written at nearly the same time
and almost, if not quite, independently.

Heaven and Earth was begun at Ravenna on the ninth of
October, 1821, according to Medwin (p. 231). "It occupied
about fourteen days." On November 14,[3] it was enclosed in a
letter to Murray (LJ. V, 473). During the next few months
Byron refers to it from time to time in his letters. "The new
Mystery is less spectacular than *Cain* and very pious" (LJ. VI,
31); "I believe the new *Mystery* is pious enough; but if anything
wants softening here and there send me an extract" (VI, 47).
He seems to have wished to publish it along with the three
plays in the *Sardanapalus* volume. Later he planned to publish
it with *Werner* and some smaller pieces. But the matter hung
fire; Murray printed the poem, but delayed publication from
month to month. Byron's growing impatience is shown in
his letters[4], but Murray continued cautious. To Medwin Byron
remarked (p. 231), "Kinnaird tells me that he can get no
bookseller to publish it. It was offered to Murray; but he is

---

[1] *Childe Harold* IV, 127.
[2] *The Prophecy of Dante* I, 158 f.
[3] Not 9, as E. H. Coleridge (P. V, 279) wrongly states. See LJ. V, 473.
[4] See, *e. g.*, LJ. VI, 50 and 54.

the most timid of God's booksellers, and starts at the title.
He has taken a dislike to that three-syllabled word Mystery
and says, I know not why, that it is another *Cain*." By the
end of October, 1822[1], Byron's patience was gone and he had
the poem transferred to John Hunt, who published it in the
second number of *The Liberal*, January 1, 1823.

As early as 1813 the first suggestion of the theme appears
in Byron's writings. "I have been thinking," he told Moore
(LJ. II, 255), "of a story, grafted on the amours of a Peri and
a mortal." This idea he abandoned because he had not the
requisite "tenderness." In *Manfred* (III, ii, 5 f.) there is a reference to —

> "the giant sons
> Of the embrace of angels, with a sex
> More beautiful than they."

The choice of the theme for dramatic treatment followed logically from *Cain*. The piece is a fragment, for Byron planned
a second part which he outlined to Medwin (if the latter can
be trusted), who printed it in his *Conversations* (p. 154 f.)[2]

Byron noted on the title-page that the Mystery was
"Founded on the following passage in Genesis, Chap. VI. 1. 2.
,And it came to pass . . . that the sons of God saw the daughters
of men that they were fair; and they took them wives of all
which they chose.'" These verses are perhaps the oldest relics
of legend embedded in the Biblical narrative. The meaning
has been disputed. One view is that "the sons of God" are
the children of Seth, who became corrupted by marriage with
the Cainites; but it is not easy to see why the offspring of
such unions should be the "giants in those days" of verse 4.
On the other hand such offspring were popularly attributed in
many Eastern tales to the marriage of women with deities and
demons; and it is certain that the phrase "sons of God" is
synonymous with "angels" in *Job* (I, 6; XXXVIII, 7) and in
Daniel (III, 25, R. V.) In any case this is the meaning accepted
by Byron. Mayn (p. 18) points out that Milton uses the ex-

---

[1] Not 1821, as E. H. Coleridge wrongly states.

[2] With the error of calling "Anah" "Adah," which Coleridge, who
reprints the outline (P. V, 321, note), fails to comment upon or correct.

pression in both senses.[1] Byron's only other direct indebtedness
to the Bible is for the names of his *dramatis personae*. Japheth
is mentioned in *Genesis* (VII, 13) as a son of Noah, but Irad
Byron gets from IV, 18, where the name occurs as that of
Enoch's father, and Anah and Aholibamah from XXXVI, 2.

The other source of *Heaven and Earth* is the apocryphal
Book of Enoch.[2] In the earliest years of our era this book
had been held in high regard by both Jews and Christians,
but because of the Messianic predictions therein contained it
was rejected by later Hebrew authorities and was rigidly
ignored by the Talmud. It fell into disfavor among Christians
also, except in Abyssinia, where it kept some of its early
prestige and where consequently some MSS were preserved.
James Bruce, the famous explorer, discovered two or three
such.[3] One he presented to the Library at Paris, another to
the Bodleian. In 1801 a "Notice du Livre d'Enoch" by
A. J. Silvestre de Sacy in the *Magazin Encyclopédique*[4] called
attention to the value and interest of the discovery, but not
till 1821 did the first translation of the book appear. This
was by Richard Laurence, at Oxford. An important fragment
of a lost Greek translation of the lost Semitic original was,
however, already well known, as it had been preserved in the
Chronographia of Georgius Syncellus, a Byzantine writer of the
eighth century. This fragment, *Concerning the Watchers*[5], Byron
certainly knew. In it occur the names Semjaza, Azazel, and
Rafael, which are of course Byron's Samiasa, Azaziel, and
Raphael. The problem as to whether Byron knew Laurence's
translation of the complete book has been answered in the
affirmative by Manfred Eimer,[6] not so much by the resem-

---

[1] *Paradise Lost* V, 447; XI, 622.

[2] See *Dictionary of the Bible*, ed. James Hastings, Edinburgh, T. and
T. Clarke: art. "Enoch, Book of," I, 705 f.

[3] In 1771 according to the *Dict. Nat. Biog.*; 1773, according to Hastings;
1785, according to E. H. Coleridge (P. V. 302).

[4] Tome I, p. 382 f. See also Richard Laurence, *The Book of Enoch
the Prophet: an Apocryphal Production*, Oxford, 1821, p. 169 f

[5] *The History of the Seventy-two Interpreters, with the History of
the Angels and their Gallantry with the Daughters of Men, written by
Enoch the Patriarch*, 1715.

[6] *Eng. Stud.* XLIV, 18 f.

blances which he finds therein to *Heaven and Earth* as by the notable parallels to *Cain*.

The flood is represented in the Old French *Viel Testament*, and in the Chester, Towneley, Coventry, and York plays; but from all these Byron is far away in matter, method, style, and purpose. I refer to them only to show the lastingness of the subject in dramatic literature.[1]

Byron's devotion to Pope makes it just possible that he may have received a suggestion as to the theme from the following note to *The Rape of the Lock*, I, 145: "Ancient traditions of the Rabbi's (*sic*) relate, that several of the fallen angels became amorous of women, and particularize some; among the rest Asael," etc.

From James Montgomery's *The World before the Flood* and George Croly's *The Angel of the World*, 1820,[2] Byron probably obtained suggestions. Montgomery accepts the interpretation of the "sons of God" as referring, not to angels, but to the descendants of Seth. Croly's poem tells the story of the angel who drank wine and revealed to a woman the secret whereby he caused his wings to grow; the woman thereupon turns into the terrible Eblis, who had assumed a seductive form to tempt the angel to sin. This story, with a different catastrophe, was used by Moore. Croly's poem is of no value, but it is likely that his unsuccessful handling of the theme suggested its treatment by three subsequent writers.[3]

The influence of *Faust* upon *Heaven and Earth* was very slight. Knobbe,[4] following Medwin, thinks that Japhet's colloquy with the evil spirits (I, iii, 55 f.) may owe something to the "Wald und Höhle" scene. Possibly; but the resemblance is slight. Eimer[5] thinks that he finds indebtedness to Goethe in the metrical form of some of the choruses.

---

[1] The first section of Mayn's monograph is a brief account of Fratricide and the Flood in Old French and Middle English Mysteries (p. 3—14).

[2] *Poetical Works*, 1820, I, 177 f.

[3] See S. C. Chew, Jr., "Byron and Croly," *Modern Lang. Notes* XXVIII, 201 f.

[4] A. Knobbe, *Die Faust-idee in Lord Byrons Dichtungen*, Stralsund 1906, p. 17.

[5] *Anglia* XXXVI, 443.

Moore's *Loves of the Angels* was published on December 23, 1822, eight days before *Heaven and Earth*. The poems were, apparently, begun quite independently, though when Moore was in Italy in 1821 he and Byron may have talked over the theme as one fit for poetic treatment. Moore at first planned a long poem, but when he heard of Byron's plans he decided to guard his thunder by restricting himself to three episodes. The work was very successful; by the middle of January Moore was turning his angels into Turks to be rid of the uncomfortable associations with religion;[1] his journal has numerous references to his success. The reviewers of the time naturally noticed Byron's and Moore's poems together, and they have remained joined in literary history, so that any study of Byron's Mystery must contain some account of Moore's poem.[2] My remarks are as restricted as possible.

The Loves of the Angels[3] is a group of three stories, all going back ultimately to *Genesis* VI, 1, 2. The first angel is most contaminated with this "sin-worn mold." His story is that of the drunken angel[4] who reveals the secret to a woman. She, instead of resolving into Eblis, as in Croly's poem, pronounces the formula and is translated to a star, thus escaping from his embrace. The second angel is of a nobler type. Against the commands of God he remains on earth where he has fallen in love with Lilis. There he discards his celestial splendor. One day Lilis begs him to appear in the cherubic garb of flame in which she first beheld him, and he, knowing that the heavenly flame is harmless, assumes his glory. Dazzled by the light, she comes to his arms. But sin has changed the pure fire to an earthly and devouring element, and at his touch, there, before his eyes, she is quickly consumed to ashes. He is doomed to remain on the earth. The career of the third angel is more edifying. He had married a woman before "religion's

---

[1] Lord John Russell, *Memoirs ... of Thomas Moore*, Boston, 1853, IV, 40.

[2] Josef Zuck, *Thomas Moore's "The Loves of the Angels" und Lord Byron's "Heaven and Earth." Eine Parallele*, Vienna 1905; Mayn, p. 42—7.

[3] *Poetical Works of Thomas Moore*, New York, n. d., p. 1—25.

[4] See E. Koeppel, "Die Engel Harut und Marut in der englischen Dichtung," *Eng. Stud.* XXXVII, 461 f.

altar," and their only punishment is the prolongation of life on earth till the end of time. In the end they will be received into heaven.

Comparison of this poem with *Heaven and Earth* is fruitful. The two writers have produced work utterly different in style, manner, attitude, and thought. Byron is definitely Biblical; "I am a great reader and admirer of those books, ... that is to say the *Old* Testament," he told Murray (LJ. V, 391). Moore's firm religious belief led to a hesitancy to treat a theme even remotely connected with religion; hence the non-Biblical atmosphere of *The Loves of the Angels*. He is content to tell his simple stories without involving in them the deep questions which occupied Byron's mightier spirit. Take, for example, the second angel's story. Rubi's mistress is suddenly destroyed in a horrible manner and her lover only exclaims *mea culpa!* An angel of Byron's creation would have asked *why* it is "in heaven a crime to love too well"; in fact Aholibamah does ask:

"And where is the impiety of loving
Celestial natures?" (I, i, 10 f.)

The setting of the two poems is different. Byron's play does not belong in the category of his Eastern Tales, though it comes from the East. Moore, on the other hand, had not forgotten Byron's advice to "stick to the East" (LJ. II, 255). In substance as in sources his poem is oriental and from the outset his angels were in a fair way to become Turks! God is Allah, Satan Eblis, the various parts of the other world have Eastern names. Maidens bathe in brooks with oriental equanimity; the customs described are of the conventional oriental kind. A third point of contrast is the tone of the two pieces; Byron's is pessimistic, Moore's optimistic. Byron's lovers all go to destruction; there is no milder fate for the meek Anah than for the defiant Aholibamah. This is a subtle attack on the justice of the Most High. Moore, by differentiating between the dooms of the several lovers, exalts the justice of Allah. In arranging their pairs of lovers Byron sought to gain dramatic contrast by giving the sterner woman to the meeker angel and *vice versa,* Moore to gain romantic harmony (except in the case of the first angel where his material was ready to hand) by "assimilating his pairs of lovers." Lilis is a worthy

mate of Rubi, Nama of Zaraph. Byron, as always, is occupied
with Nature as well as man; Moore thinks of natural scenery
as a nicely painted background for his pretty little people. In
Heaven and Earth there is, as Brandes says (IV, 223), "a glorification
of the lust of annihilation;" Moore never so much as whispers
that these sweet sinners of his are the cause of the deluge,
and much less does he exult therein! Finally, the central idea
of the two pieces is utterly different. Byron is concerned
with the littleness of man and the injustice of almighty power;
Moore shows the all-sufficing influence of holy love. Byron's
great genius reaches even in this fragment the point of view
of humanity; Moore, more thoroughly than he knew, is restricted
to three episodes. His is not a universal voice. [1]

Thomas Dale's *Irad and Adah, a Tale of the Flood,* 1821,
interprets the phrase "the sons of God" as referring to the
children of Seth, and "the daughters of men" as the posterity
of Cain. Mayn (p. 47 f.) gives a detailed outline of the poem.
It is divided into three parts: Guilt, Prophecy, and Judgment.
Irad loves Adah against the commands of God; Noah prophe-
sies the destruction of the Cainites; storm, earthquake, clouds,
are portents of the approaching evil. The third part opens
with a description of the "gradually deepening horrors of the
encroaching sea." The lovers take refuge on the highest
mountain, where they repent and pray God for pardon. In
sign of atonement they are allowed to die together before the
flood reaches them. [2] Dale's poem is full of Byronic reminiscences; much of it is in the Spenserian stanza made popular
by *Childe Harold*; but it was published considerably earlier
than *Heaven and Earth*. Hasty criticism might assume that
Byron had borrowed largely from Dale, but one must remember
that the Mystery had been long in Murray's hands. Yet the
recurrence of the name Irad is odd, if it is but a coincidence.
There are no other resemblances save of the most general nature.

---

[1] The above paragraph owes much o Mayn and Zuck, but the conclusions represent independent judgment. See also *Edinburgh Rev.* XXXVIII,
42

[2] See *Blackwood's Magazine* XII, 61 f.

The revolt of *Cain* is pushed to the extreme of defiance in *Heaven and Earth*, but Byron was too conscious of the remorselessness of universal law to have thought seriously of conveying his rebellious heroines and their angel-lovers to another star. The assertion of the individual will in opposition to the norm of things is but the prelude to destruction, everywhere and always. Had the second part of *Heaven and Earth* been written, it must have portrayed the death of the women and the condemnation of the rebel angels.

The fragment is a study of various degrees of discontent and rebellion at the inadequacy of our mortal state. The brevity of the piece hinders any development of character, but the various *dramatis personae* are differentiated one from another with more skill than Byron generally expended upon such matters. Between the positions of Noah and Aholibamah there lies an interesting gradation of motive and conduct. Noah, like Adam before him, personifies that *doctrinaire* stultification of the intellect against which Byron ceaselessly inveighs. His traits are self-confidence, self-righteousness, absolute obedience, unhesitating faith. He is portrayed with utter lack of sympathy. The same attributes are repeated in more shadowy form in the person of Shem. Then follows Irad, who loves a daughter of Cain, but who combats with that love and sternly represses it in obedience to the law of God. His brother Japhet, as Gerard (p. 99) points out, occupies a middle position in the drama. He loves Anah, a Cainite, devotedly and passionately, and he is willing to die for her; yet as one of the predestined family he must be saved. Somewhat like him in character is Anah, who would gladly make a compromise with the Almighty, but who in the end remains submissive to the behest of love. Next to her stand the two disobedient angels, whose characteristics are practically the same, who acknowledge the power of God, yet are disobedient to His will. Lastly, apart from all is the daring, resolute, proud, defiant figure of Aholibamah, true descendant of Cain, the most memorable character in the mystery.

It is necessary to dwell in some detail on her character. The scepticism and defiance of the piece are concentrated in her. Brandes says (IV, 335), "Cain's female counterpart is the proud defiant Aholibamah." Note her pride in being descended from the eldest born of Adam, her scorn of the "son of Noah," her acceptance of an angel's love, not as an honor but as hers of right, her confidence in her control over Samiasa's love. She is a noble being, willing to "dare an immortality of agonies with Samiasa." Her defiance of God is no weak murmur, but worthy of Satan. One passage includes all her attributes. Doubting the prophecy of the deluge, she asks, "Who shall shake these solid mountains, this firm earth?" (I, iii, 449 f.) to which Japhet replies, "He whose one word produced them," and she instantly asks, "Who heard that word?" Compare Lucifer's doubt as to whether God really "made us" as He has declared (*Cain* I, i, 140). Noah and Japhet have nothing in common with her. Irad has something of her spirit, but in all else is far removed. Her sister Anah moves in another sphere, for her adoration of her lover, while it leads her to destruction, makes her neither forget nor defy God. Aholibamah thinks of the joy she gives Samiasa; Anah of the happiness she receives from Azaziel. Aholibamah can face hell with Samiasa; Anah would give up all her little life rather than that Azaziel's immortality should know an hour of pain.

The reason is clear why Byron did not undertake to finish the fragment. Apart from the fact that he was occupied with other affairs, he probably saw that to continue would be to place himself on the horns of the dilemma. To tell of the destruction of the lovers would be a long anti-climax to the stirring close of the first part. To let them escape and "wing their way from star to star" would leave the whole problem hopelessly unsolved — creatures sinning yet unpunished, rebels against omnipotence yet not crushed. Wisely then he left the poem a fragment.

From the time of its publication critics have remarked on the lack of that scepticism that runs riot in *Cain*. How could it be otherwise? The characters are either marked out for special favor by God, or doomed to destruction, or angels who have stood in His presence. There is no room for the expression of doubt. Nevertheless the scepticism is there.

> "And where is the impiety of loving
> Celestial natures?"

asks Aholibamah, and the voice is the voice of Byron. The

event proves the impiety of so doing, — or shows that omnipotence can crush disobedience. But is Byron convinced? Is it not once more Cain's question of the snake-stung lamb? If it indeed be impious to love celestial natures, why suffer their approach to frail humanity? Why give weak mortals the capacity for such love?

Chapter Eight.
Werner and The Deformed Transformed.

We come now to two pieces which the world has willingly let die and which I would willingly pass over in silence. A complete study of Byron's dramas must, however, include brief accounts of *Werner* and *The Deformed Transformed.*

Werner.[1]

I have already told of the appeal of the subject of *Werner* to Byron when he was but thirteen years old, of his beginning a play on the same theme at the time of his connection with Drury Lane, and of how, after discarding and apparently forgetting it for years, he took it up for a third time in 1821. *Werner* was begun December 18, 1821, and finished January 20, 1822. It is founded upon "The German's Tale" in Sophia and Harriet Lee's *Canterbury Tales*.[2] "Founded" hardly expresses the facts of the case, for Byron followed his original with the utmost closeness, and for the most part did little more than turn the prose of the novel into very inadequate blank-verse. He attempted to forestall criticism by a frank admission of the overwhelming amount of his indebtedness (P. V, 337 f.), but this did not deter *Blackwood's*[3] from publishing two vicious

---

[1] In the following study I am indebted to Karl Stöhsel, *Lord Byrons Trauerspiel "Werner" und seine Quelle.* Erlangen, 1891, and to W. Kluge, *Lord Byron's "Werner or The Inheritance." Eine dramentechnische Untersuchung mit Quellenstudium*, Leipzig, 1913. That two elaborate studies of *Werner* have appeared shows that its importance has been greatly overestimated in Germany.

[2] There is a reprint in two volumes, Boston, Houghton, Mifflin, 1886.

[3] XII, 710 f. and 782 f. The first article is by W. Maginn, and is re-

attacks on the piece. The earlier *critique* was directed against the mediocrity of the poetry and the absolute lack of invention displayed by Byron. "There is not one incident in his play, not even the most trivial, that is not to be found in the novel from which it is taken; occurring exactly in the same manner, brought about exactly by the same agents, and producing exactly the same effects upon the plot." It is easy for Stöhsel (p. 7) to point out the exaggerations in this statement, but the facts as brought out by Stöhsel's very elaborate comparison of the play with the novel (p. 10 f.) are damning enough.

The central flaw of the piece is its almost utter lack not alone of the higher reaches of poetry but of any poetry at all. One is surprised to find E. H. Coleridge saying (P. V, 328), "If from haste or indolence Byron scamped his task, and cut up whole cantles of the novel into nerveless and pointless blank-verse, here and there throughout the play, in scattered lines and passages, he outdoes himself. The inspiration is fitful, but supreme." I have read *Werner* several times, but I have not found those passages of "supreme" inspiration wherein Byron "outdoes himself." Stöhsel (p. 18) instances Gabor's monologue in the secret passage (III, iii) and the dialogue between Ida and Josephine (V, i, 14 f.), especially Ida's description of the festival. Such excerpts shine in contrast to their surroundings, but place them beside the real glories of Byron's poetry and they are dim indeed. The versification at best is dull, at worst is execrable. With the lack of poetry there is a corresponding and, I think, related want of thought. The play is superficial and dependent on incident, like all those pieces of theatrical acceptability only among which it belongs. The typical Byronic "notes" are almost entirely absent;[1] such as occur echo the Byronic tone only in a flabby and diluted form.

Undeniably there were tragic possibilities in the theme, — the sins of the weak father reappearing in the murderous son. This appears as a key-note at the beginning of the play. Werner says:

---

printed in his *Miscellanies*, 1885, I, 189 f.; the second is by Robert Syme, under the pseudonym of "Tickler."

[1] In the Thought-Index referred to in my preface there are scarcely a dozen references to the play.

"Heaven seems
To claim her stern prerogative, and visit
Upon my boy his father's faults and follies". (I, i, 96 f.)

This is worked out in the event. Stöhsel says (p. 10), "Ver-
derblicher Leidenschaften wegen von seinem Vater verstossen,
ist Kruitzer in Not geraten und findet zuletzt, nachdem er
für seine Fehler durch Elend gebüsst hat, ein tragisches Ge-
schick, indem er bei der Verteidigung seines Erbes durch die
Wucht der Verhältnisse nicht nur selbst zu einem Verbrechen
gedrängt wird, das ihn die Ruhe seines Gewissens kostet, ohne
ihn zu retten, sondern auch durch die Verteidigung seiner
Tat, ohne es zu wollen, seinen Sohn veranlasst, den gemein-
samen Feind zu ermorden." Such a conception is excellent,
but the execution, in interest, poetry, philosophy, and technique, is entirely unworthy of it.

I will only add that I heartily wish that Mr. Leveson
Gower[1] *had* proved that the Duchess of Devonshire, and not
Byron, wrote *Werner*. Unfortunately Mr. Coleridge's reply to
this contention (P. V, 329 f.) is convincing.

The Deformed Transformed.

There is no reference to *The Deformed Transformed* in
any of Byron's letters. Is not this a sign of his slight estimation of it? The MS. is dated "Pisa, 1822," and as Medwin
(p. 151) records Shelley's unfavorable judgment of it — "it is
a bad imitation of *Faust*," July 8, the day of Shelley's death,
must be the downward limit before which the play, unless
Medwin's anecdote relates to the first scene only, must have
been completed. Since Medwin was present when Byron
showed the MS. to Shelley and since Medwin left Pisa on
March 9, Eimer shrewdly argues that that date must be taken
as the downward limit of composition, at least of the first
scene. Byron affected to be so concerned with Shelley's strictures that he threw the poem into the fire and for two years
concealed the existence of another copy. The piece was at
length published by John Hunt, February 20, 1824.

In an "Advertisement" (P. V, 473) Byron noted that the

---

[1] "Did Byron write *Werner?*," *Nineteenth Century* LXVI, 243 f.

poem was "founded partly on the story of a novel called *The Three Brothers*, published many years ago, from which M. G. Lewis's *Wood Demon* was also taken; and partly on the *Faust* of the great Goethe."

From Joshua Pickersgill's novel, *The Three Brothers*,[1] 1803, Byron borrowed the scene and motive of the transformation, and the name Arnaud or Arnold. Varnhagen (p. 12) notes that in the novel the father of Arnaud is engaged in the war between the Emperor Charles V and Francis I, and that the scene is in Italy. This would seem to have suggested to Byron the idea of associating his transformed hunchback with the Sack of Rome. The episode of the capture of Olympia is apparently his own, not very happy, invention; the name Olympia he may have taken from Shelley's *St. Irvyne*.[2]

"Ohne Goethes *Faust*," says Eimer, "wäre dies fragment gar nicht denkbar." The indebtedness to *Faust* connects the piece with *Manfred* and *Cain*. The combination Arnold-Caesar is a second and less successful study of the Faust-Mephisto or Cain,-Lucifer theme. At the beginning of the play there are two interesting divergences from the novel that aid in establishing the relationship to *Faust*. In *The Three Brothers* the devil comes in obedience to an incantation; in *Faust* the black poodle comes uncalled for, as does the Stranger in Byron's piece; and in both *Faust* and *The Deformed Transformed* a mist resolves itself into the devil. In the novel there is no express agreement between Arnaud and the devil. In *The Deformed Transformed* the Stranger deliberately rejects Arnold's offer to sign a pact, thus significantly altering the episode in *Faust*. The Stranger's attitude towards Arnold is a mingling of reverence and mockery. There are two other incidents reminiscent of *Faust*. Just as Mephisto summons the aid of an ignis-fatuus on his way with Faust up the Brocken, so the Stranger causes a "little, marshy spark of flame" (I, i, 479) to reanimate the

---

[1] *The Three Brothers, a Romance.* London, Printed for John Stockdale, 1803. E. ·H. Coleridge (P. V, 473 f.) gives extracts from it. H. Varnhagen (*Über Byrons dramatisches Bruchstück "Der umgestaltete Missgestaltete,"* Erlangen, 1905, p. 7 f.) outlines the part used by Byron.

[2] See Gillardon, p. 114.

soulless body of the hunchback.[1] The four coal-black horses brought by the page a moment later (l. 511) are a reminder of the penultimate scene of *Faust*, where the stage direction reads "Faust, Mephistopheles, auf schwarzen Pferden daher brausend."[2] Varnhagen further believes that certain of the rime-schemes of *Faust* were imitated by Byron in the incantation; this is very doubtful.

Except the first scene, there is an historical basis for the play. Byron had read Robertson's *Life of the Emperor Charles V*,[3] and a note to *The Prophecy of Dante* IV, 258, shows that he knew the contemporary accounts of the Sack of Rome, by Guicciardini and Buonaparte. He may have read also some of the lamentations in prose or verse inspired by the terrible event.[4]

The chief of many objections to *The Deformed Transformed* is that it lacks a definite plan, and such as it has is not held to consistently. The opening is inspired by bitter recollections of Byron's own childhood. In the novel Arnaud is hunchback only; Byron adds the lameness — a personal touch. The leading *motiv* is Arnold's desire for love and power and his love of beauty. These attributes he finds best summed up in the person of Achilles. With the second scene of the play the mood is changed. Arnold no longer *wishes*; he has acquired all his desires save love. From this it would seem that the Olympia incident, which fills the obvious gap, would have been made much of had the fragment been completed. Arnold has changed more than form; he is now bold, resourceful, respected, relied upon; but though bound by no contract he is none the less in the power of the devil. Nor is Caesar quite like the original Stranger: he is wittier, bitterer, more cunning. He is, however, a much less complicated and subtle character than

---

[1] As Byron refers to the ignis-fatuus eleven times in his works it is incorrect to assume that here and in *Manfred* I, i, 195 there is necessarily an echo of *Faust*.

[2] The "Raven-stone" of *Manfred* III, i (first version) and of *Werner* II, ii, 178, is a further echo of this scene.

[3] See the remarkable list of books read by Byron, compiled by him' 1807, in Moores's *Life*, I, 80.

[4] With the attack on Rome cf. *The Siege of Corinth*, l. 722 f. and the attack on Ismail in *Don Juan* (Cantos vii and viii).

Mephistopheles. He has the cynicism and mockery of Goethe's spirit, but without his sense of power and without most of his wit. Both spirits exist in evil and for evil, but whereas Mephistopheles leads Faust to seduction and murder, Caesar, in that portion of the play that Byron completed, makes no attempt to use his devilish arts to corrupt Arnold. The latter speaks of the "scenes of blood and lust" (I, ii, 20) through which he has been lured on, but they do not appear in the event. Caesar gives Arnold opportunity for advancement, but by noble means — courage, sagacity, and love. All that Caesar incites him to do it would occur to any high-minded man to undertake. There is hardly a vestige of any struggle between good and evil.

This shows that Byron had formed no very definite scheme of characterization and motivation. The two leading thoughts of the first scene do not appear again. These are, first, the willingness of Caesar to abide by the test of Arnold's deeds; second, the impressive idea of making Caesar assume the cast-off hunchback form —

"In a few moments
I will be as you were, and you shall see
Yourself forever by you as your shadow" (I, i, 447 f.)

Byron's intention would seem to have been to arrange a concrete dramatic presentation of the haunting, ever-present, watchful eye of conscience. But in the sequel he makes nothing of the idea.

It is all both puzzling and disappointing. Byron began fairly well, but his mood changed and from the second scene to the end inspiration is conspicuously absent. The action breaks off, so far as there is any development of character, and except for the introduction of Olympia, the psychological situation at the close of the fragment is just the same as at the end of the first scene. The fighting scenes are exceptionally crude, and quite unworthy of Byron.

Chapter Nine.
The Substance of the Plays.

Byron reaches the heart of the tragic idea, the rebellion
of the individual against the universal norm of things. All his
protagonists exhibit this overweening assertion of the will. The
jealousy of Faliero, the slothfulness of Sardanapalus, the "sickly
affection" of Jacopo Foscari, the dishonesty and sensuality of
Siegendorf, the misanthropy and pride of Manfred, the soaring
ambition of Cain, the rebellion of Anah and Aholibamah —
all are assaults upon eternal law. The will over-asserts itself
in one direction, and makes those determinations and desires
that in moderation are right and needful become, since pushed
too far, pernicious and perverse. Where there is exaggeration
in one direction, in another there must appear the consequences
thereof, that the balance of life be preserved. Over-insistence
upon one motive, one ideal, brings with it retribution in the
shape of the intrinsic consequences of that over-emphasis; for
Justice is even-handed. The protagonist sees one cause steadily, but at the cost of sight of the whole. He assumes this
defiant attitude for the attainment of some great end for which
he sacrifices all else. It may, or may not, be ethically justified,
but it enthrals him and blinds him to the proportional value
of things. In its noblest form this tragic singleness of purpose is an unquestioning devotion to an ethical principle. This
is the case with Brutus and Horace. In Racine and generally
in Shakespeare the choice of one impelling motive is due to
the force of passion — love, ambition, jealousy, egotism, are
the modes of operation of the will. In Byron an ethical
purpose is often mixed with the promptings of passion. Thus
Sardanapalus fights for something more than self; Faliero has
motives of patriotism mingled with those of jealousy and
revenge; Cain's discontent is with the inadequacy to the mind's
conceptions, not of *his own* state only, but of the state of all
men to come after him. In his rebellious nature, though stained
with crime, there is something of a high disinterestedness.

"Stained with crime," I say; for all Byron's heroes are
guilty in greater or less degree. The protagonist is the

representative of humanity, and as human, imperfect. Saint
Michael, who stands calm though he feels the serpent writhing
beneath his feet, is aloof from human sympathy. Man, toiling
upward towards the light, or thrust downward into darkness,
weak, struggling, sinful, aspiring, is the theme of tragedy.
Absolute wickedness, the wickedness of a Goneril or an Iago,
is not tragic. Such monsters are merely part of the machinery
of tragedy. Evil is an essential attribute in them, while in
the tragic hero it has come about through misuse of potent-
ialities for good. He is not merely an instrument in the
eternal war of good and evil; he includes within himself part
of that war. On the other hand, perfect innocence is not
tragic, but pathetic, if it go down to unmerited doom; for such
doom makes for a questioning of universal law, a denial of
eternal justice, that are hardly proper to tragedy. Yet when
we look upon the tragic loading of Othello's bed or listen to
Lear's words —

> "Why should a dog, a horse, a rat, have life,
> And thou no breath at all?"

optimism is hushed and the workings of eternal law seem blind
and purposeless. For Shakespeare often substitutes a "tragic
flaw" in lieu of actual criminality in the hero's character,
setting this flaw in the midst of virtues that put their possessor
far above those around him. In Byron's plays the crime-element
is always apparent, though upon it not such emphasis is laid
as to preclude our sympathy. Thus he writes to Hodgson
(LJ. V, 284), "I must remark from Aristotle and Rymer, that
the *hero* of tragedy and (I add *meo periculo*) a tragic poem
must *be guilty* to excite 'pity and terror,' the end of tragic
poetry." His theory may be illustrated by his practice. The
indolence, selfishness, and sensuality of Sardanapalus is not
glossed over; but he retains our sympathy by the courage
with which he defends what voluntarily he might gladly have
relinquished, by his humanitarianism, his wit, the prosperity
of the empire under his reign, and by the unworthy motives
of his opponents, who with the struggle for freedom mingle
desire for personal aggrandizement. Similarly, the Doge who
plots against the state is criminal. However worthy the cause
when undertaken by others, when Marino Faliero goes about

to free Venice from the aristocracy of which he is the titular
head, he commits a legal crime; like Orestes he is caught
between positive law and moral obligation. In *The Two Foscari*
there is rather the tragic flaw (that "sickly affection for his
native city" of which Byron spoke to Medwin; *krankhaft*
Westenholz calls it) than actual guilt, though the latter is not
lacking. Of *Werner* E. H. Coleridge writes (P. V, 328), "the
motif — a son predestined to evil by the weakness and sensuality of his father, a father punished for his want of recti-
tude by the passionate criminality of his son, is the very
keynote of tragedy." So also in the "metaphysical" plays
there is always guilt. But there is a remainder of good, or a
remembrance of past good, in the soul of the protagonist.

The protagonist is conscious of individual freedom. Tragedy presupposes not necessarily free will, but resistance to
arbitrary power prompted by *belief* in spiritual liberty. If this
confidence be ill-founded, then is the tragic irony but the
greater. Necessitarianism is compatible with tragedy only
when it does not crush human resistance. Through voluntary
action, or action that the hero *supposes* voluntary, he is placed
in opposition to the Whole. There is the liberty to choose,
there is the choice, and there is the train of consequence. "In-
centives come from the soul's self;" the stuff of tragedy comes
from events that bear the mark of causality. Nature takes no
account of the motive, and proceeds in a non-moral unconcern
to those consequences which Macbeth knew neither assassina-
tion nor any other action could trammel up.

Yet ethically the motive is everything. Of the tragic hero
there is required the choice of the higher loyalty. When he
has embraced his cause scruples arise in him; for the opposition voices the principles that must govern mankind and it
finds (paradoxical though it appear) its most ardent supporter
in the soul of the protagonist. Faliero is torn between official
duty and private patriotism; on the one side is the caste-spirit,
on the other love of country. This is the doctrine of "opposing goods" of which Lessing, following Aristotle (*Poetics* XIV),
makes so much. Sardanapalus, desiring peace, is compelled
to fight against his countrymen; Faliero plots against the state
of which he is chief; Foscari dies at the hands of his adored

Venice. Byron's heroes embrace the nobler and manlier cause, but the acceptance is not without struggle and sacrifice, for on the opposing side are dear and honorable ties of love and memory.

Hence the importance of the motive of the choice. Contemporaries[1] of Byron saw that the classical model lent itself to Byron's purposes, that his emphasis was upon motive. Of *Marino Faliero* Mr. Courthope says (VI, 261), "Plot and action, with an attendant development of character . . . are conspicuous by their absence . . . Everything depends upon motive and intention . . . The strength of the drama, therefore, lies necessarily in the speeches[2] expressive of motive." Byron here, as Mr. Courthope goes on to say, resembles Racine. The rival loyalties are weighed and contrasted. The action is not external, but psychological; the crisis is in the soul of the protagonist. Byron here points the way that many modern dramatists have followed. In Browning's[3] plays the stress is all upon the spiritual struggle. The poet is apparently unconscious of the outer world; external circumstance is nothing to him; he is concerned solely with the world of thought and passion and will, and this to an exaggerated extent which sacrifices dramatic objectivity. Browning, as to some degree Byron before him, is led astray. The combination of motive

---

[1] See *e. g. Edinburgh Review* XXXVI, 422 f. or *Jeffrey's Literary Criticism*, ed. E. Nichol Smith, London, Frowde, 1910, p. 167.

[2] This absorption in motive leads to lengthy speeches; and brevity is a requisite for stage success. In *Manfred* the lyric nature of the monologues palliates the offense. In it the longest speeches are of 49, 56, 40, 33, and 45 lines, respectively. In *Marino Faliero* there are speeches of 28, 28, 47, 80, 27, 90, 68, 58, and 78 lines. Moreover the responses in dialogue are inordinately long. For example, *Othello* with 3165 lines (Eversley ed.) has 1183 separate speeches, the average speech being thus about 2. 67 lines long. In *Marino Faliero* 3483 lines are divided among 738 speeches, an average of nearly 4. 72. This wordiness is made the more marked by several very long dialogues, e. g. Act II, Sc. i; Act V, Sc. i. In *Sardanapalus* the average is 2. 71 — a welcome decrease of verbosity with a corresponding increase in the amount of action.

[3] See further, Henry Jones, "Browning as Dramatist," *Boston Browning Society Papers*, New York, Macmillan, p. 210; C. L. Sparrow, "Browning's Dramas," *Modern Lang. Notes* XXII, 65 f.

and character should lead to action; instead the poets loiter
in the fascinating maze of conflicting purposes, intent upon

> "Thoughts hardly to be packed
> Into a narrow act,"

not realizing that such thoughts cannot be cast into a truly
dramatic form.

A barrier opposes the desires of the individual soul. Some
poets emphasize

> "the dread strife
> Of poor humanity's afflicted will
> Struggling in vain with ruthless destiny."

This, the easiest solution of the problem, relieves humanity of
responsibility by proclaiming the omnipotence of blind necessity.
I have already called attention to Byron's shifting views on
the problem of free will. *Sardanapalus* is the only one of his
plays that can be called deterministic; but there and elsewhere
is found the nobler belief that the individual must strive with
his social and political environment. This position accords
with Byron's concern for humanity in the mass, the relation
of man to his surroundings, the problems of states. And Byron
at times goes deeper yet, and accepts the position so typical
of Shakespeare, that the opposing force is *character*, that the
conflict is internal. The rottenness is not in the state of Den-
mark so much as in Hamlet's will; the witches are not objective ministers of destiny so much as the promptings of
Macbeth's own soul. They appeared to him because, as Mr.
Bradley says (p. 344), the thoughts to which they gave expression were not new to him. To this there is a striking
parallel in *Cain*. Adah who, like Gretchen — "Was steigt aus
dem Boden herauf?" — is instinctively conscious of the presence of an evil spirit, warns Cain of those

> "demons who assume
> The words of God, and tempt us with our own
> Dissatisfied and curious thoughts" (I, i, 401 f.)

Her words are justified by the event, when, later (II, ii, 352 f.),
Lucifer reminds Cain that the sacrifices of Abel are acceptable.
"So be they!" is Cain's answer; "wherefore speak to me of
this?" to which the tempter replies "*Because thou hast thought
of this ere now.*" The passage should certainly be collated with

the parallel motive in *Macbeth*, upon which it forms the essential commentary.

Since the element of crime enters into the character of the tragic hero, the element of justice is never absent from the opposing force. Tragedy becomes thus an intestinal warfare of good with good. This is exactly the Byronic position — not a clearly defined representation of the conflict of Ormuzd with Ahriman, but a commingling of the elements of good and evil in both parties of the strife. Justice is mingled with ambition and selfishness in Arbaces, with tyranny and self-will in the "Ten," with revenge in Loredano; but in no case is it absent. This fact leads us into the inmost heart of Byronism. His whole poetry is shot through with a dualistic conception of the universe. The spirit, not of Spenser only,

"down is weighd with thought of earthly things,
And clogd with burden of mortality."[1]

The sense of these lines, their very words, recur again and again in Byron. Into the characters of his poetry he is constantly inserting elements of his own spiritual experience, as when he says (LJ. III, 137), "My good and evil are at perpetual war." Almost he conceives this war as between his good and his evil genius, thus considering them as animistic entities. "Man is born passionate of body," he writes (LJ. V, 457), "but with an innate though secret tendency to the love of Good in his Mainspring of Mind. But God help us all! It is at present a sad jar of atoms." Upon this element of Byron's character Ruskin has an important comment:[2] "His deep sympathy with justice, kindness and courage; his intense reach of pity, never failing, however far he had to stoop to lay his hand on a human heart, have all been lost sight of, either in too fond admiration of his slighter gifts, or in narrow judgment of the errors which burst into the more flagrant manifestation, *just because they were inconsistent with half his soul,* and could never become incarnate, accepted, silent sin." In all Byron's characters there is this inconsistency of soul; "high thought" is "linked to a servile mass of matter"[3] which "clogs the

[1] *Amoretti* lxxii.
[2] *Works,* XIII, 143 f.
[3] *Cain* II, i, 50.

ethereal essence."[1] Byron never followed Marcus Aurelius (XI, 20) in the belief that the soul — the fiery and aerial parts — is utterly overcome by the body; hence there are in his dramas no such figures as Iago or Count Cenci, no "outrageous ranting villains," as he expresses it (LJ. V, 243). His faith in human nature is an effectual answer to the charge of pessimism. He portrays the eternal conflict of good and evil; he is himself torn and shattered by it; he knows that

"in tragic life, God wot,
No villain need be. Passions spin the plot.
We are betrayed by what is false within;"[2]

but his resolve eternally to question the mystery of evil is unalterable, and his confidence in the outcome is secure.

This confidence Byron maintains even in the face of the conclusion of tragedy. The close of his dramas accords with the belief in a divine and moral fate; his tragic theory is Hegelian. We look "with calm of mind, all passion spent" upon the logical outcome of wrongdoing, yet with a sense that the material victory is ephemeral. In *Sardanapalus* this victory is dwarfed by the moral elevation of the character of the defeated monarch. "Purged from the dross of earth and earthly passion," Myrrha and her lover remain the true victors in the fight. Yet they do not reach the spiritual heights of Faliero, for expiation, being of value not to others but only to the individual, can never rise to the dignity of sacrifice. The Doge is decapitated, but the shameful inscription that takes the place of his portrait among the doges

"Shall draw more gazers than the thousand portraits
Which glitter round it in their pictured trappings"
(V, i, 504 f.)

For "c'est la cause fait la honte et non pas l'échafaud;" "the aim, if reached or not, makes great the life." This is that paradox

"Which comforts while it mocks —
Life shall succeed in that it seems to fail."[3]

Two considerations add their weight to the spiritual triumph

---

[1] *Manfred* II, iv, 56.
[2] George Meredith, *Modern Love* xlii.
[3] Browning, *Rabbi Ben Ezra* vii.

at the close of tragedy. One is the value of suffering. "There is nothing the body suffers that the soul may not profit by."[1] Upon this Byron lays stress:

"Not in vain,
Even for its own sake do we purchase pain."[2]

The other consideration is the essential dignity of death. "Death alone can give Beauty its crown of immortality and exalt it above chance and change."[3] The king who dies rather than renounce his freedom is by death "set free forever from all faults and foes."[4]

Since the time of Aristotle it has been a commonplace to say that tragedy is concerned with the fate of great men. Art requires isolation; the tragic circumstance is separated from the generality of life. In kings and heroes "by their accidental position, the complete isolation required by art is already half accomplished."[5] But though the kingly tradition has held long, surviving not only in Byron, but in Tennyson

---

[1] Meredith, *Diana of the Crossways*, chapter 43.

[2] *Epistle to Augusta*, stanza v, P. IV, 59.

[3] William Archer, "Pessimism and Tragedy," *Fortnightly Review*, n. s. LXV, 392.

[4] I have no wish to "parade authorities" (so objectionable a feature of monograph writing), but I believe a list of the more important books used in preparation of the foregoing discussion of Byron's idea of tragedy may be of service to 'some students of the subject. Aristotle, *Poetics* (ed. Butcher); P. Berger, *Quelques Aspects de la Foi moderne dans les poèmes de Rober t Browning*, Paris, 1907; A. C. Bradley, *Shakespearean Tragedy* and *Oxford Lectures on Poetry*, both Macmillan; J. R. Colby, *Some Ethical Aspects of Elizabethan Tragedy*, Ann Arbor, 1886; Courthope, *Hist. Eng. Poetry*; W. Creizenach, *Geschichte des neueren Dramas*, Halle; Dryden, various essays; O. Elton, *Modern Studies*, London, Arnold, 1907; Hazlitt, *Lectures on the English Poets;* Henry Jones, "Browning as Dramatist," *Boston Browning Society Papers*; Lamb, *Characters of Dramatic Writers contemporary with Shakespeare, Collected Works* II, 253, and *The Tragedies of Shakespeare*, ibid. II, 232; Joseph Mazzini, *On Fatality considered as an Element of the Dramatic Art, Life and Writings*, 1865, vol. II; R. G. Moulton, *The Moral System of Shakespeare*, New York, Macmillan, 1903; Schiller, *Tragic Art, Essays Aesthetical and Philosophical*, London, Bell, 1875; D. J. Snider, *System of Shakespeare's Dramas*, St. Louis, 1877; Thorndike, *Tragedy;* E. D. West, "One Aspect of Browning's Villains," *Browning Studies*, ed. E. Berdoe, London, Allen, 1899; Woodbridge, *The Drama, Its Law and Technique*.

[5] Lascelles Abercrombie, *Thomas Hardy*, New York, Kennerley, 1912, p. 99.

and Swinburne, it is not binding. Tragic action arises among men of lowly estate;

> "the tragic Muse
> Shall find apt subjects for her highest art,
> Amid the groves, under the shadowy hills."[1]

Byron's protagonists are all men of rank. Closely allied to this is his choice of an historical setting in five of his plays. This choice is made not in order to lay stress upon public issues *as such* (tragedy is concerned with the individual), but because at such times there is an exhibition of stress of soul and depths of character that are lacking or suppressed at ordinary times.

The choice of subject involves the selection of incidents. What is of essential and permanent import is the material of art, and the true artist penetrates the tangle of incidents and grasps those factors of a situation of which the appeal is most nearly universal. Two considerations particularly weigh upon the dramatist: the presentation of the essentials of a situation within a limited time, and the giving of emphasis to the monotonous course of actuality. By rejection of the non-essential and increased distinction of relation the raw materials of life are moulded into the finished products of dramatic art, the "oozings from the mine" become the ring. The difficulties of this selective process vary in degree. Even Shakespeare seems at times — as in *Antony and Cleopatra* — dazed by the complexity of his material. Byron's limited interpretation of the unity of action makes for ease in selection. The earlier stages of the action are not presented; only the culmination and catastrophe. This elimination enables the dramatist to treat more fully such events as are reserved for portrayal. In *Sardanapalus*, for example, the audience witnesses, or hears by report, every event of any moment throughout the fatal night. Contrast this *historical* spirit with the *psychological* spirit of *Macbeth* in which we see in snatches, and from different points of view, and over a wide stretch of time, the soul of the protagonist as it goes down to ruin. In those plays where Byron discards the historical attitude the problem of selection and rejection becomes more difficult. In *Manfred* there are

---

[1] Wordsworth, *The Excursion* VI, 551 f.

but the few telling situations, showing the hero in the presence of the supernatural, of nature, of his fellow-man, of sin, of the Beloved, of orthodox religion, and of death. In *Cain* all circumstances not bearing on the central idea are similarly eliminated.

The problem of selection involves the question of episodes. The sub-plots of the Elizabethan drama do not appear in Byron's plays. That sort of episode which Dryden called a "relation," introduced to make clear some event antecedent to the play or to avoid tumult on the stage, occurs but rarely. The account of the battle in the third act of *Sardanapalus* is diversified by a certain amount of action. The desire to preserve "decorum" as well as the exigencies of the situation necessitates the arrangement of the last scene of *Marino Faliero*, an arrangement copied by Swinburne in his *Mary Stuart*. In a few cases Byron introduces episodes to aid in the delineation of character. The most important example of this is the meeting between Sardanapalus and his neglected wife. This scene emphasizes weaknesses in the king's character that help to reconcile the reader to the catastrophe; but it is hard to justify the incident; as a fragment of autobiography it is interesting but irrelevant.

The only important episodes in Byron's plays are those introduced to afford dramatic relief. He uses no scenes of "lower tension,"[1] but numerous passages of "nature poetry" get the same effect. Such passages are essentially undramatic, as Shelley knew well when, in the preface to *The Cenci*, he wrote, "I have avoided with great care in writing this play the introduction of what is commonly called mere poetry, and I imagine there will scarcely be found a detached simile or a single isolated description." Yet nothing is more characteristic of Byron than just such descriptions, nor more important, for in them appears his mature view of Nature.

In Byron's juvenile work the prevailing note is social; the interest is in men, and particularly women. Of the *Hours of Idleness* and other early poems, some eleven are addressed to men, five or six are inspired by school and college life, there are many translations and imitations, many poems of a

---

[1] See Bradley, *Shakespearean Tragedy*, p. 48—9, and cf. the exquisite interludes of Shelley's *Prometheus Unbound* (II, ii, 272 f. and III, iii).

general amatory cast, and no less than thirty-five addressed to various ladies. There is some slight interest in associations with places, with Newstead Abbey and Harrow, but there is hardly any "nature poetry" and that little of the most conventional kind. He celebrates "the steep frowning glories of dark Loch na Garr" (P. I, 173), but he had no such experiences in the presence of mountains as that recorded in the first book of *The Prelude*, lines 375—400. To this superficial view of nature *The Prayer of Nature* (1806; P. I, 224) is an exception, since it shows the influence of Spinoza, but it has come through Pope and I regard the poem as hardly more than an imitation of *The Universal Prayer*. It is significant, however, as having in germ thoughts which first found full utterance in the third canto of *Childe Harold*, and which have been generally ascribed to the influence of Wordsworth and Shelley.[1]

Byron himself records that he "learnt to philosophise" on his travels (LJ. I, 254). Such a statement should not be taken too seriously. In Portugal he delighted in the beauties of that "delicious land," but there is no pantheism in his view of nature. The prevailing interest is still social, and everywhere he concerns himself with the actions and thoughts of humanity, whether it be to comment on the beauty of the women, or to describe the national sport, or to arouse patriotism against the foreign foe. It is the same when he comes to Greece. He regards her as a "sad relic of departed worth" (*Childe Harold* II, 73), a "land of lost Gods and god-like men" (*ibid.*, 75). "Where'er we tread 'tis haunted, holy ground" (*ibid.*, 78). Mankind is the subject of the poet's thoughts and song. A good illustration of this is the description of sunset at the commencement of the third canto of *The Corsair*.[2] In Byron the sunset inspires no pantheistic fervor, but it recalls the death of Socrates; Byron's thoughts are of men. Even during the Swiss

---

[1] See M. Eimer, "Byrons pantheismus vom jahre 1816," *Eng. Stud.*, XLIII, 406.

[2] This passage was taken from the commencement of the suppressed *Curse of Minerva* where it was equally inappropriate. It seems to me to be an originally separate piece of nature-poetry, made to do service as an introductory paragraph.

period, when Byron was impregnated with Wordsworthian
metaphysics and the latent pantheism in him had been vital-
ized by companionship with Shelley, this earlier attitude, with
its emphasis upon human associations, was not discarded. The
third canto of *Childe Harold* is alive with memories of men.
Note also the sonnet to Lake Leman (P. IV. 53), which has in
it no mysticism and of which the mood is that already observed
in Spain and Greece. The poet declares that the memory of
Rousseau, Voltaire, Gibbon, and De Staël would recall to remembrance the lovely lake and that their memories have made
it lovelier. This is certainly not loving "Earth only for its
earthly sake." It is nearer to the fundamentally Byronic point
of view, admirably summed up by Lord Morley: "Nature, in
her most dazzling aspects or stupendous parts, is but the background and theatre of the tragedy of man."[1]

The "latent pantheism" to which I have referred appears
in the second canto of *Childe Harold*, stanzas xxv and xxvi;
but even here the truer characteristic is a yearning towards
man rather than towards nature. The desire is for "one to
bless us, one whom we can bless," for one "with kindred
consciousness endued," for one whose happiness and smiles
would be in some measure dependent upon him. Nevertheless
there is undoubtedly a consciousness of real fellowship with
Nature, a sensation deeper than one of mere enjoyment. It
is Faust's —

"Nicht
Kalt staunenden Besuch erlaubst du nur,
Vergönnest mir in ihre tiefe Brust
Wie in den Busen eines Freunds zu schauen" (l. 3221 f.)

Pantheism permeates the entire third canto. Trelawney (p. 8)
recorded that Byron had told E. E. Williams that "the idea of
the tragedy of *Manfred*, and many of the philosophical, or
rather metaphysical, notions interwoven in the composition of
the fourth (*sic*, almost certainly for *third*) canto of *Childe
Harold*, are his (i. e. Shelley's) suggestion; but this, of course,
is between ourselves."[2] Eimer[3] shows that such passages may

---

[1] *Byron, Miscellanies* I, 218.
[2] Byron said that Trelawney could not tell the truth.
[3] *Eng. Stud.* XLIII, 407.

be derived directly from the influence of the *Essay on Man*.
It is difficult to believe, however, that the primary influence
in this conception of the Whole which transcends the antinomy
of mind and matter, in which are all things, was not the poetry
of Wordsworth, particularly the immortal passage in the
Tintern Abbey lines in which the poet describes the sense
sublime

"Of something far more deeply interfused,
Whose dwelling is the light of setting suns,
And the round ocean and the living air,
And the blue sky, and in the mind of man:
A motion and a spirit, that impels
All thinking things, all objects of all thought,
And rolls through all things" (l. 96 f.)

This all-pervading spirit is Love,[1] a Shelleyan interpretation
of the doctrine of Spinoza. Byron cannot attain to the mystical
rapture of such lines as these —

"I know
That Love makes all things equal: I have heard
By mine own heart this joyous truth averred:
The spirit of the worm beneath the sod
In love and worship blends itself with God."[2]

With this absorption of all things in the Whole — the "One"
of *Adonais* — Byron combines a Wordsworthian mysticism,
an attempt to be "one with Nature," to grasp the ultimate
reality of things and to experience that actual community
with the Highest which is of the essence of mysticism. But
this mystical pantheism is only a passing mood of Byron's
thought, and *Manfred* is the only one of the plays which it
influenced directly.[3] When Wordsworth said,[4] with acknowledged reference to Byron, that the "words which practised
talent readily affords" were not unimpeachable evidence of

---

[1] See especially stanzas 99—104, and compare the passages cited by
Eimer, p. 408. Cf. also *Childe Harold* IV, 174, where the "fair Spirit" may
be considered as this Spirit of the Universe which is Love. Mr. Coleridge
thinks it expresses a desire for "the support and fellowship of his sister,"
which is perhaps more likely.

[2] *Epipsychidion*, ll. 125—9.

[3] The pantheism never entirely disappeared. Cf. *The Island* II, 382 f.

[4] *Poems*, ed. Wm. Knight, VII, 402: "Not in the lucid intervals
of life."

"genuine rapture," he was not gracious to Byron's memory,
but he was not far from the truth. Except in the passing
mood of 1816 there was in Byron no realization of the *Oneness*
of nature and man, no conception of man as a part of nature.
He has the sense sublime of that spirit whose dwelling is the
sunset and the ocean and the sky, but he is not conscious of
it in the mind of man. Nature and man are in essential con-
trariety. "All save the spirit of man is divine." Byron's
outlook upon nature is therefore objective. From the "hum
of human cities" he flies to her for refreshment. "Dear Nature
is the kindest Mother still." "The still, sad music of humanity" is not heard through nature; rather she affords a refuge
from its harsh and grating sounds. In the midst even of the
third canto this is shown:

> "Clear, placid Leman! thy contrasted lake,
> With the wide world I dwell in, is a thing
> Which warns me, with its stillness, to forsake
> Earth's troubled waters for a purer spring.
> This quiet sail is as a noiseless wing
> To waft me from distraction" (stanza 85).

Nature is the "balm of hurt minds." Tired of the fretful stir
and fever of the world man goes to her for relief. Thus,
gazing from his balcony over the moonlit canals Lioni
exclaims:

> "How sweet and soothing is this hour of calm!
> I thank thee, Night! for thou hast chased away
> Those horrid bodements which, amidst the throng,
> I could not dissipate."[1]

But this healing power only enforces the lesson. "What a
contrast with the scene I left," says Lioni, thinking only of
the ball he has quitted; but we, who know more, contrast the
dark conspiracy overhanging him and his fellow-nobles with
the calm and beauty of the silent, moonlit, summer night.
Such aloofness, such indifference, at such a time, reveal the
stern remorselessness of the processes of nature; they are evidence
of that "unalterable law" which drove down again the aspiring
spirit of Lucifer; they enforce the opinion that nature is indifferent

---

[1] *Marino Faliero* IV, 1, 105 f.

to the wretched strivings of humanity, a great, brooding presence, impassive, moved by laws that no man can comprehend and no man change, a disinterested and impartial witness of the tragedy of man;

"The world which was ere I was born;
The world which lasts when I am dead."

There are, then, in Byron's poetry two wholly distinct views of nature, the one subjective and intimate, the other objective and distinct from man. Of these two the latter is the characteristically Byronic attitude. Both views appear in *Manfred*.

Byron's pantheistic philosophy developed, as I have said, in 1816, and is best expressed in *Childe Harold* III. In *Manfred*, the Shelleyan "pantheism of love," and the feeling that man is a part of surrounding Nature do not exert any influence. There is a slight tendency in such passages as —

"Oh, that I were
The viewless spirit of a lovely sound" etc. (I, ii, 52 f.)

to the sentimental and mystical interpretation of nature which seeks to attain that mood in which there shall be complete harmony between nature and man, in which nature and man shall be that One which is Spinoza's God. But the pantheism of *Manfred* is rather that polytheism which peoples hills and seas and streams with the Powers of earth and air, a spiritualization of nature and her phenomena, from which, however, man stands apart. This is the theme behind the appearance of the "Spirits of the unbounded Universe" in the first scene, one of which is the spirit of the clouds, another of the mountains, a third of the waters, a fourth of the earthquake, a fifth of the wind, and a sixth of the night. Compare the phrase "the Spirit of each spot" in *Childe Harold* (III, 74, and cf. IV, 68 and 74). So also the Witch of the Alps is called "the spirit of the place" (II, ii, 11). Yet Manfred, the human being, is almost always apart from nature. Though

"the Night
Hath been to me a more familiar face
Than that of man; and in her starry shade
Of dim and solitary loveliness,
I learned the language of another world" (III, iv, 3 f.),

yet he never forgets that that "visible world," "so glorious in
its action and itself," is in splendid contrast to man —

> "We, who name ourselves its sovereigns, we
> Half dust, half deity, alike unfit
> To sink or soar, with our mixed essence make
> A conflict of its elements." (I, ii, 39 f.)

Study of Byron's plays has shown, I think, that their
value is both absolute and relative. They offer a serious consideration and reflection of life, of man in relation to his fellows,
to nature, and to the mystery that is before him and behind
and that wraps him round. But this positive worth is harmed
by Byron's lack of technical ability; the relative value is therefore of chief importance. The plays shed light upon Byron's
life and character, upon his non-dramatic work, upon the contemporary drama English and foreign, and upon the stirring
period of national awakening in the midst of which they were
composed. If I have made this clear I shall have accomplished
the task that I set myself to do.

There has been of late a considerable heightening of the
estimation in which the work of Byron is held. The long
period of anti-Byronism, which may be dated from the publication of *Sartor Resartus* and *Philip van Arteveldt,* is now
happily past. In this reaction the influence of Ruskin, Swinburne and Lord Morley has had a large share. I hope to
publish shortly an account of the development of Byronic
criticism and the philosophic basis of the recent change. Men
see that the Tennysonian tradition, inherited from Keats, is
not the final word in English poetry; and, with the break up
of the old order and rapid disappearance of the "Victorian
compromise," some have turned anew to Byron for inspiration
and stimulus. The tawdry and outworn garments of "Byronism" — dandyism, Wertherism, scandal, pose — have fallen in
rags away and can no longer hide the real man beneath.
The poet himself appears as the herald of awakening democracy, "the trumpet at her lips, her clarion, full of her cry,
sonorous with her breath;" no voice merely of disorder and
revolt, but a leader in the movement for positive upbuilding
upon new and firmer foundations.

Appendix I.
Byron and the Dramatic Unities.

On the history of the unities in England to the year 1700, see the careful study by L. S. Friedland.[1] Byron's knowledge of the criticism that has been summarized in that monograph was scanty. He had probably read Sidney's *Apologie for Poetry*.[2] He may have recognized the allusions to the unities in Shakespeare.[3] The works of Ben Jonson,[4] whom he regarded as "a scholar and a classic" (LJ. V, 330), could hardly have served as models, for Jonson's comedies only are strictly regular and Byron's concern is with tragedy. But planning a "regular" drama amid the wildest license of romanticism, he must have perceived with sympathy the analogy between Jonson and himself. Of opinions expressed by minor Elizabethans[5] Byron probably knew nothing.

With the works of Dryden Byron was thoroughly familiar. That he had studied the arguments for and against the unities in the *Essay of Dramatic Poesy*[6] is proved by a close verbal reminiscence not previously noted.[7] Byron failed to profit by

---

[1] "The Dramatic Unities in England," *Jour. Eng. and Germ. Phil.* X, 56 f.

[2] See G. Gregory Smith, *Elizabethan Critical Essays*, Oxford, 1904, I, 197.

[3] Note especially in the opening chorus of *Henry V* the references to the "wooden O" and the "hour glass." Cf. the prologues to Acts II and V of the same play, the chorus to Act IV of *The Winter's Tale*, and *Cymbeline* II, iv, 27.

[4] Note the reference in the Induction to *Every Man out of his Humour* to the rule that "the whole argument fall within the compasse of a daies efficiencie." See also the preface to *Sejanus* and the Prologue to *Volpone*. See further P. Aronstein, "Ben Jonson's Theorie des Lustspiels," *Anglia*, XVII, 479.

[5] Dekker, Marston, Middleton, Heywood, and Florio. See Friedland, p. 71 f.

[6] *Essays of John Dryden*, ed. W. P. Ker, Oxford, 1900, II, 21 f.

[7] "The universal consent of the most civilised parts of the world ought in this, as it doth in other customs, to include the rest" (Ker I, 98). Cf. "... An opinion, which, not very long ago, was the law of literature throughout the world, and still is so in the more civilised parts of it" (Preface to *Sardanapalus*, P. V, 9).

Neander's arguments in favor of the English drama. He was probably hindered in appreciation of the value of Dryden's criticism by the latter's frequent and characteristic vacillations of opinion.[1] Through Johnson's *Life of Addison*[2] he knew Dennis's strictures on *Cato*. It is highly probable that the source of Byron's one reference to Rymer is Dryden's *Heads of an Answer to Rymer* as printed in Johnson's *Life of Dryden*.[3] He may have read Rymer's two little books; at all events he was in sympathy with the school of Rymer.[4] Of other critics of the age of Dryden it is sufficient to mention Collier, Sheffield, Congreve, and Farquhar, with whose works Byron must have been acquainted. They all uphold with greater or less enthusiasm the authority of the rules.[5]

The trend of eighteenth-century criticism was away from classicism. A series of writers took the position that genius transcended rules;[6] then a few questioned the validity of any

---

[1] See Dryden's first Prologue to *The Maiden Queen* (*Works*, ed. Scott-Saintsbury, II, 422 and cf. 418). In reply to Howard's attack in *The Great Favorite* (Spingarn, *Critical Essays of the Seventeenth Century*, Oxford, 1908, II, 109) Dryden, in his *Defence* (Ker I, 116 f.), through eagerness to refute Howard, took a more "regular" position than he would else have done. See also the Prefaces to *Don Sebastian* and *All for Love* and the Dedications to *Love Triumphant* and the *Æneis*.

[2] *Lives of the Poets*, ed. J. B. Hill, II, 136 f. See also Dennis, *The Impartial Critic* (Spingarn, III, 148); Friedland, p. 458 f.; D. Nichol Smith, *Eighteenth Century Essays on Shakespeare*, Glascow, James Maclehose, 1903, p. xvi f. and 24 f.; and H. G. Paul, *John Dennis*, New York, Columbia Univ. Press, 1911, p. 173 and cf. p. 39.

[3] When Byron (LJ. V, 284) professes to quote from Rymer he in reality cites Dryden's *Heads*. Cf. *Works*, ed. Scott-Saintsbury, XV, 387.

[4] Byron's deference to the authority of Rymer may be due in part to Pope's favorable opinion (See Spence, *Anecdotes*, ed. 1858, p. 130).

[5] See Jeremy Collier, *A Short View of the Immorality and Profaneness of the English Stage*, 1698, p. 230; John Sheffield, *Essay on Poetry*, 1682, l. 177 f. (Spingarn, II, 101); Congreve, Dedication and Epilogue of *The Double Dealer*, and cf. Dryden's *To my dear Friend, Mr. Congreve. on his comedy called The Double Dealer*, l. 58 f.; Farquhar, *Discourse on Comedy*, 1702, *Works*, 1718, I, 75 f.

[6] See D. Nichol Smith, p. xv; Addison, *Spectator* No. 592; Pope, in the Preface to his Shakespeare (D. Nichol Smith, p. 50), but contrast *The Dunciad* I, 71.

rules at all,[1] and even satirized them;[2] and finally Lord Kames[3] and Hurd[4] found aesthetic justification for "Gothic," as distinct from "classical," rules of art. Thus the pathway was prepared for Johnson's influential defence of Shakespeare[5] and for the formulation by Lessing of the principles of Shakespeare's art. Johnson settled the question of the unities in England. A few pedants, aided by the influence of Voltaire, continued to criticise the loose construction of Shakespeare's plays, and as late as 1774 the anonymous *Cursory Remarks on Tragedy* shows traces of the school of Rymer. This romanticism influenced Byron negatively. With much of it he must have been acquainted; and for Johnson's critical powers he had high regard, yet he was not swayed in his allegiance by the Doctor's sledgehammer blows. Or one may say that he followed, not the precepts of the *Preface*, but the example of *Irene*.

In Byron's own age — the high-tide of romanticism — the doctrine of the unities, with all other articles of the classical creed, had been swept ever further into the background. They were no longer a question even for speculative discussion and references to them are few and almost without exception unsympathetic.[6] The exception is Byron himself. How came it

---

[1] See the *Remarks on the Tragedy of Hamlet*, 1736, anonymous, but generally attributed to Sir Thomas Hanmer (D. Nichol Smith, p. xx, note i), and Sir Thomas Upton's *Critical Observations on Shakespeare*, 1746, I, 16 and 77.

[2] Fielding, *Tom Jones*, bk. V, chap. i.

[3] *Elements of Criticism*, 1762, II, 404 f.

[4] Richard Hurd, *Letters on Chivalry and Romance*, 1762, ed. E. J. Morley, London, Frowde, 1911, p. 122 and *passim*.

[5] Especially in the Preface to his Shakespeare. Cf. S. C. Hart, *Rowe*, p. xliii; Walter Raleigh, *Johnson on Shakespeare*, London, Frowde, 1911, p. 29; and D. Nichol Smith, p. 130. See, too, *The Rambler*, No. 156 and contrast *Irene*.

[6] In the preface to the *Plays of the Passions*, vol. II (ed. 1851, p. 105) Joanna Baillie shows appreciation of the advantage of adhering in a general way to the unity of time. A like consciousness appears in the "Advertisement" to Coleridge's *Zapolya* (*Complete Poetical Works* II, 883), but Coleridge was thoroughly English and romantic. In the *Biographia Literaria* (p. 559) he refers to "the old blunder . . . concerning the irregularity of Shakespeare." Neither Wordsworth nor Keats refers to the unities, but Shelley's *Letters* contain some important strictures on *Marino Faliero*

that he, the typical romantic poet, championed so typically classical a creed?[1]

I find it explicable on several grounds. Of these his knowledge of past criticism of the subject was of least importance. I have just shown how little English theory influenced him. Continental opinions weighed more with him; "True Briton all beside, I here am French," he wrote of the drama.[2] Of Aristotle and the critics of the early Italian Renascence his knowledge, at the most, was vague; there is no evidence that he had first-hand acquaintance with any of them.[3] His information on French criticism was generally derivative. He never mentions the earlier advocates of the unities[4] and it is significant that he never appeals to the authority of Corneille whose three *Discours* he probably knew only through the medium of Dryden. He apparently knew as little of Racine for a chance remark on the lack of poetry in Racine's plays must be due to ignorance or inability to appreciate the beauties of French verse. There is nevertheless a close resemblance in method and object between Racineian and Byronic tragedy. Of Boileau he knew more;[5] doubtless he had read and drew support from the opening lines of the third book

---

(II, 888, 910, 912). Scott defends the unities at length in his preface to Dryden's *All for Love* (Scott's *Dryden*, ed. 1808, V, 287), and criticises them in the *Essay on the Drama* in the *Encyclopaedia Britannica*, 1819. Cf. also Lockhart, VI, 257 and 283. See also Milman, *Poetical Works* I, xiii and 107; Allan Cunningham, *Sir Marmaduke Maxwell*, 1822, p. vi.

[1] See especially P. IV, 340; V, 9; LJ. V, 90, 167, 217, 310, 323, 324, 347, 372, etc.

[2] *Hints from Horace* l. 271.

[3] The passages in Aristotle's *Poetics* are V, 4; VII, 3 and 6; VIII, 1, 2, and 4. Three references to Aristotle in *Don Juan* are noteworthy: I, cxx; I, cci; III, cxi. For the Italian critics it is sufficient to refer here to J. E. Spingarn, *Literary Criticism of the Renascence*, New York, Macmillan, 1899, p. 89 f.

[4] See E. Dannheisser, "Zur Geschichte der Einheiten in Frankreich," *Zeit. fran. Sprach. Litt.* XIV, 1 f. Pressure of space has forced me to omit here a discussion of Jean de la Taille, Vauquelin de la Fresnaye (*Art Poétique* II, l. 225 f.), De Laudun (Spingarn, *l. c.*, p. 209), Chapelain, Mairets, Desmarets, etc.

[5] See *Hints from Horace*, l. 183, note; *Childe Harold* IV, xxxviii; LJ. IV, 491 f.

of *L'Art Poétique.* To Voltaire Byron refers frequently; in *Don Juan* (XV, 59) he classes him with Shakespeare; to him he must have owed in part the prejudice with which he regarded the Elizabethan dramatists. He read some of Voltaire's plays; whether he met with the various *remarques* on the unities[1] I do not know, — it is likely. He may also, for he mentions both of them occasionally, have read Diderot and Marmontel on the unities.[2] The important point is that, whether deriving his knowledge at first- or second-hand, Byron knew the tenor of French criticism and recognised it as the criterion of regularity in the drama.

Signs of reaction from classical formalism are apparent in France towards the end of the eighteenth century.[3] In this change the illuminating pages of the *Hamburgische Dramaturgie,* 1767—1768, had a great part, but Byron's ignorance of German makes it doubtful whether he had read Lessing. But Lessing influenced A. W. von Schlegel, whose lectures on dramatic art and literature, 1808, were read by Mme. de Staël. In *De l'Allemagne,*[4] a book that Byron liked "prodigiously" (LJ. II, 364), she echoes Schlegel's attack upon the unities and passes on the new sentiments to Henri Beyle, whose *Racine et Shakespeare,* 1822, became a text-book of the Romantics.[5]

In my second chapter I showed how Byron grew disgusted

---

[1] See the Preface to the 1730 edition of *Œdipe, Œuvres complètes,* ed. Louis Moland, Paris, Garnier, II, 48 f.; *Discours sur la Tragédie,* prefixed to *Brutus,* 1731, ibid. II, 319; *Remarques sur les Discours de Corneille, ibid.* XXXII, 347 and cf. 366; *Remarques sur le Cid, ibid.* XXXI, 212 and cf. 328. See further L. Koelher, "Die Einheiten des Ortes und der Zeit in den Trauerspielen Voltaires," *Zeit. fran. Sprach. Litt.* XXIII, 1 f. and Lessing's Critique on *Mérope, Hamburgische Dramaturgie,* Nos. 45 and 46.

[2] See the "Premier Entretien" in Diderot's *Le Fils Naturel, Œuvres complètes,* ed. J. Assezat, Paris, Garnier, VII, 87 f. Marmontel wrote the article "Unités" in the 1777-supplement to the *Encyclopédie.* See also Lounsbury, *Shakespeare and Voltaire,* New York, Scribner, 1902, p. 336 f.

[3] Of this change Mercier's *Du Théâtre, ou nouvel Essai sur l'art dramatique,* 1773, is typical. See also Lounsbury, p. 180 f.

[4] Part II, chapter xxxi.

[5] See further, P. Nebout, *Le Drame Romantique,* Paris, Lecene, Oudin 1895, p. 68 f. The great preface to Hugo's *Cromwell* is beyond the limits of our present subject.

with the English theatre and turned more and more to a foreign, pseudo-classical standard of taste in the drama. Alfieri's influence was not without weight in this change. But of more importance was Byron's own temperament. In spite of his energetic individualism Byron was not always easy in his lawlessness. There was in him an instinctive obedience to authority. This is shown by that "classical" taste which appears in so much of his works, especially his criticisms of poetry. In his early satires and occasional verse he is a disciple of Pope[1] whom he considered "the greatest name in our poetry" (LJ. V, 274), "the moral poet of all civilization" (LJ. V, 560).[2] Eimer[3] says: "Pope war nicht nur Byrons Vorbild in der Form, in der Didaktik und Satire, sondern auch in den Grundlagen der philosophischen Anschauung;" and he has shown[4] how much the pantheism of 1816, generally (and I think rightly) ascribed to the influence of Wordsworth and Shelley, may perhaps be traced to Pope.[5] His opinion of living poets was governed by the same standard. "We are all wrong except Rogers, Crabbe and Campbell," he wrote (LJ. IV, 489). "He never recognized," says Nichol (p. 204), "the meaning of the artistic movement of his age." He always regretted "the good old style of our elders and betters" (LJ. III, 213). He had no interest in "old ballads;" he disliked that crew of "turbid mountebanks," the lesser Elizabethan dramatists (LJ. V, 218 and cf. II, 344); he condemned all the poetry of the "Lake school" save part of Coleridge's; he did not appreciate Keats; his praise of Shelley was often grudging. All this came from lack of sympathy with the romantic point of view. Similarly Byron distinguished Shakespeare the

---

[1] C. M. Fuess (*Lord Byron as a Satirist in Verse*, New York, Columbia Univ. Press, 1912, p. 69 f.) thinks that "in many respects Byron had more in common with Gifford than with Pope."

[2] Cf. LJ. IV, 304 and 486; V, 109, 154, 559, etc.

[3] M. Eimer, *Byron und der Kosmos*, *Angl. Forsch.* 34, Heidelberg, 1912, p. 195.

[4] M. Eimer, "Byrons Pantheismus vom Jahre 1816," *Eng. Stud.* XLIII, 396 f.

[5] See further C. S. Weiser, "Popes Einfluss auf Byrons Jugenddichtungen," *Anglia* I, 252 f.; F. Rover, *Lord Byrons Gedanken über Alexander Popes Dichtkunst*, Erlangen, 1886, *passim*; and the literature of the Byron-Bowles controversy.

dramatist and Shakespeare the poet. He loved and admired the poet and his verse abounds in Shakespearean echoes;[1] but the methods of the playwright were opposed to those for which Byron stood.

Byron is sweeping in his condemnation of "the detestable taste of the day" (LJ. III, 5). "I look upon this as the declining age of English poetry," he said (LJ. V, 559).[2] Self-criticism is of frequent occurrence and is evidence of his sincerity. An early couplet is:

> "From Horace show the pleasing paths of song,
> And from my own example — what is wrong."[3]

With such views it was but natural that Byron, accepting the other pseudo-classical doctrines of art, should admit the validity of the rule of the dramatic unities.

I have already pointed out that the classical model lent itself to Byron's purposes, in that he laid stress upon character and motive rather than upon action. This doubtless influenced his choice. Other considerations probably added force. Byron was tired of his own romantic license. Just as the author of *The Excursion* found it "pastime to be bound within the Sonnet's narrow plot of ground," so Byron sought in straitness relief. Moreover he wished to show what he could accomplish in a field far removed from that with which he was associated in the popular mind. In a life crowded with incidents and emotional experiences the construction of a play was, like the study of Armenian, "something craggy" to break his mind upon. Then, too, there is the appreciation of art for its own sake, a view of the value of Form, which is, says Lord Morley (p. 224), "collateral proof of the sanity and balance which marked the foundations of his character." Like all artists he desired to wrestle with Form, to bring painfully and chip by chip the statue out of the shapeless stone. For

> "l'œuvre sort plus belle
> D'une forme au travail
> Rebelle."

---

[1] See Ernst Zabel, *Byrons Kenntnis von Shakespeare und sein Urteil über ihn*, Halle, 1904, p. 56 f. and *passim*; Kölbing, "Byron und Shakespeare's *Macbeth*," *Eng. Stud.* XIX, 300 f.; and Appendix III, *post*.

[2] Cf. LJ. IV, 169 and 225; V, 554.

[3] *Hints from Horace*, l. 489 f. Cf. LJ. IV, 486 and 489; V, 559.

Finally, what amount of attention do the unities actually receive in Byron's plays?

Manfred, which, because of its irregularity, Byron called a "dramatic poem" rather than a drama, has ten scenes, no two of which are the same. The phenomenon of "double-time" is apparent as the following analysis will show, the course of time being noted in parentheses.

Act   I, Scene   i.   Midnight (1).
Act   I, Scene ii.   Morning (The following day?)
Act II, Scene   i.   The same morning.
Act II, Scene ii.   Forenoon (The same day?)[1]
Act II, Scene iii.   Moon-rise (The same evening?)
Act II, Scene iv.   The same night as II, iii. (2).
Act III, Scene   i.   The next day (Cf. *"To-morrow* ends
                      thine earthly ills," II, iv, 151).
Act III, Scene ii.   Sunset, same evening.
Act III, Scene iii.   Twilight, same evening.
Act III, Scene iv.   Night (3).

According to "short time" the action thus extends over just forty-eight hours and embraces three midnights. But in three places there is chance for analysis according to "long time." The morning on the cliffs need not immediately follow the midnight in the Gothic hall; the meeting with the witch need not occur just after the episode with the hunter; nor does the *rencontre* of the Destinies have to happen that same evening. Thus the poet produces, consciously or not, the impression of Manfred's protracted wanderings and questionings before the final release of death. This "double time" enables one to follow the life of the protagonist for an extended period without sacrificing the dramatic compression that "short time" affords. Of this *Manfred* is a good example.[2]

In *Marino Faliero* the unity of place is observed loosely;

---

[1] In this scene Byron is inconsistent, as is Shakespeare often, in indicating time. Manfred's first words are "It is not noon" and his last "The night approaches." Yet the scene is quite short.

[2] Shakespeare's employment of this device is so definite that it must have been done deliberately, e. g. in *Othello, The Merchant of Venice,* and *Twelfth Night.* See Furness, Preface to *Twelfth Night,* Variorum ed., p. xxii. For its use by other dramatists see Mable Buland, *The Presentation of Time in the Elizabethan Drama, Yale Studies* XLIV. It is not

a limited change of locality, "whither reason can be led by imagination," is permitted. There are twelve scenes, in ten different parts of Venice. The unity of time is kept strictly with some compression of actual history, but there is no loss of verisimilitude save possibly in the fifth act, where the trial follows hard upon the arrest of Faliero, and his execution hard upon the trial. In *Sardanapalus* the unities are preserved according to the most rigid French requirements. This results in some loss of verisimilitude.[1] In *The Two Foscari* Byron unbends a little; the action passes chiefly in the Hall of the Ducal Palace, but the third act is in a prison and the fifth in the Doge's private apartment. The time is within two days.

Cain of course does not observe the unity of place, but the action occupies less than three hours. Cain meets Lucifer after the morning sacrifice. The journey through the Abyss of Space and Hades occupies "scarcely two hours" (III, i, 54), and from Cain's return to the end of the play not more than an hour can elapse.[2] The unity of place is again disregarded in *Heaven and Earth*, though the time extends but from midnight to shortly after sunrise the next day.[3] *Werner* pays no attention to any unity; localities are presented that are far apart and the time extends over a period of several months.[4] So also in *The Deformed Transformed*. In both these plays Byron evinces a violent reaction from the straitness to which his championship of the unities had bound him.

---

necessary to assume conscious effort by the poet; to some degree, indeed, it follows inevitably upon a consistent indication of the passage of time.

[1] See Heber's criticism in *Quarterly Review* XXVII, 486.

[2] There is a slight oversight as to time. By no computation can it be noon, yet Adah says —

> "Ere the sun declines
> Let us depart, nor walk the wilderness
> Under the cloud of night" (III, i, 457 f.)

[3] Cf. Scene iii, l. 295: "The East is kindling" and l. 738 "The sun ... riseth."

[4] Byron's carelessness as to time appears again in *Werner*. At IV, i, 17 we are told that the reign of Count Siegendorf is "hardly a *year* o'erpast its honey-moon," whereas the narrative of Gabor (V, i, 221 f.) refers to "February last" (l. 229) an incident which occurred *before* the Count's return. The interval of a year could not have separated the two events. This error was pointed out in the *Monthly Review*, XCIX, 396. Cf. Kölbing, *Eng. Stud.* XVII, 147.

Appendix II.
Manfred and Faust.

It seems worth while to put together, with some additional comments of my own, whatever has been suggested bearing on the actual indebtedness of Byron in *Manfred* to Goethe's *Faust*.

Byron must have known the Faust-story before he became acquainted with Goethe's play, but there is no reason to doubt his repeated assertion that he knew nothing of Marlowe's *Faustus* (LJ. IV, 175 and 177). It is hardly necessary to reaffirm that Byron almost certainly knew nothing of Hroswitha's *Lapsus et Conversio Theophili Vice-domini* (tenth century), the earliest form of the legend. Any knowledge of Calderon's *El Magico Prodigioso* Byron would have obtained through Shelley, and the latter's interest in Spanish apparently did not begin until two years after the composition of *Manfred*. [1] Calderon may therefore conceivably have influenced *The Deformed Transformed,* but hardly *Manfred.*

Byron studied German as a boy,[2] but later forgot it completely and knew German literature only in translation.[3] His first knowledge of *Faust* was probably through Mme. de Staël's *De l'Allemagne*, which contains an analysis of the drama and a translation of several scenes. Brandl suggests[4] that when Byron told Medwin "All I know of that drama is from a sorry French translation," he was referring to Mme. de Staël's. This seems likely. In August, 1816, M. G. Lewis translated to Byron several scenes, or less probably the whole, of *Faust* (LJ. IV, 97 and 174). To this E. H. Coleridge (P. IV, 81) traces "the primary conception" of the poem. There is no evidence that Shelley read *Faust* to Byron at this time;[5] and judging from his letters Shelley's interest in *Faust* belongs to the last year or two of his life. In a characteristically impatient and

---

[1] *Letters* II, 719.

[2] Medwin, p. 125.

[3] On Byron's relations to Germany see M. Eimer, "Byrons Beziehungen zur deutschen Kultur," *Anglia* XXXVI, 313 f. and 397 f.

[4] "Goethes Verhältnis zu Byron," *Goethe-Jahrbuch* XX, 30.

[5] See *Eng. Stud.* XLIV, 300; *Anglia* XXXVI, 440.

emphatic mood Byron exclaimed, "The devil may take both
Faustuses, German and English — I have taken neither" (LJ. IV,
177), but in the phrase already quoted — "much more than
Faustus" — he acknowledged the debt.

How large this debt was has been a matter of dispute.
Koeppel[1] goes so far as to declare that *Faust* was the dramatic form
on which Byron modeled *Manfred.* Groag says,[2] "Die Ähnlichkeit
der beiden grossartigen Dichtungen ist gar nicht zu verkennen.
Ja manche Stellen in *Manfred* klingen sogar wie eine etwas
freie Übersetzung des deutschen Originals." He qualifies this
broad statement, however, by applying it especially to the first
act. It is certain that the chief resemblances occur early in
the dramas. These have been pointed out by Brandl (p. 7—8)
and others, and shall be resumed here with comments and
certain qualifications. Byron himself admitted that the opening
scenes were much alike (LJ. V, 37). Manfred is discovered in
"a Gothic gallery;" Faust, "in einem hochgewölbten, engen,
gothischen Zimmer." There is in each case a long opening
monologue, the theme being the ceaseless striving after knowledge, the further penetration into recesses of thought, with ever
the same result, — the realization of the falsity of the promise
"Eritis sicut Deus, scientes bonum et malum." The despairing
cynicism of Faust's cry:
> "Da steh ich nun, ich armer Thor!
> Und bin so klug, als wie zuvor" (l. 358 f.)

is the burden of Manfred's soliloquy. It is Byron's indebtedness
to Goethe for this theme — that Man possesses
> "Of knowledge — just so much as shows that still
> It ends in ignorance on every side"[3] —

that makes Mr. Coleridge trace the primary conception of the
character to *Faust.* Byron has motived the conventional
misanthropy, which had already been portrayed in a long
line of heroes.

Manfred, like Faust, has power over spirits and conjures
them up. Instead of the Spirit of the Earth, who appears to
Faust, Manfred summons the "Spirits of the unbounded Uni-

---

[1] Emile Koeppel, *Lord Byron,* Berlin, Hofmann, 1903, p. 110.
[2] J. G. Groag, *Lord Byron als Dramatiker,* Linz, 1877, p. 24.
[3] Browning, *Parleyings, With Francis Furini,* l. 283 f.

verse;" that is, the all-embracing Earth-spirit is represented
by spirits of the various and individual phenomena that together
make up earth. In both cases the pantheism is fundamentally
the same.

These spirits are at first invisible to Manfred, and when
one of them appears "in the shape of a beautiful female figure"
he is unable to endure the sight and falls senseless. Brandl
compares this to Faust's cowering fear in the presence of the
Earth-spirit — "Soll ich dir, Flammenbildung, weichen?" (l. 499)
— and there is certainly an analogy, but the conception is
common to many scenes in which a mortal beholds a spirit,
and I believe that this "Seventh Spirit" who appears to Manfred was suggested by quite another incident in *Faust*. The
identification of this figure has been disputed. Mr. Coleridge's
note (to I, i, 187) is, "It is evident that the female figure is
not that of Astarte, but of the subject of the 'Incantation'." Mr.
Edgcumbe writes (p. 293), "The Spirit, which appeared to Manfred
in the form of a beautiful female figure, was Mary Chaworth."
That is, putting to one side the autobiographical meaning
which underlies the poem, Mr. Edgcumbe identifies this figure
with Astarte. Gillardon[1] says, "Dieser Geist ist der Genius
Manfred's. Er erscheint hier als wunderschöne Frauengestalt,
später in Akt III, Scene iv, als furchtbarer unterirdischer
Dämon." And again: "Der 7. Geist in Manfred Akt I, Scene i,
der Dämon in Akt III, Scene iv, und *first destiny* in Akt IV,
Scene iii [*sic* for II, iv] sind ein und dasselbe wie sich aus
einem Vergleich der betreffenden Stellen ergibt." This last
view may be dismissed without comment, because of the lack
of evidence of any such identification and the *a priori* im-
probability of so un-Byronic a conception. Nor is Mr. Coleridge's
explanation more plausible. The certainty that in the *Incantation* there is direct reference to Lady Byron contradicts this
view, as do the words of passionate longing uttered by Manfred
before he falls senseless. These words are a support to Mr.
Edgcumbe's theory that the figure and Astarte are the same,
but her introduction here would be an inartistic anticipation

---

[1] Heinrich Gillardon, *Shelley's Einwirkung auf Byron*, Heidelberg,
1899, p. 98.

of the climax of the drama. My own belief is that the apparition of the "beautiful female figure" with whom Manfred "yet might be happy" is an indistinct reminiscence of "das schönste Bild von einem Weibe," which Faust sees in the Witch's mirror (l. 2436). Manfred's exclamation at the sight of the figure recalls Faust's final aspiration:

"Lass mich nur schnell noch in den Spiegel schauen!
Das Frauenbild war gar zu schön!" (l. 2599 f.)

But whereas in *Faust* the figure represents the temptations of sensual delight that will make him see a Helen in every woman, Manfred's vision is more nearly analogous to that of Marlowe's Faustus. He catches a fleeting glimpse of the Ideal towards which in youth he had striven, but which had long since vanished. Hence his exclamation. The influence of Shelley is apparent. Compare lines 13—17 of the *Hymn to Intellectual Beauty:*

"Spirit of Beauty, that dost consecrate
With thine own hues all thou dost shine upon
Of human thought or form, — where art thou gone?
Why dost thou pass away and leave our state,
This dim vast vale of tears, vacant and desolate?"

In *Epipsychidion* (l. 22 f.), this Ideal is invoked as —

"Veiling beneath that radiant form of Woman
All that is insupportable in thee
Of light, and love, and immortality."

Thus a suggestion from *Faust* has been given a new meaning through contact with Shelley.

After the departure of Wagner, in the same First Study Scene, Faust falls into a train of meditation that leads to a determination to put an end to his life, and as he is about to drink from the deadly phial the Chorus of Angels breaks in upon him (l. 737 f.) and frustrates his design. This may have lent a suggestion to the second scene of *Manfred,* where a like suicidal purpose is thwarted by the intrusion of piety, in the person of the Chamois-hunter, but Byron had already conceived the contrast of the devotee of *doctrinaire* religion and the seeker after absolute truth; and in Manfred's revery there is as much of Hamlet and Prometheus as of Faust. Brandl has suggested, with some hesitation, that the Witch of the Alps (Act II, Scene ii) may owe something to the *Hexen-küche*. The contrast is here more striking than the resemblance. Ruskin,[1] telling of his delight in Byron, says that Byron "sympathized with me in reverent love of beauty and indignant recoil from ugliness. The witch of the Staubbach in her rainbow was a greatly more pleasant vision than Shakespeare's, like a rat without a tail, or Burns's, in her cutty sark," or, he might have added, Goethe's with her family of apes. There is a nearer resemblance to *Faust* in the offer by the Witch of the Alps of her power if Manfred will be her servant (II, ii, 156). The same theme is repeated, with a like refusal of the offer, in *Cain* (I, i, 303 f.) In both the motive is that of the contract with Mephistopheles, which is certainly copied in *The Deformed Transformed* (I, i, 140). All, however, go back to *Matthew* IV, 9; *Luke* IV, 7.

There are other scattered passages later in *Manfred* reminiscent of *Faust*. The mention of the "great festival" in the Hall of Arimanes (II, iii, 15) recalls the *Walpurgisnacht*, especially as the First Destiny is at the Summit of the Jungfrau on her way to the festival. Compare the toilsome climb of Faust and Mephistopheles, guided by the Ignis-fatuus. The position of the Hall of Arimanes, high in the clouds, may have been influenced by the *Hexenelement* on and around and above the Brocken.[2] The song of the demon Ashtaroth, in the first version of the third act of *Manfred* (P. IV, 122, l. 17 f.), is influenced by the same Witches' Sabbath, and the reference (l. 18) to the "Raven-stone" is obviously drawn from the penultimate scene of *Faust*. The final scene of *Manfred* has little in common with the close of *Faust*, especially if Byron knew of the promise of final salvation contained in the Prologue, but it is closely related to the legendary form of the story (reproduced in Marlowe's terrible conclusion), and to the catastrophe of *Don Juan*.[3]

---

[1] *Praeterita* I, viii, *Works* XXXV, 150.

[2] On the position of the Hall, see Kölbing, "Zu Byrons Manfred," *Eng. Stud.* XXII, 140.

[3] Other minor resemblances have been suggested. Eimer (*Anglia* XXXVI, 441) thinks certain metrical peculiarities betray the influence of *Faust*. This is very doubtful. H. Kraeger (*Der Byronische Heldentypus*, Munich,

Appendix III.

Shakespearean Echoes in Marino Faliero.

Marino Faliero.	*Shakespeare.*
"His taking off" (I, ii, 227).	"His taking off" (*Macb.* I, vii, 20).
The Doge takes up the ducal crown: "Hollow bauble," etc. (I, ii, 259 f.)	Prince Henry with the crown: "O polished perturbation! golden care," etc. (*Henry IV, Pt. I,* IV, v, 23).
"There's blood upon thy face" (I, ii, 334).	"There's blood upon thy face" (*Macb.* III, iv, 12).
"Will not my great sires leap from the vault, Where lie two doges who preceded me, And pluck me down among them?" (I, ii, 583 f.)	Juliet's speech before taking the sleeping potion (*R. and J.,* IV, iii, 24 f.)
The scene between Faliero and Angiola (II, i, 173 f.)	The scene between Brutus and Portia (*Jul. Caes.* II, i, *ad fin.*)
"The same sin that overthrew the angels" (II, i, 207 — *i. e.* pride).	"By that sin fell the angels" (*Henry VIII,* III, ii, 441).
"Milkiness of spirit" (II, ii, 80).	"Milk o' human kindness" (*Macb.* I, v, 18).
"*Cal:* But if we fail — *Ber:* They never fail who die In a great cause."	"*Macb:* If we should fail? *Lady M:* We fail! But screw your courage to the sticking place And we'll not fail" (*Macb.* I, vii, 59).

1898, p. 89) compares Faust's and Manfred's fatal love — a vague resemblance. Brandl (p. 8) compares the exclamation of the spirits, "Crush the worm!" (II, iv, 49) to that of the Earth-spirit, "Ein furchtsam weggekrümmter Wurm" (l. 498).

Marino Faliero.	*Shakespeare.*
"Their spirit walks abroad" (II, ii, 97.)	"O Julius Caesar, thou art mighty yet! Thy spirit walks abroad" (*Jul. Caes.* V, iii, 94 f.)
"Make our assurance doubly sure" (II, ii, 156).	"I'll make assurance double sure" (*Macb.* IV, i, 83).
"Covetous of brief authority" (II, ii, 188).	"Dressed in a little brief authority" (*Meas. for Meas.* II, ii, 118).
"I have set my little left Of life upon this cast" (III, i, 54 f.) (Compare also *Corsair*, ll. 337 and 1543).	"I have set my life upon a cast" (*Rich. III,* V, iv, 9).
"Their new swords well flesh'd" (III, ii, 15). (Compare *Corsair*, l. 623).	"Full bravely hast thou flesh'd Thy maiden sword" (*Hen. IV, Pt. I,* V, iv, 133).
"As far among the foe as any he That hears me" (III, ii, 61).	Shakespearean use of *he, e. g.* — "I am that he, that unfortunate he" (*As You Like It* III, ii, 414).
"A thing of robes and trinkets" (III, ii, 188).	"A king of shreds and patches" (*Hamlet* III, iv, 102).
"We will not scotch, But kill" (III, ii, 268).	"We have scotched the snake, not killed it" (*Macbeth* III, ii, 14).
"I blame you not — you act in your vocation" (III, ii, 456).	"'Tis no sin for a man to labour in his vocation" (*Hen. IV, Pt. I,* I, ii, 116).
"That horrible incarnadine" (IV, ii, 147).	"The multitudinous seas incarnadine" (*Macbeth* II, ii, 62).
"Tremendous bodements" (IV, ii, 185).	"Sweet bodements" (*Macbeth* IV, i, 96).
Calendaro spits at him (V, i, 134).	"And spit upon my Jewish gaberdine" (*Mer. of Ven.*, I, iii, 113).

Marino Faliero.	*Shakespeare.*
"Who would have foreseen That Nature could be filed to such a crime" (V, i, 192). (Compare *Childe Harold* III, 113).	"For Banquo's issue have I filed my mind" (*Macbeth* III, i, 65).
"Fortune is female: from my youth her favors Were not withheld" (V, i, 267).	"Fortune . . . Shown like a rebel's whore" (*Macbeth* I, ii, 14). "Fortune . . . is a strumpet" (*Hamlet* II, ii, 239).
"Look to the Lady" (V, i, 325).	"Look to the Lady" (*Macbeth* II, iii, 131).
"Alas! Signor, He who is only just is cruel; who Upon the earth would live were all judged justly?" (V, i, 362).	"In the course of justice none of us Should see salvation" (*Mer. of Ven.*. IV, i, 199).
"Noble Venetians, many times and oft" (V. i, 479).	"Signior Antonio, many a time and oft" (*Mer of Ven.*, I, iii, 107).
"Thy good are confiscate unto the state" (V, i, 486).	"Thy lands and goods Are, by the laws of Venice, confiscate Unto the state of Venice" (*Mer. of Ven.*, IV, i, 310).
"To pull in resolution" (V, ii, 50).	"I pull in resolution" (*Macbeth* V, v, 42).
"The Greek Walks o'er thy mart, and smiles on it for his" (V, iii, 59).	"Banquo smiles upon me And points at them for his" (*Macbeth* IV, i, 123).
"A barbarian Vice of Kings" (V, iii, 66).	"A vice of kings" (*Hamlet* III, iv, 98).
"All the ills of conquer'd states shall cling thee" (V, iii, 84). (Compare *Darkness*, l. 50)	"Till famine cling thee" (*Macbeth* V, v, 40).